Na

Eu

THIRD

Dylan

HODDER
EDUCATION
HACHETTE UK COMPANY

9780340986982

Study Guide authors: Angela Leonard (Edexcel) and Martin Jones (OCR)

The publishers would like to thank the following individuals, institutions and companies for permission to reproduce copyright illustrations in this book: © Bettmann/CORBIS, page 26; Bibliothèque des Arts Décoratifs, Paris, France/Archives Charmet/The Bridgeman Art Library, page 81; Bibliothèque Nationale, Paris, France/Giraudon/The Bridgeman Art Library, page 31; © Burstein Collection/CORBIS, page 126; Chateau de Versailles, France/Lauros/Giraudon/The Bridgeman Art Library, page 131; © The Gallery Collection/Corbis, page 125; Hulton Archive/Getty Images, page 24; © INTERFOTO/Alamy, page 50; © Lebrecht Music and Arts Photo Library/Alamy, page 9; © The London Art Archive/Alamy, pages 63, 127; Louvre, Paris, France/The Bridgeman Art Library, page 72; Louvre, Paris, France/Giraudon/ The Bridgeman Art Library, page 165; Mansell/Mansell/Time & Life Pictures/Getty Images, pages 133, 167; Musée de la Ville de Paris, Musée Carnavalet, Paris, France/Lauros/Giraudon/The Bridgeman Art Library, page 90; Private Collection/The Bridgeman Art Library, page 28; Private Collection/Ken Welsh/ The Bridgeman Art Library, page 13; Dylan Rees, pages 161, 170; JOEL ROBINE/AFP/Getty Images, page 46; © Walker Art Gallery, National Museums Liverpool/The Bridgeman Art Library, page 166; Time Life Pictures/Mansell/ Time Life Pictures/Getty Images, page 8.

The publishers would like to acknowledge use of the following extracts: Cambridge University Press for an extract from *Revolution and Reaction: Europe 1789–1849* by A. Matthews, 2001; Fontana Press for an extract from *France 1789–1815: Revolution and Counterrevolution* by D.M.G. Sutherland, 1985. Every effort has been made to trace all copyright holders, but if any have been inadvertently overlooked the Publishers will be pleased to make the necessary arrangements at the first opportunity.

Hachette UK's policy is to use papers that are natural, renewable and recyclable products and made from wood grown in sustainable forests. The logging and manufacturing processes are expected to conform to the environmental regulations of the country of origin.

Orders: please contact Bookpoint Ltd, 130 Milton Park, Abingdon, Oxon OX14 4SB. Telephone: (44) 01235 827720. Fax: (44) 01235 400454. Lines are open 9.00–5.00, Monday to Saturday, with a 24-hour message answering service. Visit our website at www.hoddereducation.co.uk

© 1993 Andrina Stiles and Dylan Rees
First published in 1993 by
Hodder Education,
An Hachette UK Company
338 Euston Road
London NW1 3BH

Second Edition published in 2004.
This Third Edition published in 2009.

Essex County
Council Libraries

Impression number   5   4   3   2   1
Year   2013   2012   2011   2010   2009

Cover image: *Napoleon Crossing the Alps on 20 May 1800*, 1803 (oil on canvas), Chateau de Versailles, France, courtesy of the Bridgeman Art Library/ Getty Images
Typeset in 10/12pt Baskerville and produced by Gray Publishing, Tunbridge Wells
Printed in Malta

A catalogue record for this title is available from the British Library.

ISBN: 978 0340 986 769

Contents

Dedication

Keith Randell (1943–2002)

The *Access to History* series was conceived and developed by Keith, who created a series to 'cater for students as they are, not as we might wish them to be'. He leaves a living legacy of a series that for over 20 years has provided a trusted, stimulating and well-loved accompaniment to post-16 study. Our aim with these new editions is to continue to offer students the best possible support for their studies.

1 Napoleon: Background and Rise to Power

POINTS TO CONSIDER

The French Revolution was one of the most dramatic events in modern European history. In 1789 the old order, or *ancien régime*, started to collapse. Over the course of the next six years until 1795, the Revolution steadily became more extreme and chaotic, at which point a measure of stability was restored with the setting up the Directory. Of the many important figures to emerge out of the Revolutionary period none equalled the extraordinary career of Napoleon Bonaparte. He not only made a lasting impact on France but, over the course of his reign, altered the map of Europe. This chapter will explore his background through the following sections:

- Synopsis of Napoleon's career 1796–1815
- Background and character
- Napoleon and the early years of the Revolution
- Napoleon and the Directory

Key dates

1769	August 15	Napoleon born in Ajaccio, Corsica
1778	December 15	Napoleon left Corsica to be educated in Brienne
1785	September 1	Napoleon graduated from the *École Militaire* as an artillery officer
1789	July 14	The storming of the Bastille
1792	August 10	French monarchy overthrown
1793	June 11	Napoleon and his family fled Corsica
	September 16	Napoleon appointed Commander of Artillery at the siege of Toulon
1795	October 1–5	Vendémiaire uprising in Paris
1796	March 2	Napoleon appointed Commander of the Army in Italy
	March 9	Napoleon married Josephine de Beauharnais
1798	May 19	Napoleon set out for Egypt
1799	November 9–10	*Coup* of Brumaire
1821	May 5	Death of Napoleon on St Helena

A new calendar and dating system was adopted by the French Republic in October 1793 to mark what it considered was a new era in human history. Year I started in September 1792 when the Republic came into existence. The second month in the new Revolutionary calendar was Brumaire – the month of fog. On 18–19 Brumaire in year VIII of the Revolution (9–10 November 1799) a *coup d'état* in Paris unexpectedly brought a young General, Napoleon Bonaparte, to power in France. In the event, it also led to his assuming power in most of the rest of Europe over the course of the next 15 years. Who was he and what was he like, this man who was to dominate Europe until 1815, and to live on in legend long after his death?

Before Napoleon became Emperor in 1804 he should be referred to as Bonaparte or General Bonaparte. It was not until 1802 that his full name appeared for the first time in official documents, when it was given as 'Napoleone Bonaparte'. (He had much earlier abandoned the Italian spelling of his surname, Buonaparte.) Soon after 1802, the Italian version of his baptismal name was also dropped, in favour of the French, Napoleon Bonaparte. It was to be a source of conflict with his British gaolers on St Helena that, having been deprived by the allies of his imperial title at the time of his second abdication in 1815, they addressed their prisoner as 'General Bonaparte'. The argument continued even after his death in a very undignified way. The British officials on the island would not agree to the name 'Napoleon' being put on the coffin, and as the French representatives there would accept nothing else, he was buried anonymously. (For the sake of simplicity, Napoleon, the anglicised form of his name, is used throughout this book.)

1 | Synopsis of Napoleon's Career 1796–1815

Key question
What were the main features of Napoleon's career?

At the beginning of his ascent to power in the 1790s, Napoleon was still slim and active, although not particularly prepossessing in appearance according to eyewitness accounts. These describe him as untidily, almost shabbily dressed, with lank, greasy shoulder-length hair and a sallow complexion. A rather serious young man, he had little sense of humour and seldom laughed. In 1796 two events of great importance in his life occurred – he married the widowed society beauty, Josephine de Beauharnais, and he was appointed commander of the Army of Italy. It was as a result of his military campaigns in Italy (1796–7) and afterwards in Egypt (1798–9) that in 1799 he came to power in the *coup d'état* of Brumaire, making him **First Consul** and undisputed ruler of France.

First Consul
The most important of the three consuls who headed the government after the 1799 *coup*.

Key term

Domestic affairs

As First Consul (1799–1804) and then as Emperor until 1814, Napoleon's government was highly **centralised** and his authority as sole ruler of France was not effectively disputed. His regime was basically a dictatorship, although, despite the fact that the head of state was also head of the armed forces, it was not a military one. By a mixture of bribery (through the liberal use of gifts of land, titles, official appointments and money to buy support) and a ruthless suppression of freedom of thought, word and deed (through the widespread use of indoctrination, intimidation and propaganda to make opposition difficult), Napoleon maintained himself in power for 14 years.

Foreign affairs

Napoleon's relations with most of the great powers involved war at some time or other. Apart from the short period of peace in 1802–3 France was almost continuously at war during the Napoleonic period. Indeed, the Peace of Amiens (1802) can be seen as little more than a truce in a long succession of wars, begun during the Revolution and continued under Napoleon. France fought these wars against a succession of European coalition armies. Until 1807, Napoleon led France to a series of brilliant victories on land, extending the borders of France far beyond their '**natural frontiers**' of the Rhine, the Alps and the Pyrenees, into Germany and Italy. At the beginning of 1811 the Empire reached its greatest extent (see the map on page 104), but its collapse was already threatened by the lengthy Spanish conflict begun in 1807 and made certain by Napoleon's ill-judged invasion of Russia in 1812. Even Napoleon's most strenuous efforts failed to save the Empire in the campaign of 1813 and with the fall of Paris to the allies of the Sixth Coalition in March 1814 he was forced to abdicate, and was exiled to **Elba**. His return to France the following year during the 'Hundred days' campaign that ended in his defeat at the Battle of Waterloo, brought his reign and the Napoleonic era to a close.

St Helena and after

Exiled again in 1815, this time to **St Helena** (a remote island in the south Atlantic from which escape proved impossible), Napoleon occupied the remaining years of his life in dictating his own version of events to a group of companions on the island. He died, most probably from stomach cancer, on 5 May 1821, shortly before his 52nd birthday. From these records, and from the accumulated propaganda of his years in power, his many followers in the years after his death, carefully constructed the Napoleonic legend.

Key question
What factors contributed to the downfall of the Napoleonic Empire?

Key date

Death of Napoleon on St Helena: 5 May 1821

Key terms

Centralised
Political power dispensed from one central location or through one individual.

Natural frontiers
Natural features, such as rivers, mountains, lakes or the sea.

Elba
A small island off the north-western coast of Italy.

St Helena
A tiny British island in the south Atlantic over 1000 miles off the coast of Africa.

2 | Background and Character

Family background

Napoleon was born on 15 August 1769 in the town of Ajaccio on the island of Corsica and was christened Napoleone di Buonaparte. Although he was born a French citizen, Corsica had only been part of France since 1768. In that year it was ceded to France from the Republic of Genoa. The Buonaparte family were minor nobility with a fierce, independent pride in all that was Corsican. Napoleon's father, Carlo Maria Bonaparte (1746–85), had been a passionate nationalist. Carlo was a supporter of the Corsican nationalist leader Pasquale Paoli, and his attempts to gain independence from Genoa. When France became involved in the conflict, Carlo fought against them. Following the final defeat of the Corsican rebels, Carlo decided that further resistance was futile and made his peace with the new ruling power.

Key question
What impact did Napoleon's Corsican background have on his career?

Napoleon born in Ajaccio on the island of Corsica: 15 August 1769

Key date

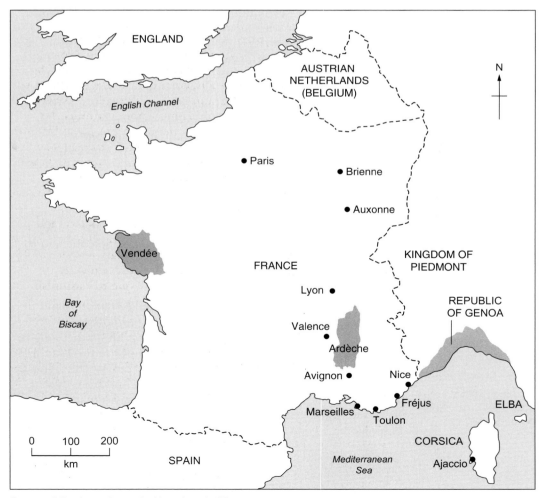

Some of the key places in Napoleon's life.

Key terms

Cidevant
List drawn up during the Revolution of former members of the nobility.

Counter-revolutionaries
All who were hostile to the Revolution.

La patrie
The fatherland – with which all passionate revolutionaries closely identified.

Popular sovereignty
A belief that political power rests with the people and their chosen representatives.

Key dates

Napoleon left Corsica to be educated in a college in Brienne: 15 December 1778

Napoleon graduated from the *École Militaire* as an artillery officer: 1 September 1785

The acceptance by Carlo of an amnesty saw him change sides. There were advantages to be gained for his growing family of five sons and three daughters by attaching himself to the French administration of the island (see Napoleon's family tree on page 177). One of these advantages was the acquisition of the documentary proof of his status as a nobleman, which he needed in order to send Napoleon, his second son, to be educated at the French government's expense at a military academy on the mainland. Fortunately perhaps for Napoleon, the Corsican nobility was considered by most Frenchmen to be much inferior in status to that of France, and his name was never entered in the '*cidevant*' lists at the time of the Revolution. This might have proven difficult for him as following the abolition of the nobility in 1790 many noblemen were suspected of being **counter-revolutionaries**.

Napoleon's education

On 15 December 1778 at the age of nine, the young Napoleon, whose first language was Italian, was sent by his father to study in France. When he returned to Corsica in 1786 after an absence of eight years he met for the first time his younger brothers and sisters. Before starting his studies he was given an intensive course in French to prepare him for any future career. He never lost his Italian accent, and never learnt to write grammatically correct French – this latter fact may have been the reason why he dictated all official documents and correspondence, leaving it to his secretaries to correct the grammar. It is difficult to know how far he ever felt himself to be truly French, however much he spoke of 'France, first and always'. Some historians go so far as to suggest that France for him was never *la patrie* – that he was always, at least emotionally, a Corsican. It is certainly true that he initially thought of the Revolution as an opportunity for the Corsicans to gain freedom from France as they had once dreamed of gaining freedom from Genoa.

During the opening years of the Revolution, Napoleon was strongly influenced by the philosopher Rousseau, who developed a theory of **popular sovereignty** whereby ordinary people would exercise political power. For a while he was obsessed with Rousseau's view '… that this little island will one day astonish Europe'. Much later during his life, when Corsica ceased to dominate his thoughts in the same way, and he came to denounce Rousseau as 'a madman', the Corsican sense of family loyalty remained with him, and would influence many of his subsequent political appointments (see Napoleon's family tree on page 177).

The first formal education Napoleon received in France was at a small preparatory school of 110 students at Brienne. The school was run by monks to a very strict routine. The young Napoleon was not allowed to leave until his education had been completed, a period of six years. Part of the aim of the strict upbringing was to produce boys who were tough and self-reliant. In October 1784, his education at Brienne completed, he left for Paris where he entered the *École Militaire*, to train as an artillery officer. This was one of the few branches of the military where promotion was strictly on the basis of merit rather than upbringing. He became the first Corsican to graduate, 42nd out of a class of 58, as a sub-lieutenant of artillery on 1 September 1785.

Napoleon's character and personality

Napoleon's character and personality were very complex and certainly evolved over the course of his career. There are a number of essential features that can be identified:

Key question
What were the essential features of Napoleon's character and personality?

- As a Corsican whose first language was Italian, he was clearly perceived as an outsider during the years he spent in France being educated. While at school he kept himself very much to himself and could certainly be described as a loner.
- Napoleon's youth was far from normal and it suggests that during these early years he was very adaptable. When confronted with difficult and trying circumstances, he was able to overcome them and flourish.
- With friends, he could be charming and amusing. But he did not always choose to be so, and his rages and his cold displeasure could be terrifying to those around him. He recognised the fact that his mood could change suddenly: 'I am two different men', he once said of himself. The artist Antoine-Jean Gros, who painted him in 1796, described him as cold and severe.
- He was fiercely ambitious and driven to achieve his potential. As the well-known French historian Georges Lefebvre pointed out, the young Napoleon possessed an '… irresistible impulse towards action and domination which is called ambition'. Napoleon himself clearly recognised and fully acknowledged this trait: 'It is said that I am ambitious, but that is an error: or at least, my ambition is so intimately allied to my whole being that it cannot be separated from it.'
- As a native of Corsica, Napoleon placed great emphasis on family loyalty. The **clan system** on the island encouraged the reward and promotion of relatives. This goes some way to explaining Napoleon's tendency as Emperor to appoint close relatives he could trust to powerful positions in government.
- Napoleon possessed enormous energy. He was, for much of his adult life, a workaholic, sometimes working 18 or more hours a day, and was able to exist on very little sleep. As Emperor, he was determined to oversee personally all aspects of the state and would dictate his official communications often to half a dozen secretaries at once. It has been estimated that he 'wrote' more than 80,000 documents during his 15 years in power.
- It is a historical myth that Napoleon was unusually short and that his enormous energy and overweening ambition are explained by a need to compensate for his lack of height. At a time when the standard height for adult enrolment in the French army was 5 feet (approximately 150 cm), reduced by 1813 to 4 feet 9 inches (approximately 142 cm), Napoleon at 5 feet 2 inches (approximately 155 cm) was in fact above average height for a Frenchman.

Clan system
A group of people, related in some way, who protect and look after one another.

Key term

- Given that he lived on his nerves Napoleon sometimes became anxious and fearful – especially in crowds, or when called upon to speak in public (which he did very badly). Despite this failing he possessed enormous charisma and inspired fanatical devotion among his closest followers – particularly those soldiers he had commanded.
- From 1807 onwards officials, friends and servants noticed a change in Napoleon, which became more marked after his return from the ill-fated Russian campaign of 1812. Although only 43 in 1812 his previously excellent memory began to decline, he became much more arrogant, more intolerant of others' points of view and more brutally contemptuous of the rest of the human race: 'power comes through fear', he said at this time. He began to put on weight, becoming lethargic and slow, and ageing prematurely into the balding, paunchy figure beloved of cartoonists then and since.

3 | Napoleon and the Early Years of the Revolution 1789–93

Key dates

The storming of the Bastille – usually taken as marking the start of the French Revolution: 14 July 1789

French monarchy overthrown: 10 August 1792

At the age of 16, the newly commissioned Napoleon was posted to the town of Valence in southern France to continue his training as an artillery officer. During this time he studied and read widely, and became particularly interested in history. In 1788 he was sent to Auxonne, one of the best military bases in France, to complete his training. France by this time was in the throes of a deep financial crisis. The King's inability to deal with it created a political crisis which ultimately developed into a revolution. The summoning of the **Estates-General** in 1789, for the first time since 1614, was an indication of the gravity of the crisis. The storming of the Bastille on 14 July 1789 confirmed this. Royal authority by that summer was breaking down across the whole country.

As Louis' hold over the country was weakening, the power of his opponents was increasing. This would have been visible in Paris and other cities, by the large numbers of people wearing the **cockade**, an early symbol of the Revolution. Louis was reluctantly forced to make significant changes in the way France was governed. The most important of these was conceding an elected law-making Assembly. Many who opposed the Revolution left France and sought the help of Austria and Prussia to regain for the King the powers he had lost. France went to war in 1792 to defend its revolution from foreign interference. The disastrous performance of its army and the threat of defeat led to a political crisis in Paris which resulted in the overthrow of the King on 10 August 1792 and the establishment of the first French Republic.

Key terms

Estates-General
Elected representatives from the clergy, nobility and everyone else.

Cockade
A tri-coloured cloth rosette comprising the red and blue of Paris and the white of the uniform of the French guards.

Napoleon, Corsica and the Revolution

Napoleon returned to Corsica in September 1789 on leave, to find the island in turmoil. He joined a political club that was actively supporting the Revolution and worked tirelessly to further both its cause and the interests of his family. The return of

Key question
What impact did the Revolution have on Napoleon?

Paoli to the island after over 20 years of exile was at first widely acclaimed by the Bonapartes, although they did not share in the distribution of offices and favours which the nationalist leader showered on supporters who had been loyal to him during his lengthy absence. In 1791, shortly before returning to his regiment in France, Napoleon became an active member of the newly formed Patriotic Club, which was affiliated to the **left-wing Jacobin club**. When he returned to Valence his younger brother Louis accompanied him, and Napoleon assumed responsibility for his education. As far as Napoleon's political views and loyalties were concerned he was clearly sympathetic to the ideals of the Jacobin club, becoming secretary of the branch in Valence. It is likely that it was at this time that he became an active republican.

Political events back in Corsica were occupying his mind and he was hoping to travel back there in 1792. With war against Austria looming, the only way he could return to the island was if he transferred to the Corsican National Guard and was elected to the rank of Lieutenant-Colonel. This he achieved with some effort.

Key terms

Left wing
A position supporting extreme change to benefit the majority of the population.

Jacobin club
'The Society of the Friends of the Constitution', the most extreme of the political clubs in Paris.

An early portrait of the young Napoleon Bonaparte serving as Lieutenant-Colonel of the first battalion of the Corsican National Guard during the pre-Consul period.

Very shortly after his appointment, he became embroiled in an incident that threatened to damage his career when a riot in Ajaccio got out of hand and resulted in the National Guard laying siege to the town. Napoleon was accused of abusing his position to favour pro-revolutionary groups. Evidence from an inquiry was sent to Paris for consideration and Napoleon decided to travel to the capital to hear the outcome.

Relations between the Bonaparte family and Paoli had not been easy since Carlo Bonaparte's abandonment of the nationalist cause and subsequent collaboration with the French. Increasing disillusionment with Paoli's policies, particularly his hostility to France, led to a deterioration in relations between him and the Bonaparte clan. Napoleon and his family were forced to flee the island for mainland France on 11 June 1793. With their assets seized, the family were penniless refugees who managed to

Key date

Napoleon and his family fled Corsica for the French mainland: 11 June 1793

Napoleon at the siege of Toulon 1793.

survive through the help of some of Napoleon's political friends, especially Cristoforo Saliceti, one of the Corsican deputies to the National Assembly.

The siege of Toulon 1793

Growing hostility to the Republican government, which was perceived to be increasingly under the influence of the Jacobins, prompted many of the towns and regions outside Paris to reject its authority. The **federal revolt**, as it was known, erupted in a number of areas, particularly in central and southern parts of France. Lyon, Marseilles and Toulon all broke away from the control of the central government (see the map on page 4). Republican armies were dispatched to restore order. **Representatives on mission** were attached to these armies to supervise their operations. The situation in the great naval base of Toulon was much more serious than in most other areas because counter-revolutionary forces had handed over control of the port to the British, who entered the war on 1 February 1793.

The occupation of Toulon by the British had the potential to undermine the survival of the Republic. Recapturing the port was essential but this was no easy task given that its fortifications were among the most formidable in Europe. The task of recapturing the port was given to General Carteaux, whose forces started to occupy the surrounding area and began a siege. His army, in common with all those of the Republic, had suffered from the mass emigration of officers who were members of the nobility. It is estimated that between 1789 and 1792 as many as 6000 commissioned officers left the country and joined the ranks of the *émigrés*. This provided plenty of opportunities for able and energetic, but not particularly well-born or well-endowed, career-soldiers to advance rapidly up the ladder of promotion in a way undreamed of during the *ancien régime*.

Napoleon's role in the siege of Toulon

Napoleon's involvement in the siege occurred by chance. When the commander of the artillery was wounded, Napoleon was offered his position on 16 September 1793, by one of the representatives on mission in the area, his friend and fellow Corsican, Saliceti. General Carteaux was not consulted regarding the appointment. The lack of suitable officers, Napoleon's availability and his political connections undoubtedly contributed to his appointment. With the rank of major, he used his enormous energy and great skill as an artillery officer to build up the numbers of guns and resources at his disposal. His grasp of the nature of the terrain and how capturing certain key positions could close the port to the British and render the port worthless to them, was an indication of his considerable technical skill as a soldier. Although the plan to capture the key British position defending the port was not his own he was more than willing to accept all the credit for it. The city finally fell on 19 December 1793. Napoleon's role in recapturing the port was crucial. It advanced his career in a number of ways:

Key question
Why was the recapture of Toulon so important?

Key terms

Federal revolt
The rejection of the authority of the government in Paris in favour of regional authority.

Representatives on mission
Highly placed politicians sent from Paris with the authority of the government to ensure that generals were actively carrying out their orders.

Émigrés
Former members of the aristocracy, royalists and priests who fled France fearing for their safety.

Key question
What role did Napoleon play in the siege of Toulon? What impact did it have on his career?

Key date

Napoleon appointed Commander of Artillery at the siege of Toulon:
16 September 1793

- The skill with which he deployed the artillery to such great effect marked his emergence as an important commander.
- His success at Toulon brought him to the attention of a number of powerful men in Paris.
- His role in the siege was rewarded with his promotion to the rank of Brigadier General in addition to his being appointed commander of the artillery of the Army of Italy.

Key question
Who helped
Napoleon's career
during the period
1793–4?

Friends in high places

In addition to his friendship with Saliceti, Napoleon acquired a number of other powerful friends and allies during this period. His military abilities and staunch commitment to the republican cause marked him out as a soldier whose support was worth cultivating. There were two politicians in particular who supported him at this time. The first was Paul Barras, an influential politician and one of the most powerful representatives on mission in southern France. Napoleon's career was clearly helped by Barras' patronage, and whose former mistress Josephine he would later marry. During this period, Napoleon published many pamphlets which were very sympathetic to the extreme Jacobin government, whose leading figure was Maximilian Robespierre. This brought him to the notice of Augustine Robespierre, Maximilian's brother. In a letter to his brother, Augustine mentioned favourably the young soldier:

> I add to the names of patriots I have already mentioned citizen Buonoparte, general in command of artillery, a man of transcendent merit. He is Corsican, and brings me the simple guarantee of a man of that country who resisted the blandishments of Paoli and whose property has been destroyed by that traitor.

Napoleon and the Terror

By the summer of 1794 the authority of the Republic had been restored over most of France and its armies were poised to take the offensive against its external enemies. The system of Revolutionary government (or Jacobin dictatorship as opponents labelled it) that had secured these victories is known as **the Terror**. With republican authority restored, many were questioning the need for the highly centralised and ruthless system that was governing the country. In the **coup d'état** of **Thermidor**, 27–8 July 1794, Robespierre and his closest allies (including his brother) were overthrown and executed. As someone who was closely identified with the Jacobins, Napoleon was arrested and briefly imprisoned. That Napoleon was able to survive the overthrow of the Jacobins says a great deal about his political skills and the shortage of talented soldiers in the republican armies at this time.

In May 1795 Napoleon was ordered to assume command of the artillery, attached to the Army of the West, which was engaged in suppressing the **Vendée rebellion**. He viewed fighting internal rebels as beneath his abilities and refused to take up the post. The consequence of such a flagrant disobeying of orders was his

Key terms

The Terror
A ruthless system of government created by the Jacobins between 1793 and 1794 to defeat the enemies of the Republic.

Coup d'état
Overthrowing a government and seizing power.

Thermidor
One of the months in the new Revolutionary calendar, 9 July–17 August.

Vendée rebellion
Anti-republican revolt covering several departments in western France including the Vendée.

removal from the list of active officers. His whole career appeared in jeopardy and he even contemplated offering his services to the **Ottoman Empire**. That his career was rescued owed a great deal to being in the right place at the right time and the powerful friends he had in high places.

4 | Napoleon and the Directory

With the overthrow of the Jacobins, there was a return to a less extreme system of government. In 1795, a new and more moderate Constitution was adopted. It aimed to secure the position of the *bourgeoisie* over all other groups in the political life of the nation. This was to be achieved in the following ways:

- ensuring that political power was in the hands of the propertied classes who paid high levels of taxes
- heading up the government with an **executive** of five Directors
- having a two-chamber legislature comprising the Councils of Five Hundred and a Council of Ancients.

These arrangements were intended to prevent a dictatorship, as no single person or body had overall control of the state. The new system was characterised by a series of conflicts and disputes. While the Directory, which lasted for four years, was the longest lasting regime of the First Republic, it failed to deal with the deep divisions in French society that were a legacy of the early years of the Revolution. The most significant of these divisions were religious (those for or against the Catholic Church), social (between the poor and the rich middle and upper classes) and political (republicans and royalists).

The Vendémiaire uprising 1795

From the very outset the new regime was faced by opponents on the left and **the right**, who wished to overthrow it. Its response when confronted with opposition was to ignore the will of the people and resort to force. Faced with a royalist uprising in Paris between 1 and 5 October 1795, the Directory was determined to use all methods available to preserve order. The Commander of the Army of the Interior, General Menou, was dismissed because of his reluctance to open fire on the rioters. Barras assumed control of the situation. He appealed for any officers in the city without postings to come to the aid of the government.

Napoleon, who had been removed from the army list, immediately answered the call and Barras made him one of his commanders. Once again he proved to be in the right place at the right time. The decisive incident in the crisis was the killing of a large number of rebels, possibly by **grapeshot**, in the narrow streets near the Church of Saint-Roche. It is generally asserted that Napoleon gave the order to fire on the rebels with devastating effect – possibly 400 were killed. Whether or not he delivered the 'whiff of grapeshot' on the rebels is unclear. What is clear is that he took the credit for it, and when his friend Barras was appointed one of the Directors, Napoleon was promoted to

The Vendémiaire Uprising, an engraving by Louis Blanc (1811–82). The artillery commanded by Napoleon open fire on a crowd near the Church of Saint-Roche.

Command the Army of the Interior. At the age of 26, without ever commanding a significant force on a battlefield, Napoleon found himself in charge of the largest army in France. His ascent had been nothing short of meteoric, but he was not entirely satisfied with his new role. Napoleon's eyes were very firmly set on a field command and the one he had in his sight was the Army of Italy.

Marriage and war 1796

Napoleon was compelled to bide his time to gain command of a fighting army. As commander of the Army of the Interior he was active in suppressing the Jacobin Club, whose politics he now rejected. It was during this time that he met and fell in love with Josephine de Beauharnais, the widow of a republican politician and soldier who had been executed in 1794. She was seven years older than Napoleon and well known in Parisian society. They married on 9 March 1796.

Napoleon's desire to prove himself on the battlefield was well known to his political masters in the Directory. Despite the fact that his duties were confined to securing the Republic from its internal enemies, this did not stop him from commenting on the campaign that was taking place rather ineffectually in Italy. He was particularly critical of the commander in charge of the campaign, General Scherer. There were three decisive factors that led the Minister of War, Carnot, to appoint Napoleon on 2 March 1796 to Command the Army in Italy, following Scherer's resignation:

Key question
How did Napoleon come to command the Army in Italy?

Key dates

Napoleon appointed Commander of the Army in Italy: 2 March 1796

Napoleon married Josephine de Beauharnais: 9 March 1796

- The support of Napoleon's friend Saliceti, who had been sent to visit the army and report on its position. Saliceti argued convincingly that Napoleon be appointed.
- Napoleon's knowledge of the area obtained from a number of postings and missions following the siege of Toulon.
- Napoleon's confidence that he could reverse the fortunes of what was to all intents and purposes a dispirited army whose morale was at rock-bottom.

When Napoleon arrived to take up his command, he discovered an army made up of both experienced professional soldiers and Revolutionary volunteers. Not only was morale low but the attitude among many was also mutinous. Over the following years Napoleon was able to reverse the fortunes of this army, which says a great deal about his powers of leadership and great abilities as a commander. His position as Commander of the Army of Italy laid the foundation of his military reputation and paved the way for his own political ambitions. (For an account of the campaign in Italy see pages 79–83.)

Disillusionment with the Directory

During the next two years, Napoleon's standing rose dramatically as his Italian army won a series of impressive victories. Following a treaty with Austria (see page 82) in 1797, he returned to Paris. His status was in marked contrast to the standing of the Directory, which became increasingly discredited as it resorted to illegal means to cancel election results it did not agree with. During the **coup of Fructidor** in September 1797, Napoleon helped Barras to expel the recently elected right-wing royalist majority. The following year, 1798, the Directors once again resorted to military support and annulled that year's elections because they produced a left-wing Jacobin majority. Napoleon was becoming increasingly suspicious of the motives of the Directors and disillusioned with their approaches to government. In addition, he was concerned that plans to invade Britain appeared to have stalled.

Napoleon proposed an alternative scheme to undermine Britain by disrupting its trade route with India, thereby inflicting damage to its economy. His plan was to take an army to the eastern Mediterranean where the Ottoman Empire had territory in what is now modern-day Egypt and Syria. The Directors backed his campaign, and were probably relieved that such an ambitious and popular general would be out of the country. Napoleon set off for Egypt on 19 May 1798. After initial successes the campaign failed, leading to his abandonment of the army and his return to France in 1799. (For an account of the campaign see pages 83–5.) Back in France, he now became much more directly involved in the politics of the Directory and ultimately helped bring about its overthrow during the **coup of Brumaire**, 9–10 November 1799.

Key question
How did Napoleon's relations with the Directory change?

Key terms

Coup of Fructidor
Napoleon deployed the army on behalf of Barras to expel newly elected royalists from the Assembly.

Coup of Brumaire
Brought about the overthrow of the Directory.

Key dates

Napoleon set out on a military expedition to Egypt: 19 May 1798

Coup of Brumaire: 9–10 November 1799

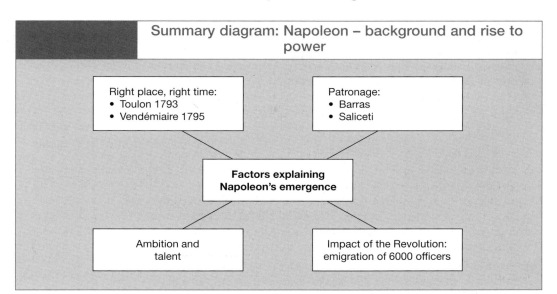

Summary diagram: Napoleon – background and rise to power

Right place, right time:
- Toulon 1793
- Vendémiaire 1795

Patronage:
- Barras
- Saliceti

Factors explaining Napoleon's emergence

Ambition and talent

Impact of the Revolution: emigration of 6000 officers

Study Guide: AS Question

In the style of OCR

How far do you agree that Napoleon's rise in the years to 1799 was due primarily to the influence of Barras?

Exam tips

The cross-references are intended to take you straight to the material that will help you to answer the question.

The instruction 'How far …?' tells you how to approach the question – you must weigh up the evidence one way and then the other before coming to an informed judgement. To score high marks, your argument and your judgement must be backed up with evidence (if they are not, your essay will be only a list of assertions).

Barras' importance is to be seen in his active patronage in 1793–4 and especially from 1795 after the Vendémiaire uprising – perhaps most notably in his securing for Napoleon command of the Army of the Interior. Against that, there is a range of evidence that could be used, for example:

- Napoleon's other important patrons (page 11)
- Napoleon's own military ability (especially from Toulon onwards) (page 10)
- Napoleon's own ambition (political as well as military) (page 6)
- Napoleon's luck – surviving the *coup* of Thermidor, his disobedience over the Vendée, his failure in Egypt (pages 11 and 83–5).

Avoid a straight 'yes he was/no he wasn't' type of answer. A good answer always looks to identify and explain complexities. You might argue that Barras' help was very important in launching Napoleon, but that in the key period from 1796 he was no longer the core influence, for example Barras did not secure Napoleon command of the Army of Italy. Further, once in Italy, it was Napoleon who made his own name. Napoleon himself had to have the talent – to deliver victory after victory, and to get himself noticed.

The *Coup* of Brumaire 1799

POINTS TO CONSIDER

The event that brought Napoleon into power and overthrew the Directory was the *coup* of Brumaire. This transformed his career from that of a successful republican general into a major political leader. Brumaire paved the way for Napoleon's domination of France and led to the establishment of his empire. These events are considered by looking at a number of themes:

- The political background to the *coup* of Brumaire and why it occurred
- The events of the *coup* of Brumaire
- Why was the *coup* of Brumaire successful?

Key dates

1795	August 22	Constitution of Year III
	October 1	Royalist Vendémiaire uprising
1796	March 26	Napoleon assumed command of the Army of Italy
1798	May 11	*Coup d'état* of Floréal
	May 19	Napoleon set sail for Egypt
1799	October 9	Napoleon landed at Fréjus
	November 9	Start of the *coup* of Brumaire
	November 10	Councils met at Saint-Cloud and abdicated power

1 | The Political Background to the *Coup* of Brumaire

Establishing the Directory

Key question
Why was the Terror introduced?

Following the overthrow of the monarchy in August 1792, France became a republic. The subsequent trial and execution of Louis XVI alarmed the other major powers in Europe and the war which France had been involved in since 1792 was extended. By the summer of 1793, the Republic was confronted by significant internal and external opposition. There was a strong possibility that it would be defeated. In order to prevent this, the government waged a policy of repression against its internal opponents while at the same time preparing the country to defeat its external enemies. Between 1793 and the summer of 1794, the

Terror was organised by the Committee of Public Safety (CPS), whose key figure was the Jacobin politician Maximilian Robespierre.

By the summer of 1794, the Republic had defeated most of its internal enemies. The crisis facing the army, which had seen the emigration of 6000 officers from noble families, provided opportunities for soldiers from humble backgrounds to be promoted. It was during the Terror that Napoleon came to the attention of prominent politicians in Paris, such as Paul Barras and Augustine Robespierre (Maximilian's brother). His role in the siege of Toulon marked him out as an ambitious and able officer who fully supported the Republic (see pages 10–11). During this phase of his career he was a firm supporter of the Jacobins. Through a combination of good fortune and good connections Napoleon was able to survive the overthrow of Robespierre. In the reaction following Thermidor, Napoleon as a staunch Jacobin was arrested, and thrown into prison. After two weeks behind bars he was released on the orders of his friend Saliceti.

The *coup* of Thermidor which overthrew Robespierre also marked the end of government by Terror. It occurred for a number of reasons:

- Robespierre's opponents believed that he wanted to create a new religion – the Cult of the Supreme Being.
- Moderate republicans considered that the Terror had achieved its aim of preserving the Republic from the threats posed by its internal and external enemies.
- There was no longer any need for the repressive laws passed by the CPS.
- The *bourgeoisie* were alarmed with the influence the **sans-culottes** appeared to have over the CPS.

During the Thermidorian reaction that followed the *coup*, there was a wave of violence against those who had supported the Terror. Many of the policies of the CPS had been influenced by their working-class supporters, the *sans-culottes*. Following Thermidor, the property-owning *bourgeoisie*, who had been marginalised during the Terror, sought to reassert their control over the Republic. They aimed to do this by drawing up a new and more moderate Constitution. The Constitution of Year III was approved on 22 August 1795. One of its central aims was to secure the position of the *bourgeoisie* over all other groups in the political life of the nation. This was to be achieved by ensuring that political power was in the hands of the propertied classes who paid high levels of taxes.

The Constitution of Year III

The main features of the new Constitution were:

- The government was headed by an executive of five Directors who had no control over legislation.
- Law-making powers were granted to two councils.

Key term
Sans-culottes
Working-class people living in towns and cities.

Key date
Constitution of Year III: 22 August 1795

Key question
What were the main features of the Constitution of Year III?

- The first of these councils, the Five Hundred, could initiate legislation but not vote on it. They could then send it on for consideration to the second council.
- The second council was known as the Ancients (250 men all aged at least 40), who could not discuss any proposed laws, merely accept or reject them.
- The Directors could not insist that the Councils pass a particular law, nor could they veto any laws that they did pass. They could not dissolve the Councils.
- Every year one-third of the members had to retire and stand for re-election.
- Each Director would hold office for five years, although one, chosen by lot, would have to retire every year.

Napoleon and the Vendémiaire uprising

Key question
What led to the Vendémiaire uprising and what was Napoleon's role in it?

Key term
Conventionnels
Members of the Convention between 1792 and 1795.

Key date
Royalist Vendémiaire uprising: 1 October 1795

The new Constitution was intended to prevent dictatorship, by ensuring that no single person or body was in overall control of French political life. However, the new structure led to a series of political conflicts and disillusion among many and paved the way for its overthrow. Having drawn up the new Constitution, the members of the Convention argued that there ought to be a measure of continuity between it and the new assemblies. To ensure this, they passed a law that preserved two-thirds of the seats in the new legislature for members of the old Convention. While the *conventionnels* argued that this would preserve continuity, opponents saw this as a cynical attempt to hang on to power. Royalists in particular were incensed at the law of the two-thirds. Their opposition led to the Vendémiaire uprising on 1 October 1795. Napoleon, who was in Paris, assisted the government in its attempts to maintain order (see pages 12–13). His reward for helping to suppress the Vendémiaire uprising was to be given command of the Army of the Interior.

Methods used by the Directory to maintain power

Key question
How and why did the Directory ignore the will of the people between 1795 and 1799?

The Directory, which lasted for four years from 1795 to 1799, was the longest lasting regime of the First Republic, yet it failed to deal with the deep divisions in French society that were a legacy of the early years of the Revolution. The most significant of these were:

- the hostility between supporters of the Catholic Church and those citizens who were anti-clerical
- differences in society between the poor, mainly urban, *sans-culottes* and the richer property-owning *bourgeoisie*
- political divisions between those who were passionately committed to the Republic and those royalists who favoured a restoration of the monarchy.

Almost immediately following its establishment, the Directory showed its determination to resist opposition, by force when necessary, when it used the army to put down the royalist Vendémiaire uprising in the autumn of 1795. Napoleon's willingness to support the Directory with his artillery raised his standing with the politicians in Paris. They considered him a reliable and trusty general who could be called upon to support the government with force, as and when the need arose. It appeared that when confronted with opposition, from either the right (royalist) or the left (Jacobin), the Directors were willing to resort to unconstitutional methods to secure majorities in the Councils. The army was used in 1797 in a *coup* to expel the newly elected royalist majority. Although Napoleon was in Italy, he sent the pro-Jacobin General Augereau to Paris to defend the three ex-Jacobin Directors from royalist elements in the legislative councils. When elections in 1798 produced significant numbers of Jacobin deputies, the Directors on 11 May 1798, during the *coup d'état* of Floréal, appealed once more for military support and annulled that year's elections. Once again it seemed that the Directors were showing their contempt for the wishes of the electors.

Key dates

Coup d'état of Floréal – Jacobin deputies excluded from the Council:
11 May 1798

Napoleon assumed command of the Army of Italy: 26 March 1796

Napoleon and the Army of the Orient set sail for Egypt: 19 May 1798

Napoleon during the Directory

It was during the Directory that Napoleon was able to enhance further his military reputation and commitment to maintaining the survival of the Republic. Following the Vendémiaire uprising, he was rewarded with promotion and on 26 March 1796 assumed command of the Army of Italy (see pages 79–83). His great success in reversing the fortunes of a demoralised and ill-equipped army in the Italian peninsula, to a point where they were able to defeat the Austrians and negotiate a peace, marked him out as one of the ablest and most popular of the Republic's generals. On his return to France, he was given the task of supervising the invasion of England, although his own inclination was to attack Egypt. Napoleon managed to persuade the Directors of the advantages of disrupting British trade in the Mediterranean, and also the possibility of attacking the most important part of Britain's empire – India. For their part, the Directors were quite willing to support the venture as it guaranteed Napoleon's removal from France where his mounting popularity was a potential threat to their own survival. He set sail for Egypt on 19 May 1798.

Key question
What did Napoleon do during the Directory and how did it contribute to his development?

The Egyptian campaign proved to be a mixed blessing for Napoleon (see Chapter 3, pages 83–5). While it added to his reputation as the best known of the Republic's generals, who was now involved in an exotic campaign in the Orient, his military reputation had been damaged. There was no escaping the fact that he had abandoned the army in Egypt to return to France with a view to pursuing a political career.

When the Directory was established, Napoleon was a relatively unknown artillery officer who, following his role in the siege of Toulon, was ascending the promotional ladder. Four years later in 1799, on the eve of the Directory's overthrow, he was the best known of the First Republic's generals. It was during this important period that he learnt a number of lessons that would help him later in his career. These were:

- The great value of self-publicity and self-promotion. Whenever an opportunity presented itself for enhancing his reputation, he seized it. Regular dispatches were sent back to France from Italy and then Egypt, publicising his military achievements (and glossing over any setbacks). Enormous quantities of looted art were sent back to France for public display – all courtesy of Napoleon.
- As a general, he realised the value of ensuring the loyalty of his men and he sought to maintain their support by promising that their material interests while campaigning would ultimately be rewarded.
- Belief in his own destiny. Napoleon possessed enormous drive and energy. He also came to believe that he alone could rescue France.
- As a general on active service in foreign theatres, he was able to develop and perfect his military tactics, which helped to make him one of the greatest soldiers of his generation.
- Following the expulsion of Austrian forces from northern Italy he established himself as the virtual ruler of the territories under the control of his forces. It was during this time that he deliberately set himself apart from his other commanders and started to adopt the traits of a ruler.

Table 1: Uprisings and *coups d'état* 1794–9

Year	Event	Cause
1794	*Coup* of Thermidor	Overthrow of Robespierre
1795	Vendémiaire uprising	Royalists try to overthrow Assembly
1797	*Coup* of Fructidor	Royalists expelled from Assembly
1798	*Coup* of Floréal	Jacobin deputies expelled from Council
1799	*Coup* of Prairial	Removal of ineffective Directors
1799	*Coup* of Brumaire	Overthrow of the Directory

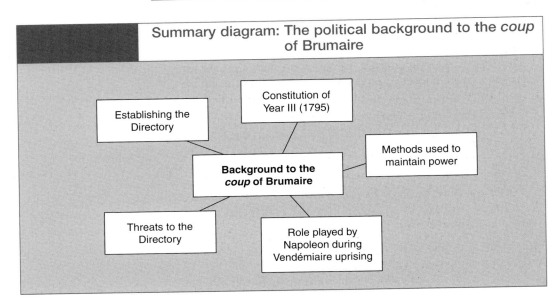

Summary diagram: The political background to the *coup* of Brumaire

2 | The Events of the *Coup* of Brumaire

The condition of France, early 1799

The year 1799 would prove to be a momentous one for
Napoleon, France and Europe, albeit in differing ways. As far as
France was concerned the year started off badly. There were a
number of problems:

Key question
What was the political
situation in France
during the early part
of 1799?

- The re-emergence of a powerful anti-French alliance – the
  Second Coalition in 1799, partly due to Napoleon's Egyptian
  campaign. Tsar Paul of Russia was particularly incensed when
  Napoleon seized Malta. Paul considered himself as the
  protector of the Knights of St John who occupied the island.
  Austria, the Ottoman Empire, Naples, Portugal and Britain
  made up the other members of the alliance.
- By early 1799 French forces had suffered a number of defeats
  in Germany, Switzerland and Italy.
- In southern and western parts of France there were a number
  of uprisings among local people against conscription. As many
  were farmers they did not want to leave their farms to join the
  army.
- The 1799 elections once again showed the unpopularity of the
  Directory. Only 66 of the 187 government candidates were
  elected. Among the rest were about 50 Jacobins, including
  some who had been purged during Floréal.
- The Directory's inability to deal with the economic, political
  and military crises that it faced led to the purge of three of the
  Directors in the **coup** of Prairial (18 June 1799). Significantly, a
  leading role in the *coup* was played by Napoleon's younger
  brother Lucien, who was a member of the Council of the Five
  Hundred.

Key terms

Coup **of Prairial**
The removal of two
Directors who were
considered to be
ineffective.

Draconian measure
A severe or extreme
law or policy.

With the Republic once again under severe threat, a number of
draconian measures were introduced to try and restore the
military, political and economic situations. These were:

- A forced loan from the rich which was intended to raise
  100 million *livres*.
- Law of Hostages – passed on 12 July 1799. Any areas resisting
  the government's laws could be declared 'disturbed'.
  Authorities in those areas were then given the power to arrest
  relatives of *émigrés*, nobles or rebels, who could be imprisoned,
  fined and their property confiscated to pay for the damage
  done by those causing the disturbances.
- Jourdan's Law – proposed the reintroduction of conscription
  with the aim of raising more than 400,000 men for the army.
  Of the first draft of 230,000 conscripts only 74,000 reached the
  armies. Most men either ignored the call or left their home
  areas to avoid the draft.

These measures appeared to be a return to the arbitrary arrests
and harassment of the Terror of Year II (1793–4). Yet, by
November, only 10 million *livres* of the forced loan had been
collected. Although conscription was planned to raise 400,000

troops, there was widespread resistance as there had been in 1793 and only 248,000 men eventually joined the army. Many became draft-dodgers or joined the royalist rebels to avoid being called up. The Law of Hostages was hardly ever applied because of opposition from local officials.

The Directory in the provinces

Key question
How effective was the authority of the Directory in the provinces?

By the summer of 1799 government administration in the provinces was in a state of virtual collapse. There were many reasons for this:

Key terms

Non-juring priests
Priests who refused to take the oath to the Civil Constitution of the Clergy.

Brigandage
Outbreaks of lawlessness and violence by armed groups of bandits.

- The Directory could not persuade local notables to accept office and were able to call on few loyal troops to enforce their decrees.
- Local authorities were often taken over by royalists who refused to levy forced loans, persecute **non-juring priests** or catch deserters.
- The National Guard was not large enough to keep order in the absence of regular troops, so substantial areas of the countryside were not policed at all.
- Government commissioners were killed as quickly as they were replaced.

The result of this administrative collapse was **brigandage**. By the autumn of 1799 there was civil war in the Ardèche region in southern France (see the map on page 4).

The return of Napoleon

Key question
How was Napoleon greeted on his return from Egypt?

Despite the many difficulties which he had faced during the Egyptian campaign, as far as the French public were concerned the numerous dispatches which he had sent back to France served only to enhance his reputation in the country. With France once again in crisis and the Directory largely blamed for it, Napoleon's return was greeted by many as that of a saviour. Napoleon left Egypt and abandoned his army on 23 August and set foot once again on French soil at Fréjus on 9 October 1799. On his way to Paris he was welcomed with enthusiasm by crowds who gathered everywhere he went. There were ecstatic popular demonstrations at Avignon and Aix as he progressed towards Paris. The civilian population knew of his past victories in Italy and Egypt and greeted him as a hero, while the army hailed him as the leader needed to overthrow a weak government of which they were tired and that had lost touch with its revolutionary roots. He wrote later of his triumphal journey to Paris:

Key date
Napoleon landed at Fréjus following his return from Egypt:
9 October 1799

> The joy was universal. It was not like the return of a citizen to his country or a general at the head of a victorious army, but like the triumph of a sovereign restored to his people. The people seemed to say, We want a leader to direct us; we now behold him and our glory will once more shine forth. I was … resolved to possess myself of authority and restore France to her former glory.

Planning the *coup*

Clear tensions were emerging within the Directory. One of the newly chosen Directors – Sieyès (see profile below) – decided to plan a *coup* aimed at strengthening the executive at the expense of the more unpredictable legislative assembly. Once again, it was decided to make use of the army. The plotters began looking for a popular and successful general who could organise the military support they needed to force through changes in the constitution, and who would be willing to retire gracefully from political life afterwards. Although he was not their first or even second choice, they eventually settled on Napoleon as a suitable candidate and he was recruited to the ranks of the conspirators. The selection, though, did not turn out to be what they expected – or wanted. Napoleon was chosen for the following reasons:

- His 'Jacobin' background made him appear a safe general as he was not a royalist.
- His military disasters had occurred far away in Egypt; in Europe he was seen as a successful general who commanded the loyalty of all who had served under him.
- His military record to date did not appear to suggest that he might be a general with political ambitions.

Key questions
Why was it decided to plan a *coup*? How did Napoleon become involved in the plot?

Profile: Abbé Emmanuel Sieyès 1748–1836

1748 – Born in Fréjus into a *bourgeois* family
1773 – Ordained as a priest
1787 – Elected as a clerical representative at the provincial Assembly of Orleans, where he was particularly interested in issues relating to taxation, agriculture and poor relief
1789 – Published a highly influential pamphlet *What is the Third Estate?*, in which he argued that it was the most important part of the nation
Represented the Third Estate of Paris in the Estates-General
Drew up the Tennis Court Oath and contributed to the Declaration of the Rights of Man
1792 – Elected to the Convention and voted for the King's execution but took no active part in the Terror
1793 – Following Thermidor he served on the **Committee of Public Safety**
1794 – Elected to the Council of 500
1798 – Appointed ambassador to Berlin
1799 – Elected Director and plotted the *coup* of Brumaire with Bonaparte. Left public office during the Napoleonic Empire and retired from public life

Committee of Public Safety Effectively, the government of France during 1793–4 and one of the twin pillars of the Terror along with the Committee of General Security. — Key term

Sieyès was one of the main constitutional planners of the revolutionary period. When asked what he had done during the Terror he declared 'I survived'. He helped to draw up the constitutions linked with the Revolution and was one of its most influential political thinkers.

Key questions
What was the plan for the *coup*? What role was Napoleon to play in the *coup*?

Key dates

Start of the *coup* of Brumaire:
9 November 1799

Councils met at Saint-Cloud and abdicated power: 10 November 1799

Key terms

Anarchists
In the context of the Revolution those who wished to create chaos and disorder.

Saint-Cloud
A royal palace on the outskirts of Paris.

Events of the *coup*

Once in Paris, Napoleon had a series of secret meetings with Sieyès, to discuss tactics. By early November, detailed preparations were complete for a *coup* to introduce a new Constitution. A meeting of the Council of Ancients was to be called early on the morning of 9 November 1799 at which the members would be 'persuaded' that there was a plot by **anarchists** and foreigners to destroy the Republic. They would then agree that the government's only safety lay in moving themselves and the Council of the Five Hundred out of Paris into the suburbs once again. The command of the Paris garrison of some 8000 troops and the government defence force of 1500 grenadiers would be given to Napoleon. He would then be able to 'take all measures necessary for the safety of the nation's representatives', who 'in the shelter of his protecting arms may discuss peacefully the changes which the public interest renders necessary'.

The Ancients met as arranged and, after agreeing to the move from Paris, summoned Napoleon before them to swear a prepared oath of loyalty to the government. When he arrived at the council chamber, he made a speech instead, concluding with the words: 'What we want is a republic founded on true liberty, civil liberty and national representations; and we are going to have it. I swear it, in my name and in that of my comrades in arms.' Despite not being exactly what they had asked for, the Ancients accepted these words and allowed Napoleon to leave. Once outside the building, he harangued his troops with the same words as he had used to the Ancients and issued an Order of the Day expressing his belief that the army would support him 'with the energy, steadfastness and confidence' that he had always found in it before.

Napoleon at Saint-Cloud

Key question
What was Napoleon's role in the events that took place at Saint-Cloud?

The following day, 10 November 1799, after considerable delays in finding suitable furnishings for the makeshift council chambers hastily prepared in the palace of **Saint-Cloud**, the Ancients and the Five Hundred began their deliberations just after noon. News soon reached them that all the Directors had either resigned or were under arrest, and that, without an executive, the Directory was, therefore, at an end. The way was open for the deputies to set up a new, provisional government. As the meetings of the two Councils continued without any decisions being reached, Napoleon, waiting in an outer room, became impatient. Without warning, and uninvited, he burst into the Council of the Ancients and began to speak.

Exactly what happened next is disputed. Napoleon's secretary, declared that 'he made no speech to the Ancients unless a conversation held without nobility and without dignity can be called a speech. Only a few words could be heard, "brothers-in-arms", "plain-speaking of a soldier" … repeating several times "That is all I have to say to you" – and he was saying nothing'. The official version of the speech, probably provided by

Napoleon and the Council of Five Hundred at Saint-Cloud, an engraving by Bouchot c1860.

Napoleon himself, and published the following day, was very different. Far from the 'incoherent babbling' usually attributed to him on this occasion by historians, he was represented as delivering a reasoned and statesmanlike account of his part in events to date. He denied that he was an intriguer or a political opportunist, urged the Ancients 'to act in saving liberty, saving equality', and promised that when this was done he would act as 'nothing more than the arm to support what you have established'. The report continued:

> Yesterday I was staying quietly in Paris, when I was summoned by you to provide military support for the transfer to Saint-Cloud. Now I am attacked as a new **Caesar** … and there is talk of a military government. But I am only acting through and for you. The Republic has **abdicated** – the Directors have resigned or are under police protection – the Five Hundred is at sixes and sevens. Everything depends on the Ancients …
>
> I am not an intriguer: you know me well enough for that: I think I have given sufficient pledges of my devotion to my country. If I am a traitor it is for each of you to be a **Brutus**. But if anyone calls for

Key terms

Caesar
A reference to the Roman general Julius Caesar, who seized power in ancient Rome and was considered by many a military dictator.

Abdicated
Gave up power.

Brutus
One of Julius Caesar's assassins.

my outlawry, then the thunderbolt of war shall crush him.
Remember that I march hand in hand with the god of fortune and
of war!

Napoleon was not an effective public speaker and the printed
report probably represents what he afterwards wished he had
said, rather than what was actually said.

Leaving the Ancients to continue their debate, Napoleon,
accompanied by four grenadiers, went to where a stormy meeting
of the Five Hundred was being held. The Jacobin majority was
arguing fiercely against a proposal that the Directory should be
replaced by a stronger executive body when Napoleon entered
the room. Again it is not clear exactly what happened, as there
are once more a number of conflicting accounts. However, it
seems that many of the Five Hundred suspected Napoleon of
plotting to make himself military ruler of France under a new
constitution forced through the Councils with the help of the
army. Napoleon was immediately greeted with cries of 'Outlaw
the dictator'. This was a dangerous development, for if a **decree
of outlawry** were agreed, it would mean summary execution by a
firing squad.

The role of Lucien Bonaparte

The recently appointed president of the Five Hundred,
Napoleon's brother, Lucien Bonaparte, was unable to quell the
disorder that immediately broke out in the chamber, or to prevent
the demand that a debate be held on the proposed outlawry.
Meanwhile, after being much jostled and roughly handled by
some of the deputies, Napoleon was rescued by the four
grenadiers who managed to escort him to safety outside to the
courtyard where other soldiers were waiting. Once there, pale and
shaken, near fainting and incapable of action, he could say only 'I
simply went to inform the deputies of the means of saving the
Republic, but they answered me with dagger-blows', pointing to
his face that had a slight smear of blood, probably made
accidentally by his own finger nails. This theme of the daggers
was quickly taken up by Lucien, who had hurried from the
Council to join his brother:

> The president declares that the vast majority of the Council is for
> the moment living in terror of several representatives with **stilettos**
> … confronting their colleagues with the most dreadful threats.
> These brigands are no longer representatives of the people, but of
> the dagger. The Five Hundred is dissolved.

Lucien then staged a dramatic scene for the benefit of the waiting
troops. After denouncing 'the minority of assassins' among the
deputies, he drew his sword and swore to kill his brother with it if
Napoleon ever threatened the liberty of the French people. He
then called on the army to follow their general and 'employ force
against these disturbers'. Napoleon, now recovered from his
fright, ordered the soldiers to advance against the Five Hundred.

Key terms

Decree of outlawry
Anyone accused of
outlawry could be
immediately
arrested and
summarily executed
without a trial.

Stiletto
A dagger with a
very thin blade.

Key question
What role did Lucien
Bonaparte play in the
coup of Brumaire?

A contemporary British cartoon depicting Napoleon as a crowned crocodile.

Led by an officer shouting 'Kick them all out', the men marched with fixed bayonets, and to the sound of a drum the Five Hundred were driven out of the room in less than five minutes, many of them escaping through the windows. When the Ancients heard what had happened, they quickly agreed to the formal abolition of the Directory, the creation of a three-man executive, and the replacement of the two legislative Councils by two provisional Standing Committees of 25 members each.

By evening, according to a contemporary account, 'the agitators, intimidated, had dispersed and gone away' while 'others [of the Five Hundred] protected now from the [dagger] blows, came freely back to the Council room, and propositions necessary to the safety of the public were heard'. Under the chairmanship of the tireless Lucien, 'The salutary resolution which is to become the new and provisional law of the Republic was discussed and prepared' by a **rump** of 100 or so deputies. This 'Law of Brumaire', in addition to accepting the proposals of the Ancients, named as the three provisional **consuls** Sieyès, the nonentity Ducos (another former Director), and Napoleon.

On the 11 November 1799 the three Consuls issued the following Proclamation to justify their action.

The Constitution of Year III (1795) was dying. It was incapable of protecting your rights, even of protecting itself. Through repeated assaults it was losing beyond recall the respect of nations. Selfish factions were despoiling the Republic. France was entering the last stage of general disorganisation. But patriots have made themselves heard. All who can harm you have been cast aside. All who can serve you, all those representatives who have remained pure have come together under the banner of liberty … Frenchmen,

Key terms

Rump
A group of sympathetic deputies who remained after the others had been expelled or had fled.

Consul
The title given to the three new executive members.

the Republic strengthened and restored to that rank in Europe which should never have been lost, will realise all the hopes of her citizens and will accomplish her glorious destiny. Swear with us the oath which we have taken, to be faithful to the Republic, one and indivisible, founded on equality, liberty and the representative system.

The *coup* was over. The Napoleonic era was about to begin.

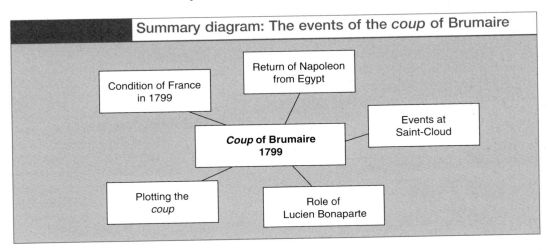

Summary diagram: The events of the *coup* of Brumaire

- Condition of France in 1799
- Return of Napoleon from Egypt
- **Coup of Brumaire 1799**
- Events at Saint-Cloud
- Plotting the *coup*
- Role of Lucien Bonaparte

3 | Why was the *Coup* of Brumaire Successful?

Key question
What was de Tocqueville's interpretation of the *coup* of Brumaire?

Over the years there has been much analysis of the *coup* of Brumaire. One of the best known is by the famous nineteenth-century French historian Alexis de Tocqueville, who wrote that it was 'One of the worst conceived and worst conducted *coups* imaginable, which succeeded only by virtue of the all powerful nature of its causes – the state of mind of the public and the disposition of the army.' To what extent was de Tocqueville right in this judgement and were there any other factors at work in helping to explain the success of the *coup*?

The *coup* was certainly a confused affair, in terms of both its organisation and its execution. While there was agreement between the two central figures beforehand on their political aims, in reality this was more apparent than real. Sieyès said afterwards that he had intended Napoleon to destroy the Directory and then quietly withdraw, leaving the field clear for him to take control at the head of a new executive. Napoleon later admitted that in the days before the *coup*, he had promised that Sieyès' own 'wordy constitution would be put into effect'. It seems unlikely that he made such a promise without being offered something in return; but he never admitted it. The following are the main factors that can be identified in explaining the success of the *coup*.

The roles of Sieyès and Napoleon

It is possible that Sieyès wanted a *coup* that would bring about change by peaceful means, and strengthen the executive without disturbing a system where the *bourgeoisie* dominated political life. Events on 18 Brumaire went in accordance with Sieyès' plans and represent the first act of the *coup*, with him in charge. There was no public reaction and all was quiet in the capital that night. Sieyès was confident that the Councils would agree to his proposals in the morning, but delays in starting the meetings gave the opposition group in the Five Hundred time to formulate their objections to changes in the constitution. This, combined with Napoleon's impatience for action, changed the whole nature of the *coup* and marked the beginning of its second act, with Napoleon in charge. Did Napoleon intend all along to seize control of events? It seems probable that he did. His triumphal progress through France on his return from Egypt, his speeches at the time, and his later assertion that, during the weeks of discussion before the *coup*, he was always following 'the interest of his own plans', all suggest it.

Key question
What were the respective roles of Sieyès and Napoleon in the *coup*?

The state of public opinion towards the end of 1799

Alexis de Tocqueville wrote that 'the state of mind of the public' was a prime cause of the *coup*'s success. Opinions are divided about the condition of France at the end of 1799. At one time, it was fashionable to accept unquestioningly that France was socially and economically at a very low ebb towards the end of the 1790s. Roads were like 'ploughed fields', travel was dangerous because of robbers. Everywhere there was poverty and depravity resulting from a widespread decline in trade and industry and a breakdown of law and order. With royalist risings in the west causing civil war at home and the armies of the Second Coalition threatening an invasion of France, there was defeatist talk of a Bourbon **restoration** and an accompanying fear that the achievements of the Revolution would be destroyed. This ultra gloomy picture is now largely discredited for it is known to have been based on reports sent in to Napoleon by his newly appointed officials in the provinces. *The Great Survey of Year IX* and numerous pamphlets, such as *The State of France at the end of Year VIII*, constituted a determined government effort to blacken the record of the Directory and justify the *coup d'état*, to the advantage of the officials and of Napoleon himself. It was an early example of the Napoleonic propaganda machine at work.

Key question
What was the mood of public opinion in 1799?

Restoration
The return of the Bourbons to the throne of France.

Key term

Disillusionment with the Directory

It would be wrong to suggest that the period of the Directory was a complete disaster and that it failed to deal with the immediate problems – military, economic and political – facing it. Yet it was to an extent tolerated rather than accepted. The government was confronted by a wide range of opposition from both royalists and extreme republicans to Catholics and property owners. It had, despite disregarding the constitution, failed to quash its

Key question
To what extent was there disillusionment with the Directory?

opponents. Although it was the longest lasting of regimes set up during the Revolution, it was inherently unstable and certainly did not command universal affection from the **body politic**. Napoleon had considerable insight into how weak the Directory was in reality, and how its reliance on the army in the past had provided him with an opportunity to advance his career. The extent to which he saw himself as the saviour of France and the Revolution is one of the issues you will need to consider over the following chapters.

The support of the property-owning classes

A vast amount of property changed hands during the Revolution. Much of it was taken from the church or former nobility. This property was mainly acquired by two groups of people:

- Existing property owners, including large landowners and wealthy urban *bourgeoisie* who had bought up the **biens nationaux**.
- Rural peasants and small farmers. The Revolution freed peasants from having to pay tithes to the church and feudal

Key question
Why did property owners support Napoleon during the *coup*?

Key terms

Body politic
The political nation – those groups and individuals who were active in the political life of the country.

Biens nationaux
Royalist and church lands seized by the state early in the Revolution and sold off to anyone able to pay.

A contemporary print depicting France as a woman being dragged into an abyss by two figures representing fanaticism and anarchy. Napoleon is attempting to draw her back towards justice, unity, peace and plenty. According to this print, what is Napoleon's role in the history of the Revolution?

dues to their landlords, and in some cases they had been able to buy small quantities of land. Existing farmers were able to expand their holdings by borrowing money to purchase land.

By 1795, when the Directory came to power, the constitution already embodied the principle of ownership of private property as one of the rights guaranteed by the Revolution. Many of the new property owners, especially the *bourgeoisie*, feared that a Jacobin revival or a Bourbon restoration would result in a government seizure of their recent acquisitions. Either of these events might occur, they believed, under the weak government of the Directory. They welcomed, therefore, the chance of strong government that they associated with Napoleon, It seemed likely that he would protect them against Jacobins and royalists alike.

Political apathy

Napoleon's seizure of power does not seem initially to have aroused much public interest or enthusiasm in any class of society, property owning or otherwise. What some historians have called a cloud of **political apathy** had settled down heavily over France during the Directory, after the great upheavals of the early years of the Revolution. It even became difficult in the late 1790s to persuade candidates to come forward for election as local officials. When the *coup* came there was little or no political reaction, probably because it appeared at first to most people to be just another of the Directory's temporary manoeuvres – a mere cosmetic substitution of consuls for directors. Not until Napoleon's policies became clear did the property owners rally to his side and his interests become theirs.

Key question
What was the role of political apathy in the success of the *coup*?

Political apathy
A lack of interest in politics.

Key term

The role of the army

By 1799 the use of the army in civilian politics had become an accepted fact – the Directory had called on them successfully in 1797 and 1798 to maintain itself in power – but in 1799 the situation was different. The Directors realised too late that they had lost control of events when they put the Paris garrison of 8000 or so regular troops under Napoleon's command, especially when they failed to extract from him the very specific oath of loyalty they had at first demanded. The soldiers knew Napoleon as the General who had arranged for the Army of Italy to receive half their wages in gold and silver, not in depreciated paper money, a decision that had made him personally enormously popular, even before he won a single victory. With the glory of his Italian and Egyptian campaigns still upon him, they were well disposed to do whatever he ordered, particularly after he promised on 19 Brumaire to remedy their grievances against the government. These were mainly concerned with a lack of decent footwear, a shortage of tobacco and delays in payment of their wages. The *coup* could not have been carried out successfully without the intimidating presence of the army at Saint-Cloud, nor without its help in dispersing the opposition members of the Five Hundred.

Key question
How important was the role of the army to the success of the *coup* of Brumaire?

Key question
How important was the role played by Lucien Bonaparte in the *coup*?

The contribution of Lucien Bonaparte and support among the Ancients and the Five Hundred

A small but highly important and influential group of supporters of the *coup* were to be found among the Ancients and the Five Hundred. In the weeks before the *coup*, the conspirators worked hard on the deputies, and by various means, mostly financial, bought the allegiance of many of them. Many of the Ancients were apparently given advance information on the *coup* and agreed to support it. There was no real opposition raised to moving the Councils to Saint-Cloud, thereby enabling the *coup* to take place in relative seclusion. Even more significant was the election, immediately prior to the *coup*, of Napoleon's brother, Lucien, to be President of the Five Hundred, where he acted as a counter-balance to the Jacobin majority. His presence there proved invaluable and his role in the later stages of the *coup* was crucial to its success. Without his decisive action, his brother's bid for power would have ended prematurely, almost certainly in death, shot as an outlaw.

It is possible to argue, as Geoffrey Ellis does, that Napoleon was the great beneficiary of the *coup* of Brumaire but Lucien was its true hero. Napoleon emerged from the events of the *coup* as a figure who was hesitant and indecisive. These facts, though, were speedily disguised by Napoleonic propaganda, and Lucien – after a short spell as Minister of the Interior, when he made himself useful to his brother in manipulating the results of the first plebiscite – was removed from the government and sent out of the limelight into near exile as ambassador to Spain.

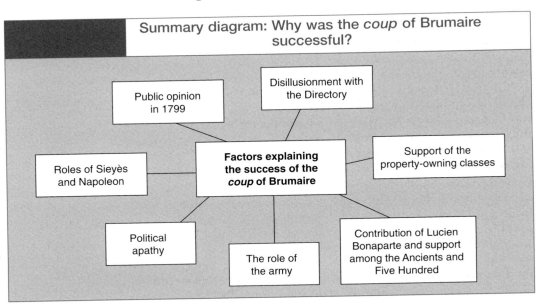

Summary diagram: Why was the *coup* of Brumaire successful?

- Public opinion in 1799
- Disillusionment with the Directory
- Roles of Sieyès and Napoleon
- **Factors explaining the success of the *coup* of Brumaire**
- Support of the property-owning classes
- Political apathy
- The role of the army
- Contribution of Lucien Bonaparte and support among the Ancients and Five Hundred

4 | The Key Debate

The *coup* of Brumaire was a decisive event in the history of the French Revolution. On the one hand it brought an end to the longest lasting regime of the Revolutionary period and in the process marked a decisive shift in the Revolution, while on the other hand it signalled the emergence into political prominence of Napoleon Bonaparte. Brumaire was the event that brought Napoleon international as well as national prominence.

> How have historians interpreted this dramatic event that was so central to the history of the Revolution?

R.S. Alexander

In an important study in 2001, R.S. Alexander sought to focus on how Napoleon's reputation had changed over the years. He argued that when Napoleon returned to France in 1799 his main motive was personal ambition. According to Alexander, Napoleon did not make a significant contribution to planning the *coup*. Sieyès was much more involved in organising Brumaire than was Napoleon. Indeed when the plotters were considering sympathetic generals that they could approach, Napoleon was at best third on the list. Lucien on the other hand did play a significant part in the events that unfolded. In Alexander's view, Napoleon did not particularly distinguish himself by his actions during the *coup*.

Geoffrey Ellis

Ellis, in his profile of Napoleon (1997) in power, stresses that when Napoleon returned to France in October 1799 he found the Directory in 'terminal discord', lacking direction and clear leadership, and afraid of a Jacobin resurgence. Any *coup* would need a strong military figure with a high profile and popularity with the army. Napoleon clearly fitted the profile. Yet as the events of the *coup* unfolded the true hero of Brumaire according to Ellis was Lucien, although his brother would undoubtedly be the great beneficiary of the dramatic events of 9–10 November 1799.

Peter Taaffe

Over the years the Revolution has been studied by many left-wing historians and writers. Peter Taaffe is part of this tradition and his focus is very much on how the Revolution betrayed the interests of ordinary people. He argues that during the Directory the *bourgeoisie*, having lost confidence in their own political capacity, took refuge in the regime's corruption. According to Taaffe, it was the *bourgeoisie* who were the main beneficiaries of the Revolution and to preserve these gains they supported the *coup*. The conspirators turned to Napoleon because he was enormously popular, with an outstanding military record and a Jacobin past that would give the plotters a measure of Revolutionary authority. Yet they ended up with a military dictatorship that did not serve their interests.

Clive Emsley

In his overview of Napoleon's career, Emsley stresses his rapid rise to prominence under the Directory. He notes that the regime was deeply unpopular and that the conspirators of Brumaire knew this. It had failed to bring an end to the interminable wars of the Revolution, but even more serious in the eyes of the men of property, according the Emsley, who had benefited from the early upheavals of the Revolution, it had failed to establish internal security. The Directory was prone to *coup* and counter-*coup* which to all intents and purpose legitimised instability. In Emsley's opinion the *coup* of Brumaire as an event was not particularly exceptional, and Napoleon did not distinguish himself during it.

Some key books in the debate
R.S. Alexander, *Napoleon: Reputations* (Hodder Arnold, 2001).
Geoffrey Ellis, *Napoleon: Profiles in Power* (Longman, 1997).
Clive Emsley, *Napoleon* (Longman, 2003).
Peter Taaffe, *1789–1815* (Fortress Books, 1989).

Study Guide: AS Question
In the style of OCR

'Disillusionment with the Directory was the main reason why the *coup* of Brumaire was successful.' Assess this claim.

Exam tips

The cross-references are intended to take you straight to the material that will help you to answer the question.

This question does not ask you to assess reasons why an event happened – it asks why it was successful. 'Assess' means weighing up the relative importance of a series of causal factors and so your task is to sort them into a rank order of importance. One cause is given in the question and you must examine it seriously, even if you are going to reject it in favour of a cause you believe to have been more important. You might divide your answer into two separate sections: longer term reasons and short-term reasons. Alternatively, you might decide from the start your rank order and examine the relative significance of individual factors throughout your essay. Try not to look at each reason in isolation. Important events usually happen when several factors combine to create a new dynamic – look for ways to explain how some reasons influenced, and were influenced by, others.

Brumaire was one of a series of *coups* in 1797–9. What does that tell us? Was the Directory a failure? What was the mood of public opinion in 1799? As you think about these questions, decide whether disillusionment with the Directory was anything more than a background factor opening the way for a bold new regime. Against whatever you decide, you must then assess the weight to be given to other causal factors, for example:

- the roles played by key individuals like Sieyès and Lucien Bonaparte (pages 24 and 27)
- the ambition of the army (page 32)
- the support of the well-to-do (page 31)
- the support of core elements of the political élite (pages 31–2).

As you weigh up their relative importance, there is one other factor to consider: the driving ambition of Napoleon himself. Do not sit on the fence. Work out which reason you think was the most important and explain why to justify your argument.

Study Guide: A2 Question

In the style of Edexcel

'The *coup* of Brumaire owed little to Napoleon Bonaparte.' How far do you agree with this opinion?

Exam tips

The cross-references are intended to take you straight to the material that will help you to answer the question.

This question requires you to examine the interplay of factors and events responsible for the overthrow of the Directory in the *coup* of Brumaire. The main beneficiary of the event was Napoleon Bonaparte, but how central was he to its success?

You should consider each of the following before reaching a judgement:

- the state of public opinion in 1799 and the unpopularity of the Directory (page 30)
- the influence of the property-owning classes (page 31)
- the role of Sieyès (page 30)
- the decisive intervention of Lucien Bonaparte (page 33).

However, you must take account of:

- Napoleon Bonaparte's personal prestige in 1799 (page 23)
- the power conferred by his relationship with the army (page 32)
- evidence which suggests he had intended all along to seize power (page 30).

How significant were these factors in setting the *coup* in train and in determining its outcome? Set against these factors, should much significance be attributed to the accounts of hesitancy and the temporary overshadowing of Napoleon by his brother during the events of 10 November (page 27)? In coming to your conclusion, remember also to consider how much weight should be given to the circumstantial factors that contributed to the ease with which the Directory was overthrown.

---

3 Establishing Power

POINTS TO CONSIDER

Following the seizure of power in 1799 during the *coup* of Brumaire, Napoleon embarked on a series of measures designed to ensure that his position was firmly established and that there would be no significant challenge to his power and authority. He did this through a combination of constitutional change and domestic reforms. This chapter will consider the following aspects of his policy:

- Constitutional and political changes
- Economic reforms
- Legal and judicial reforms: the Civil Code
- Education reforms
- Relations with the Catholic Church: the Concordat

Key dates

1799	November 10	Three consuls sworn in
	December 25	Constitution of Year VIII came into force
1800	January 6	Creation of the Bank of France
	February 7	Plebiscite for new constitution
1801	July 16	Concordat with the Pope
1802	May 1	Education law set up *lycées*
	May 19	Legion of Honour established
	August 4	Constitution of Year X approved by plebiscite
1804	March 20	Execution of the Duc d'Enghien
	March 21	Introduction of the Civil Code
	May 18	Senate proclaimed Napoleon Emperor
	December 2	Napoleon crowned himself Emperor of the French
1808	March 17	Imperial University founded
1810	April 2	Napoleon married Marie Louise of Austria

1 | Constitutional and Political Changes

Success in the *coup* of Brumaire was only the beginning for Napoleon. He had gained political power, but needed to consolidate it if he were to make himself undisputed ruler of France. He began with the constitution.

The Constitution of 1799

Late in the evening of 19 Brumaire year VIII (10 November 1799) the three newly elected provisional consuls (Napoleon, Sieyès and Ducos) swore an oath of allegiance to the Republic. At the same time Napoleon issued his first Proclamation:

> On my return to France I found that the Constitution was half destroyed and no longer capable of maintaining our liberty ... The Council of Ancients called on me – I answered the appeal ... I offered myself to the Five Hundred, my head uncovered, alone, unarmed ... twenty assassins rushed upon me, aiming at my breast ...

Within a few hours of the *coup* there were expressions of anxiety among the **philosophes**, particularly when it became known that, under the Law of Brumaire, the two legislative councils had been adjourned. On 20 Brumaire, **Benjamin Constant** warned Sieyès that:

> This step appears disastrous to me in that it destroys the only barrier against a man with whom you associated yesterday but who is threatening the Republic. His proclamations, in which he speaks only of himself and says that his return has given rise to the hope that he will end France's troubles, have convinced me more than ever that in everything he does he sees only his own advancement.

In the **Luxembourg Palace** in Paris the consuls set to work on the new constitution, bypassing the two Standing Committees that were supposed to draw up the draft plans. In a series of long and often heated discussions, Sieyès proposed that Napoleon should occupy the role of a figurehead in the new constitution. Napoleon refused to countenance the idea. There must, he argued, be a First Consul as head of state with complete control, in peace and in war, at home and abroad; and he himself must be that consul. The roles of the second and third consuls also caused argument. Sieyès wanted them each to have **voix deliberative**. Napoleon, however, insisted they should have only **voix consultative**. In all matters, his decision would be final. Faced with Napoleon's domineering personality, Sieyès was eventually forced into the humiliating position of having to make the official nomination of Napoleon as First Consul. All three consuls would serve initially for ten years.

The negotiations had taken about six weeks to complete. In this time the government of France had been transformed from one where political responsibility was spread as widely as possible to one where it was centralised in the hands of a single man – a

---

dictator. Sieyès was compensated for the ruin of his plans and the loss of his consulship by being given the presidency of the Senate and a large estate in the country. 'Gentlemen, you have got yourselves a master', he is reported to have said of Napoleon at the end of the negotiations, 'a man who knows everything, wants everything, and can do everything'.

In a proclamation, Napoleon explained to the French people his reasons for seizing power:

> To make the Republic loved by its own citizens, respected abroad and feared by its enemies – such are the duties we have assumed in accepting the First Consulship

and he added reassuringly that the new constitution was

> based upon the true principles of representative government and on the sacred rights of property, equality and liberty. The powers it sets up will be strong and lasting.

Features of the new constitution

Napoleon's own words claimed that the new constitution which came into force on 25 December 1799 was based on the true principles of representative government. But was this true? Careful examination of the system indicates that this was not the case.

- The electoral system adopted at the beginning of the Consulate was Sieyès' invention and certainly provided for '**universal suffrage**', unlike the property-based vote of the 1795 constitution. But this suffrage was too indirect to fulfil the idea of popular sovereignty.
- There were about six million 'Frenchmen of the age of 21 with a year's domicile' named as voters on the commune registers in 1799. Women were not given any role in the new political system. The six million men chose 10 per cent of their number to form a communal list (from whom local officials would be drawn), and that was as far as the direct vote went. These 600,000 in turn chose 10 per cent of their number to form a departmental list. They in turn selected from among themselves 6000 to form a national list 'of persons fit for public service' (see diagram on page 42).
- From this national list of '**notables**' the Senate chose the members of the two legislative bodies – the Tribunate of 100 members aged 25 or more who could discuss legislation but could not vote on it, and a Legislature of 300 members aged 30 or more who could vote on legislation by secret ballot but could not discuss it.
- The Senate (some 60 distinguished men aged 40 or more, and holding office for life) was itself nominated by the First Consul, who also presided over the Council of State of 30 to 40 men, who were chosen by him.

Key question
Was the new constitution based on representative government?

Key date

Constitution of Year VIII came into force: 25 December 1799

Key terms

Universal suffrage
A vote for every man over a certain age regardless of wealth.

Notables
The most prominent men in any community.

- The Council nominated all major central and local government officials, and initiated all legislation (see diagram on page 42).

Democratic involvement in the elections was minimal. While there was the appearance of adult male suffrage, there were no *elections*, only *presentations* of candidates suitable for appointment as deputies, and the choice of candidates was restricted to notables – men of wealth, usually landowners or existing government officials. Power was firmly in the hands of one man (the First Consul), who headed the new structure.

The role of the First Consul

In the new constitution, the First Consul had a vast amount authority. He was able to dominate the political system through exercising the following powers:

- He controlled government appointments, made and unmade ministers, whom he closely supervised and to whom he allowed no freedom of action.
- He initiated all legislation through the Council of State or the Senate.
- He declared war and made peace.

Sieyès intended the Senate to act as a brake on the executive. Napoleon turned it into an instrument of his personal power. The Senate had available to it the procedure of *senatus-consultum* which would allow it to act as the guardian of the existing constitution. Napoleon used this procedure extensively from January 1801 onwards in order to thwart the wishes of the Tribunate and the Legislature. He also ruthlessly exploited his power to appoint members of the Senate. Senators were appointed for life, given a substantial salary and suitably rewarded with gifts of land and money. Membership of the Senate increased from the original 80 to about 140 by 1814, most of the extra members being Napoleon's direct nominees or 'grand dignitaries' of the Empire, used to **pack the Senate**. As a result it developed into a largely consultative body anxious to please its benefactor and president, Napoleon.

The plebiscite of 1800

Under the Law of Brumaire, the new constitution, in order to become legal, had to be 'submitted to the acceptance of the French people'. On 7 February 1800, a **plebiscite** was held and the electors were given a month in which to vote in their communes for or against the constitution. The official results showed 3,011,007 voting in favour with 1562 against. This was not quite as overwhelming a display of public approval as the figures suggest. Voting took place at different times in different places, and the ballot was not a secret one. Voters simply wrote 'yes' or 'no' against their names on an open list. Not surprisingly, malpractice and intimidation affected the results in some areas. The government, made aware of the problem of possible later victimisation, promised to burn all lists when the votes had been

Key question
What measure of control did the First Consul have under the new constitution?

Key terms

Senatus-consultum
A procedure that allowed the Senate to preserve and amend the constitution and to approve constitutional change and new laws.

Pack the Senate
Napoleon appointed his own nominees whose loyalty and support he could guarantee.

Plebiscite
A vote on a single issue where electors are asked whether they support or reject a proposal.

Key question
Why was a plebiscite necessary and what was its outcome?

Key date
Plebiscite held to secure approval of the new constitution: 7 February 1800

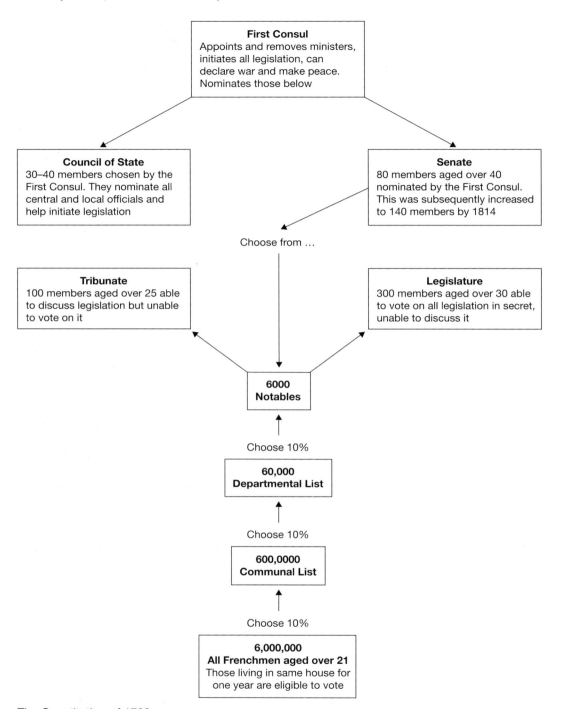

The Constitution of 1799.

counted. However, this promise was not kept and in many parts of France the lists are still available for study.

As the constitution had already been put (illegally) into operation, there was very little point in voting 'no', especially as many people feared that to do so might lead to trouble afterwards. Although a favourable vote would merely ratify what had already occurred it was important to the government's credibility that the constitution should appear as widely accepted as possible. There is little doubt that before the voting figures were published, they were adjusted by Lucien as Minister of the Interior in order to ensure a large majority for the government. He almost doubled the total number of 'yes' votes, rounding up the figures by about 900,000 and then adding in another 500,000 to represent the unanimously favourable votes it was alleged would have been cast if they had been included in the plebiscite. The real 'yes' vote was, therefore, probably only about 1,500,000.

Moreover, recent research has suggested that the number of those eligible to vote in the communes was probably much nearer 8,000,000 than the figure of 6,000,000 previously accepted by historians. The 'yes' votes, therefore, represented not over 50 per cent of the electorate, as once appeared, but only something under 20 per cent. Even if it were argued that the large number of abstentions ought to be considered as 'not opposed' to the new regime, it does not appear that public opinion was genuinely inclined towards Napoleon and the new constitution at the beginning of 1800 to justify his regarding the result as a vote of confidence. The results of the plebiscite would appear to indicate public apathy rather than committed support.

Changing the electoral system

The whole electoral system proved extremely cumbersome when it was eventually put into operation in 1801. Napoleon abolished it the following year even before all the lists were complete. He introduced a new arrangement that lasted until the end of the Empire and which reduced still further the element of popular choice. It was intended to produce groups who would act as intermediaries between government and people. All adult males met to elect life members to departmental 'colleges', or boards. However, electors had only a limited choice of candidates, as life members had to be selected from a list of the 600 richest men in the **department**. Every five years the colleges produced lists of candidates for election to vacancies on the legislative bodies, but their main function was to provide readily available groups of wealthy property owners (notables) for Napoleon to court with offers of central or local government posts or other benefits. In return for these favours, he expected them to bring their wealth and influence to bear on behalf of the regime. It was an

Key questions
Why did Napoleon replace the electoral system? What method did he replace it with and how did it operate?

Key term

Departments
The local government divisions established by the National Assembly.

Table 2: Plebiscites held during the Consulate and Empire 1800–15

Year	Purpose of plebiscite	Voting yes	Voting no
1800	Constitution of Year VIII	1,550,000	1562
1802	Plebiscite on Life Consulate	3,653,000	8272
1804	Plebiscite on Empire	3,572,329	2569
1815	Plebiscite on *Acte Additionnel* (see page 141)	1,552,942	5740

arrangement by which Napoleon not only rewarded the property-owning classes for past support but also secured their loyalty for the future. It was to remain a favourite political manoeuvre until his final defeat.

In a number of ways the new constitution established a framework for ensuring that the main social gains made during the French Revolution were secured. Among the most important of these changes was the vast transfer of land that had taken place largely at the expense of the Catholic Church and the French nobility. It was necessary to bind the beneficiaries of these transfers to the new regime. This was achieved by creating a political system which favoured the propertied classes. Power in the new regime was far more centralised than it had been under the Directory. In a way it was a reversion back to the Jacobin phase of the Revolution (1793–4) when France was governed by a dictatorship. By cultivating the support of notables, Napoleon was seeking to incorporate and consolidate the new élite of talent that had emerged since 1789.

The hereditary principle: constitution of 1802

Napoleon only narrowly escaped assassination in December 1800, making the Senate acutely aware of the fragile nature of a regime dependent for its continuation upon one man. Partly because of this, and partly as a demonstration of gratitude to the First Consul for his achievements at home and abroad, it was decided to offer him the Consulship for life, with the right to nominate his successor. It was the first step towards the reintroduction of the **hereditary principle** and rule, which had been abandoned with the overthrow of Louis XVI in 1792. A new constitution was drawn up to formalise the change (the Constitution of Year X, 1802). Napoleon accepted 'if the will of the people demands it', and, so, on 4 August 1802, another plebiscite was held. The result was similar to that of 1799 (an alleged 3,600,000 in favour of making Napoleon Life Consul and 8272 against). While there is no evidence that the central government tampered directly with the figures, it is known that local officials often sent in results which they thought would be pleasing to their superiors, sometimes even recording a unanimous 'yes' vote when, in fact, no poll had been held at all.

In his speech of thanks to the Senate for his appointment to the Life Consulship, Napoleon remarked that much still remained to be done to strengthen the constitution. One thing that was done almost immediately was to increase Napoleon's personal power through his control of an enlarged Senate, which became responsible for 'everything not provided for by the constitution, and necessary to its working'. This arrangement was greatly to the detriment of the representative bodies, the Tribunate and the Legislature. They lost much of their importance, and met less and less frequently. The Tribunate was severely **purged** in 1802 for daring to criticise the Civil Code (see pages 50–1), and with a much reduced membership became little more than a rubber stamp for the remainder of its existence,

Key question
Why was Napoleon offered the Consulship for life?

Key date

Constitution of Year X approved by plebiscite with Napoleon as Consul for life: 4 August 1802

Key terms

Hereditary principle
A system where an individual is succeeded by his nearest male relative – usually the eldest son. Such a system is used in monarchies.

Purge
The forced removal of political opponents.

while the Legislature's credibility was reduced by being 'packed' by Napoleon with 'safe' men who would not oppose his wishes.

By 1803 Napoleon was riding in splendour around Paris and holding court in royal style. State ceremonies multiplied, etiquette was formalised, and official dress became more elaborate. The **Legion of Honour** (see pages 67–8) had been introduced on 19 May 1802, and there were hints that a nobility was to be re-established, the rumours fired by Napoleon's granting permission for a large number of *émigrés* to return to France. In 1804, a series of disasters, royalist plots and counter-plots culminated in the affair of the Duc d'Enghien, a member of the Bourbon royal family alleged to be involved in a plot to overthrow Napoleon by murdering him and taking over the government. The Duke was kidnapped on Napoleon's orders while on neutral territory, tried and, on very inadequate evidence, found guilty of conspiracy. There was very little time between the end of the trial and the execution on 20 March 1804 in what amounted to judicial murder. This was justified by Napoleon on the grounds that he was entitled by the Corsican laws of vendetta to kill an enemy who threatened his personal safety:

> The great number of plots which are woven against my life inspire no fear in me. But I cannot deny a deep feeling of distress when I consider the situation in which the great people would have found itself today had the recent attempt [at assassination] succeeded.

Napoleon becomes Emperor: constitution of 1804

In the wake of these events Napoleon began to prepare the people for his next step. Others apart from Napoleon were considering what would happen to France if he should be murdered. The property owners took seriously the Bourbon pretender's recent threat to return all 'stolen properties' to their 'rightful owners' as soon as he regained the throne, and most were convinced that only Napoleon stood between them and the loss of all they had gained by the Revolution. There was widespread talk of making the Consulship hereditary in the Bonaparte family, in the hope of providing for a smooth succession and the survival of the constitution should Napoleon meet an untimely death. On 18 May 1804, a motion was approved by the Senate that 'Napoleon Bonaparte at present First Consul be declared Emperor of the French, and that the imperial dignity be declared hereditary in his family.'

A third plebiscite was held in November 1804 for the Constitution of Year XII. Electors were asked to confirm Napoleon as hereditary emperor of the French. The wording of the plebiscite was chosen to overcome the difficulty that Napoleon and his wife Josephine had no children, by allowing for a successor to come from within the Bonaparte family – an important point for a Corsican. The plebiscite achieved the desired result (3,572,329 'yes' and 2569 'no' votes). Remembering that in the previous plebiscite 40 per cent of the no votes came from the army, the government took no chances this time and did

Key dates

Introduction of the Legion of Honour: 19 May 1802

Execution of the Duc d'Enghien: 20 March 1804

Senate proclaimed Napoleon Emperor of the French: 18 May 1804

Key term

Legion of Honour
An élitist organisation created by Napoleon to bind powerful men to his regime through a system of rewards and titles.

Key question
Why was it decided to make Napoleon an Emperor?

The French artist Jacques-Louis David's (1748–1825) depiction of the coronation of Napoleon at Notre Dame shows Napoleon crowning Josephine as Empress. This was painted between 1806 and 1807.

not actually poll the soldiers. They simply added in about half a million 'yes' votes on their behalf.

At a sumptuous ceremony in the cathedral of Notre Dame in Paris held in the presence of the Pope on 2 December 1804, Napoleon, as previously arranged, took the imperial crown and placed it on his own head, before he himself crowned Josephine as Empress. In his coronation oath Napoleon swore:

Napoleon crowned himself Emperor of the French: 2 December 1804

Key date

> to uphold the integrity of the Republic's territory, to respect and impose the laws of the Concordat and the laws of equal rights, political and civil liberties, the irrevocability of the sale of national property, to raise no duty and establish no tax except through the law, to uphold the institution of the Legion of Honour, and to rule only in the interests of the happiness and glory of the French people.

Changes to government

During the next two or three years the Tribunate and the Legislature were hardly consulted at all. The Tribunate was finally abolished in 1808 and, although the Legislature survived, it was able to do so only by maintaining its subservient attitude to Napoleon's demands. Government was increasingly conducted through the Senate and the Council of State, both of which were firmly under Napoleon's personal control. In theory, the Senate acquired important new powers in 1804 with the formation of two

Key question
How did the government of France change after 1804?

standing committees, one concerned with preserving individual liberty and the other with safeguarding freedom of the press. From the outset, however, these committees were rendered impotent by Napoleon. Neither was allowed any real opportunity to consider complaints, and only a handful of cases were dealt with in ten years. The committee on freedom of the press was further handicapped by being prevented from considering anything connected with the publication of newspapers or periodicals.

Divorcing Josephine

Key question
Why and how did Napoleon divorce Josephine?

Only one thing more was needed to establish the Napoleonic dynasty beyond question – the production of a legitimate son and heir. Napoleon went about it in his usual determined way. Despite his continued fondness for her, Josephine, now past child-bearing age, would have to be divorced, and a new wife selected; but first the church had to be persuaded that Josephine should be set aside. This was not easy, for although their original marriage had been a civil one, the church had insisted on a second, Catholic ceremony as a necessary preliminary to the coronation in 1804. Eventually, on the grounds of alleged irregularities in the conduct of the religious marriage, the church reluctantly agreed to an annulment, leaving Napoleon free to remarry. A list of eligible princesses was drawn up for him. On 2 April 1810, at the age of 40, he married 18-year-old Marie-Louise of Austria, a niece of Marie-Antoinette (Louis XVI's wife, who had been executed during the Revolution). In the following year the hoped-for son, Napoleon, King of Rome, was born. The succession seemed assured, the dynasty secure. 'I am at the summit of my happiness', Napoleon is reported to have said.

Key date
Napoleon married Marie-Louise of Austria: 2 April 1810

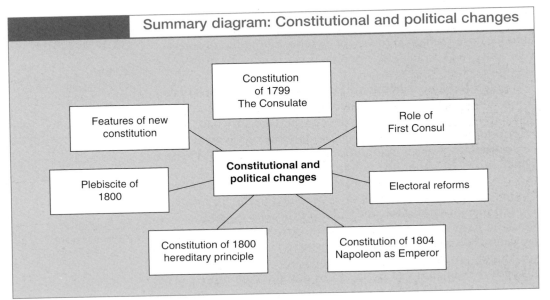

Summary diagram: Constitutional and political changes

- Constitution of 1799 The Consulate
- Features of new constitution
- Role of First Consul
- Plebiscite of 1800
- **Constitutional and political changes**
- Electoral reforms
- Constitution of 1800 hereditary principle
- Constitution of 1804 Napoleon as Emperor

2 | Economic Reforms: Establishing Financial Stability

Of the many problems confronting the new government, possibly the most pressing was the need to establish financial stability and secure an adequate revenue stream. There was very little money available in the treasury in November 1799 – only a few thousand francs. Napoleon introduced a series of major financial reforms that went a considerable way to transforming the situation. As Napoleon himself lacked the technical skills to overhaul the financial system, he appointed a number of very able and efficient ministers to undertake this task. Among the key appointments were Gaudin, who was appointed Minister of Finances in 1799 (a position he retained until 1814), and Barbe-Marbois at the treasury (1801–6). Both these appointments brought a measure of stability to state finances.

Key question
Why did Napoleon need to establish financial stability?

Tax reforms

The early financial reforms introduced were:

Key question
What reforms were introduced to improve the financial situation?

- a much clearer division of roles between the ministry of finances (which oversaw collection of taxes and revenues) and the treasury (which dealt with government expenditure)
- the reorganisation of both **direct** and **indirect tax** collection
- the first steps in establishing a public banking system.

One of Gaudin's most important reforms was to remove the assessment and collection of direct taxation from the control of local authorities and form a central organisation to undertake the task. The main source of government revenue continued to be the land tax. A much more detailed tax register detailing those eligible to pay was drawn up. More efficient land registers listing ownership helped to ensure that the amount paid was spread more evenly. Although the system was reformed and stabilised the amount raised remained constant at some 250 million **francs** a year until 1813, which represented 29 per cent of government revenue.

A more dramatic increase in revenue came from indirect taxes. Many of these had been abolished by the Constituent Assembly. Faced, however, with mounting deficits the Directory had reintroduced indirect taxes on certain goods. Napoleon centralised the collection of duties by creating a Central Excise Office in 1804. Among the goods and services taxed were tobacco, alcohol, items made from gold and silver, playing cards and public transport. In 1806 salt was added to the list, which revived memories of the hated *gabelle* of the *ancien régime*. Revenue from indirect taxes increased by over 400 per cent between 1806 and 1812 and was considered a much easier way of making up any shortfalls in government revenue from direct taxes. It is estimated that by 1813 revenue from all indirect taxes accounted for possibly 25 per cent of the government's revenue.

Key terms

Direct taxes
Taxes imposed on all by the state, usually based on income or the ownership of property.

Indirect taxes
Taxes levied on selected goods.

Franc
On 7 April 1795 the Convention introduced the silver franc as the official unit of currency, replacing the *livre*.

Key question
Why was the Bank of France created?

Key date

Creation of the Bank of France: 6 January 1800

Napoleon on a gold 20-franc coin portrayed as a Roman Emperor.

The Bank of France 1800

One of the most important reforms introduced by Napoleon (which survives to this day) was the creation of the Bank of France on 6 January 1800. Although the bank was a private bank with its own shareholders it was given a range of public functions such as the sole right to issue paper notes. The aim was to improve the efficiency of the state's finances. A risky business venture in 1805 threatened the stability of the new bank. In order to boost state finances, a scheme aimed at importing silver from Mexico to Spain and then on to France was arranged. It even involved agreement from the British. When the scheme ended in failure, Napoleon, in order to avert a more serious crisis, imposed stricter controls on the bank.

An important indicator of the financial health of a country is the stability of its currency. The inflation linked to the *assignat* was a clear reminder to Napoleon of the problems an unstable currency could pose. On 28 March 1803, he introduced the *franc de germinal*, which became the basis of his monetary system. The new gold and silver coins established a standard ratio of gold to silver at 1:15.5. Each one-franc coin would weigh five grams of silver. Other denominations would be minted in strict proportion to this (so, for example, a five-franc coin would contain 25 grams of silver and so on). This reform gave France the most stable currency in Europe at that time. It would remain the basis of France's currency for the next 120 years.

Key question
To what extent did Napoleon's reforms achieve financial stability?

Conclusion

The extent to which Napoleon achieved financial stability is difficult to assess. When compared with the financial chaos of previous regimes, both the Consulate and the Empire were much more successful. The currency was stabilised, public debts were honoured and the wages of public officials and the army were paid. But while greater efficiency was brought to the government's finances, greater burdens were placed on it. State spending increased steadily as a result of increasing military expenditure from around 700 million francs in 1806 to over 1000 million in 1813. The widening gap between the government's income and its expenditure was made up by forcing defeated countries to pay a financial penalty. The military defeats of 1813–14 removed this source of income and marked a renewed period of financial instability.

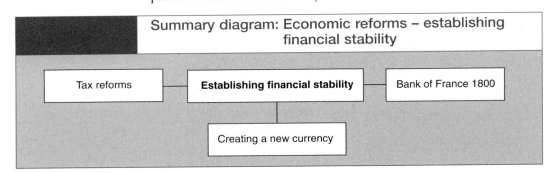

Summary diagram: Economic reforms – establishing financial stability

Tax reforms — Establishing financial stability — Bank of France 1800

Creating a new currency

3 | Legal and Judicial Reforms: The Civil Code

The basis of the legal system, the Civil Code, which was introduced on 21 March 1804 and later known as the *Code Napoléon*, was founded on the work of successive Revolutionary governments that had tried to organise some sort of acceptable nationwide legal system out of the conflicting customary laws of the north and the **Roman law** of the south. The early 1790s had seen a bias towards a system based on the liberal customary law with its acceptance of the equality of persons, civil marriage, divorce and the equal division of property between heirs; but from 1795 there had been a reaction

Key questions
On what was the Civil Code or *Code Napoléon* based? How liberal was the new Civil Code?

Introduction of the Civil Code: 21 March 1804

Roman law
A legal system created in ancient Rome over 2000 years ago which listed crimes and punishments in a series of tables.

CODE CIVIL

DES

FRANÇAIS.

ÉDITION ORIGINALE ET SEULE OFFICIELLE.

GRAND JUGE ET MINISTRE DE LA JUSTICE.

À PARIS,

DE L'IMPRIMERIE DE LA RÉPUBLIQUE.

AN XII.   1804.

The cover of the Civil Code 1804.

in favour of the more authoritarian Roman law that emphasised male authority and the father's rights. The Civil Code was strongly influenced by the principles of Roman law – they fitted in well with Napoleon's own views on society and the inferior status of women – and although it was the work of professional lawyers, Napoleon himself took a very active interest in its formulation. He presided personally over nearly half the sessions of the Senate that were devoted to its discussion.

The Code has been praised as the most impressive of all the legislative measures carried out by Napoleon. Yet while it is an important reform for its clear and understandable presentation of the law, the Code itself was in many ways illiberal and restrictive in outlook, even by the standards of the day. The main areas where it can be considered illiberal are:

- Individual male rights to ownership of property were maintained and the civil rights of Frenchmen were assured, but married women fared badly under its double standards. A man had total authority over his wife and family – he could send an adulterous wife or a defiant child to prison – and divorce, although permitted in theory, was made very difficult and expensive to obtain.
- There was a lack of liberty, too, in the treatment of black people and workers. Slavery was reintroduced in the French colonies 'in accordance with the laws current in 1789', and workmen were made subject to close police supervision through use of the **livret** (see page 68).

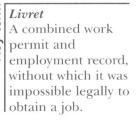

Key term

Livret
A combined work permit and employment record, without which it was impossible legally to obtain a job.

The Code did, however, give legal sanction to some of the important developments of the 1790s – confirming the abolition of feudalism, and giving fixed legal title to those who had earlier purchased confiscated church, crown and *émigré* property (the *biens nationaux*). It also followed the Revolutionary principle of *partage*, that is, equal division of estates among male heirs instead of primogeniture (whereby the eldest son inherited everything).

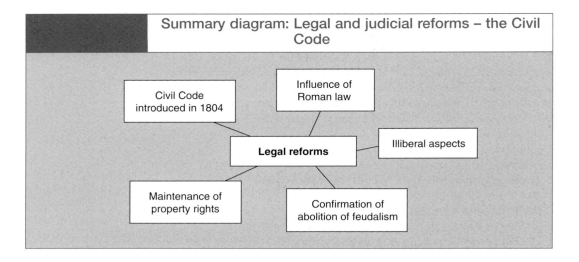

Summary diagram: Legal and judicial reforms – the Civil Code

Civil Code introduced in 1804

Influence of Roman law

Legal reforms

Illiberal aspects

Maintenance of property rights

Confirmation of abolition of feudalism

4 | Education Reforms

Napoleon believed that there were two main functions to an education system:

- First, it was to provide the state with a ready supply of civilian officials and administrators and loyal and disciplined army officers. He intended to recruit these from among the sons of the property-owning classes.
- Second, education had a clear role in binding the nation closer together – an aim that could only be fulfilled if the government took direct central control over the system.

Education for the ordinary people was neglected by Napoleon, as it had been by the governments of the *ancien régime* and of the Revolution. All that was considered necessary for ordinary people was a simple 'moral education' and basic literacy and numeracy. This was provided in primary schools run by the church, by the local community or by individuals. Napoleon often declared his belief in equal opportunities for all according to ability and irrespective of birth or wealth, what he called '**careers open to talents**', but he generally failed to ensure that this was carried out in practice.

Careers open to talents
Any person of ability irrespective of social status should be able to progress in their chosen field.

Lycées
Élite schools for the sons of the wealthy organised on strict military lines.

Key terms

Secondary education

Secondary education was almost entirely restricted to the sons of *notables*, who were educated, often free of charge if their fathers were army officers, in the 45 highly selective, militarised *lycées* established by the education law of 1 May 1802, and to a lesser extent to boys attending the rather less high-powered secondary schools established three years later. The system was highly centralised and government-appointed teachers would all teach to a common syllabus from identical textbooks. So uniform was the system that Napoleon boasted that he knew exactly what every pupil in France was studying from the time of day. The *lycées* were one of Napoleon's permanent legacies.

Neglected areas

Some areas of education were neglected. A similar provision was not made for the education of girls. Napoleon had a poor view of women, who 'should not be regarded as the equals of men; they are, in fact, mere machines to make children. I do not think we need bother about the education of girls … Marriage is their destiny'. They did not, therefore, need to think and should not be taught to do so. Scientific education and research was also neglected. The *Polytechnique*, which had been founded during the Revolution to promote scientific research, was converted by Napoleon into a military academy in 1805.

The Imperial University

In order to ensure that his wishes concerning education were complied with, Napoleon founded the Imperial University on 17 March 1808. This was not a university in the ordinary sense, but a kind of Ministry of Education developed from Napoleon's earlier 'Order of Teachers' and was invested 'with sole responsibility for teaching and education throughout the Empire'. As Napoleon told the Council of State:

> Of all our institutions education is the most important. It is essential that the morals and the political ideas of the generation which is now growing up should no longer be dependent on the news of the day or the circumstances of the moment. We must secure unity; we must be able to cast a whole generation in the same mould. There will be no stability in the state until there is a body of teachers with fixed principles. Let us have a body of doctrine which does not vary and a body of teachers which does not die.

The University controlled the curricula and appointed all the teachers of the state secondary schools, which operated only by its permission and under its authority. Under Napoleon, the French education system was very tightly controlled. Both parents and teachers had a number of concerns about the educational system. Among these were:

- Total obedience was demanded by the University from its member teachers, who had to take an oath of loyalty to their superiors and were subject to many petty restrictions – a visit to Paris without special permission, for instance, would mean a spell in prison.
- Lessons were standardised, and what was taught was dictated in accordance with the needs and demands of the government.
- There was no room for freedom of choice within the state system, or for freedom of thought or expression by pupils or staff. For this reason many parents preferred to send their children, if they could, to the more expensive private church schools, especially when these became more easily available after the Concordat with the Pope in 1801.

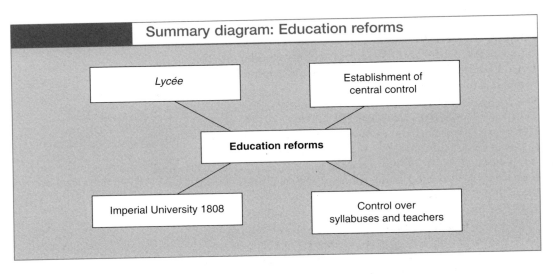

Summary diagram: Education reforms

5 | Relations with the Catholic Church: The Concordat

As early as the summer of 1800, Napoleon was making proposals to improve relations with the Catholic Church in France, which had been in conflict with the state since 1790. Under the Directory, many parish churches had already been reopened and priests persuaded to officiate. Following the repression of the Revolutionary period there had been a revival of Catholic public worship. No government that hoped to attract popular support could ignore this revival and it is likely that Napoleon's motives for seeking a *rapprochement* with the Pope were practical. Catholicism had become identified with the royalist cause. It needed instead to be identified with the people as a whole. If it could then be reunited with the State, loyal in its support of the head of State and under his control, it would be a force for peace and stability in the country, and draw Catholics away from their Bourbon allegiance.

Key terms

Rapprochement
When former enemies seal their differences and improve their relations.

Schism
A deep division.

Napoleon's views of the Catholic Church

Napoleon had been born and brought up a Catholic but, as a good Jacobin, he had become if not exactly an atheist at least an agnostic. Although the Napoleonic legend was to have him die in the Catholic faith, he paid it no more than lip service during his adult life, and that only so that his coronation could follow the imperial tradition of Charlemagne (c742–814, King of the Franks and Holy Roman Emperor). However, he appreciated the power of religion to act as the 'social bond' cementing together a divided people. In addition he understood the importance that its official re-establishment would have in bringing an end to the **schism** between clergy who had sworn allegiance to the Revolution and those who had not. Religious peace would help to bring political and social peace to France. His opinion was that:

> No society can exist without inequality of fortunes; and inequality of fortunes cannot exist without religion. When a man is dying of hunger beside another who is stuffing himself with food, he cannot accept this difference if there is not an authority who tells him, 'God wishes it so' ... It is religion alone that gives to the state a firm and durable support.

The terms of the Concordat

Having decided that 'the people need a religion', Napoleon set about 'rebuilding the altars', but with the proviso that 'this religion must be in the hands of the government'. Discussions with the papacy lasted many months and 21 different drafts were drawn up before the Concordat was finally signed on 16 July 1801. The Concordat was one of the most controversial policies initiated by Napoleon. The main terms of the agreement were:

- Confirmation that the separation of church and state, which had been one of the main policies of the Revolution, was to end.
- The Catholic Church would recognise the Revolution and agreed that no attempt would be made to recover church lands lost since 1789.
- A state-controlled church was established, and its clergy became paid civil servants, appointed by the government and bound to it by oath.
- It was agreed that Catholic worship, 'the religion of the great majority of the citizens', should be 'freely exercised in France', and that public worship should be 'in conformity with police regulations which the government shall deem necessary for public peace'.
- Other religious faiths were tolerated under the Concordat.

The Concordat was published by Napoleon in April 1802 as part of a wide-ranging ecclesiastical law on to which he tacked the so-called 'Organic Articles'. These were a series of clauses limiting Papal control over French bishops while increasing state control over the clergy. 'The Head of the Church', Napoleon announced, 'has in his wisdom and in the interests of the church considered proposals dictated by the interests of the state … What he has approved the government has listened to, and the Legislature has made a law of the Republic.' He went on to urge the clergy:

> See that this religion attaches you to the interests of the country. See that your teaching and your example shape young citizens in respect and affection for the authorities which have been created to protect and guide them. See that they learn from you that the God of Peace is also the God of War, and that He fights on the side of those who defend the independence and liberty of France.

The imperial catechism

In 1806 Napoleon went a step further. By standardising the numerous existing church **catechisms**, he was able turn a necessary church reform to his own political ends. The questions and answers of the new official catechism, as amended by Napoleon personally, were taught in all schools and carried a very clear message, one that was not at all agreeable to the Pope. The following examples illustrate this:

> Q. What are the duties of Christians towards princes who govern them? In particular what are our duties to Napoleon, our Emperor?
>
> A. Christians owe to the princes who govern them, and we, in particular owe to Napoleon I, our Emperor, our love and respect, obedience, loyalty and military service, and the taxes ordered for the defence of the Empire and his throne …
>
> Q. Why are we bound in these duties to our Emperor?
>
> A. … because God creates Empires and apportions them

Key question
What was Napoleon's purpose in amending the catechism?

Key term

Catechism
A set form of question and answer, used by the church to teach the key aspects of its faith.

according to his will, and has set him up as our sovereign and made him the agent of his power, and his image on earth. So to honour and serve the Emperor is to honour and serve God himself …

Relations between Napoleon and the Catholic Church following the Concordat were frequently tense. He managed to anger Pope Pius VII by ordering, without consultation, that the Church throughout the Empire should celebrate 16 August (the day after his own birthday) as St Napoleon's Day, unceremoniously removing from the list of saints the existing occupant of that date. The cult of the Emperor had reached its peak. Such blatant interference in church affairs for political and personal advantage made it obvious that Napoleon's religious activities were intended solely to produce loyal soldiers and civil servants. It was clear that the church was no longer the privileged First estate it had been under the *ancien régime* with its tax exemptions and vast landed estates. There appeared to be very little prospect that either would ever be restored. According to Nigel Aston, Napoleon achieved '… what no previous Revolutionary regime had really wanted to bring about – the acceptance by the leadership of the Catholic Church of a government that was not led by a legitimate Bourbon prince'.

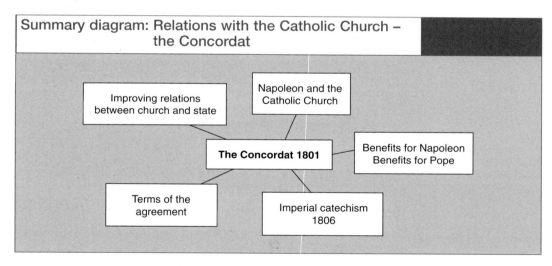

Summary diagram: Relations with the Catholic Church – the Concordat

- Improving relations between church and state
- Napoleon and the Catholic Church
- The Concordat 1801
- Benefits for Napoleon
  Benefits for Pope
- Terms of the agreement
- Imperial catechism 1806

6 | The Key Debate

The event that formed the backdrop to Napoleon's seizure of power was the French Revolution. As a young and highly ambitious soldier the Revolution gave him an opportunity to advance his career first in the service of the King and then in the Republic. The Revolution made great changes to people's lives in a variety of areas, yet the governments that introduced them were essentially unstable. One of the great debates surrounding

Napoleon's career is the nature of his relationship with the Revolution. A question frequently asked is:

> Did Napoleon preserve or destroy the gains of the Revolution?

Albert Vandal

One of Napoleon's staunchest supporters was Albert Vandal, whose two-volume work *The Advent of Napoleon* appeared between 1903 and 1907. One of the many charges made against Napoleon by his critics was that he destroyed the liberties established by the Revolution. Vandal responded to this by asserting that, 'Bonaparte could not suppress something which did not exist'. He argued that the death of liberty occurred under the Directory during the *coup* of Fructidor in 1797 when the resurgent royalists were crushed. By ending the instability that had characterised the first Republic, Napoleon, according to Vandal, was able to consolidate many of the most important aspects of the Revolution. He was also able to represent the opinion of those working people who had benefited very little from the Revolution and who saw in him, 'the embodiment of their hopes'.

George Rudé

In his book *Revolutionary Europe 1783–1815*, Professor George Rudé suggested that Napoleon was a man of strange paradoxes and contradictions. The greatest of these, according to Rudé, was that as an upstart soldier of the Revolution he carried the principles of 1789 to half the countries in Europe, yet built a new despotism and new aristocracy on the ashes of the old. Of the many myths that surrounded the Emperor, often generated from St Helena, Rudé believed that the most enduring was that of his work as the soldier of the Revolution. While some domestic reforms, particularly the legal reforms of the *Code Napoléon* of 1807, enshrined the gains made since 1789, his religious policy suggested a return to aspects of church–state relations more familiar with the *ancien régime*. During the Empire the egalitarianism of the Revolution was abandoned and privilege was restored.

Alfred Cobban

Alfred Cobban was not an admirer of Napoleon. In his opinion, during the 15 years that he held power, the country was at the mercy of a gambler, who according to Cobban, 'fate and his own genius had dealt all the aces'. By way of emphasising his disdain for the Emperor he noted that he cheated at cards and that his carriage concealed a cache of diamonds in case he had to flee the country at short notice. Yet unlike Rudé, Cobban conceded that under Napoleon the great gains of the Revolution were preserved. These in essence were: equality before the law, religious toleration, and the abolition of privileges and *seigneurial* burdens. Napoleon also strictly maintained property rights and there was a clear emphasis on the interests of the small owner.

Cobban drew particular attention to the Civil Code, which he believed was the '… most effective agency for the propagation of the basic principles of the French Revolution that could have been devised'.

D.M.G. Sutherland

Sutherland argues that by 1790 the French Revolution had achieved its goals. It had defeated despotism and it had defeated privilege. The Constituent Assembly, according to Sutherland, had created a society that had mobilised the masses to assume responsibilities in a range of institutions across a variety of levels. Over a million citizens volunteered to help in the national regeneration of France. The contrast with the Napoleonic regime could not have been greater. The Empire paid only lip service to democracy. All the important officers in the state were appointed, often out of the ranks of a new élite – the notables. This was a clear breach with the Revolution, as was its deliberate attempt to control opinion. Whereas ideas flourished during the Revolution they were discouraged by Napoleon. The Concordat was close to a restoration of the refractory church, the destruction of which had been a central feature of the great reforms of the National Assembly. On balance, Napoleon did not preserve the gains of the Revolution.

Some key books in the debate
Alfred Cobban, *A History of Modern France. Volume 2, 1799–1945* (Penguin, 1961).
George Rudé, *Revolutionary Europe 1783–1815* (Penguin, 1964).
D.M.G. Sutherland, *The French Revolution and Empire* (Blackwell, 2003).
Albert Vandal, *The Advent of Napoleon. Volume 1* (Paris, 1903).

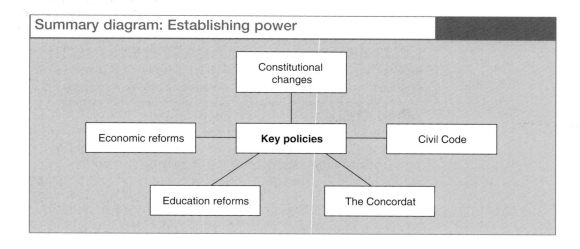

Summary diagram: Establishing power

Study Guide: AS Question

In the style of OCR

'Napoleon's main aim in domestic policy was to win the support of the middle classes.' How far do you agree with this view of the Consulate (1799–1804)?

Exam tips

The cross-references are intended to take you straight to the material that will help you to answer the question.

The question is about the possible motives behind Napoleon's domestic policy and asks you to evaluate the historical validity of a given statement. Your answer must keep its focus on the given elements (domestic policy aims, win middle-class support) in the given time period (the Consulate). There is no set answer – it is up to you to argue your case, but you must address the question. If you do not evaluate policy aims in relation to winning middle-class support, you will not score well.

You will need also to consider what 'middle classes' means in this context. Here you could use a narrow definition (the '*bourgeoisie*') or a broader classification (the 'notables'). That does not matter either because the point is debatable, as long as you apply what you know to the question focus.

A range of evidence is available to you supporting the claim. For example:

- constitutional and administrative reforms that gave prominence to the notables/middle classes as mayors and prefects (pages 40–1)
- education reforms that favoured the able sons of the notables/middle classes (page 52)
- legal reforms and the Concordat that guaranteed notables possession of lands acquired during the Revolution and property rights generally (pages 51 and 55)
- the emphasis on order and efficient government (page 41).

But you must give a balanced answer, which means that alternatives must be considered. Some examples would be:

- Was security in power a more important priority for Napoleon? He may have appeased the notables/middle classes, but not to the extent of allowing freedom of speech/the press or effective middle-class democracy (constitutions).
- Did educational reforms suit the notables/middle classes? They preferred private education to the indoctrination at the *lycées*.

Decide how to interpret the balance between these possibilities and pull your answer together to judge the matter clearly – do not sit on the fence.

Study Guide: A2 Question

In the style of Edexcel

'In the process of consolidating his power, Napoleon had, by May 1804, destroyed the gains of the Revolution.' How far do you agree with this judgement?

Exam tips

The cross-references are intended to take you straight to the material that will help you answer to the question.

You should first remind yourselves, using Chapter 3, what the main gains of the Revolution were in terms of liberty, equality and fraternity. Then consider how far these were undermined by Napoleon's measures as First Consul.

You could consider some key social and political gains of the Revolution to be:

- an end to royal despotism
- the ending of the powers and privileges of the church
- abolition of noble privileges and seigniorial burdens on the peasantry (page 51)
- equality before the law (page 51).

How far did the following undermine those reforms?

- the powers of the First Consul (page 41)
- the hereditary principle (page 44)
- the Concordat (page 54)
- the influence of an élite in the institutions of government and in society.

How far did the following reflect those gains and principles?

- the Civil Code (page 50)
- education reforms (page 52).

Before reaching a conclusion you should also examine the extent to which the constitutional changes of the period to 1804 undermined the progress towards democracy and liberty achieved during the Revolution. Here the debate is more complex. Given the authoritarian and arbitrary powers exercised by the Directory you might conclude on the point that was made on page 58 that 'Bonaparte could not suppress something which did not exist'.

4 Consolidating Power

POINTS TO CONSIDER
Following the *coup* of Brumaire, Napoleon set out by various means to consolidate his power. He went to considerable lengths to ensure that the system he was creating would survive. This chapter will deal with the various methods he used to ensure the survival of the Empire. His approach was a combination of repression and reward, supported by propaganda. The main focus will be on the following themes:

- Coercion and control
- Patronage and bribery
- Censorship and propaganda

Key dates

1800	January 17	Censorship of the press decreed
	February 17	Creation of the role of prefect
1802	May 19	Creation of the Legion of Honour
1803	December 1	*Livret* established
1808	March 1	Creation of new Imperial nobility

1 | Coercion and Control

The restriction of individual liberty was an important element in Napoleon's policy of consolidating and maintaining his grip on the French state. In order to do this, he used many measures, some more subtle than others. During his period in power he built up a system of supervision and control worthy of a modern **dictator**.

Law enforcement and the police

In late eighteenth-century France the word 'police' had a rather different meaning to the modern usage of the word. During the Napoleonic era it referred to the people entrusted with the administration and operation of the entire system of rules and regulations for the maintenance of public order and state security. Napoleon's police system was an important part of his centralised administration and a key element in his attempt to consolidate his power.

Napoleon took a close personal interest in the legal system and the structures for maintaining law and order in France. His interest was directly linked to his need to consolidate his regime and ensure that any potential threat was identified and then stifled. From the beginning of his regime, he made a number of changes to the judiciary in order to ensure its loyalty and deter any potential threats. The most important of these related to judges and courts. The key changes were:

- Judges, apart from local justices of the peace, instead of being elected as under the Directory, were appointed by the government for life and were kept subservient and loyal by a combination of close supervision and a system of 'purges'.
- A whole new hierarchy of judicial tribunals was set up. The Criminal, Commercial and Penal Codes were updated in a similar way to the Civil Code. The Criminal and Penal Codes were essentially concerned with punishment – perpetual hard labour, loss of the right hand and branding were among the penalties laid down. Special new courts emerged – there were military courts and tribunals for political offenders presided over by 'magistrates for public security'.

In 1810, a system of arbitrary imprisonment without trial (similar to the *lettres de cachet* used in pre-Revolutionary France) was reintroduced. This was never extensively used, as the authorities favoured imposing a form of **house arrest** imposed on those considered to be potential threats to the state. A number of extra prisons were built in France and it is estimated that in 1814 they were occupied by about 16,000 ordinary convicts (more than three times as many as in 1800).

The general police

The general police operated under the control of the Minister of Police. For much of the Napoleonic era, this was a position held by Joseph Fouché (see the profile on page 63). In Paris, one of their main functions was to monitor the state of public opinion in the city and to report daily on variations in food prices. The following example dating from after 1808 illustrates this:

> Today everyone is very concerned about Spain and what is going on there. As usual it is all exaggerated. The Ministry of Police has taken measures to quash false rumours. People are no longer complaining about the high price of coffee and sugar; many people go without them.

The general police under Fouché's control focused much of their efforts on surveillance and gathering intelligence on those suspected of being a threat to the security of the state. In their capacity as trained spies, they had a range of functions, principally:

- the imposition of censorship
- the surveillance of possible **subversives**
- the search for army deserters
- the organisation of raids on areas believed to be sheltering **draft dodgers** or enemy agents.

Key terms

Lettres de cachet
A detention order signed by the King and a minister authorising the imprisonment without trial of a named individual.

House arrest
When an individual is confined by the state to his or her house.

Subversives
Those wishing to overthrow the state.

Draft dodgers
Men attempting to avoid conscription to the army.

Profile: Joseph Fouché, Duke of Otranto 1763–1820

1763	– Born near Nantes, son of a sea captain
1792	– Elected to the Convention for the Department of Loire-Inférieure – voted for the execution of Louis XVI
1793	– Appointed representative on mission to Nantes and the West – actively supported the Jacobin policy of **dechristianisation**
1794	– Helped defeat rebels in Lyon. Responsible for mass killings, *mitraillades* – blasting prisoners in to pits using grapeshot. Recalled to Paris
1798	– Became a protégé of Barras and was sent as ambassador to the Cisalpine Republic
1799	– Appointed Minister of Police
1802	– Ministry closed and Fouché dismissed following argument with Napoleon
1808	– Created Duke of Otranto and Minister of the Interior
1809	– Dismissed because of suspicions regarding his loyalty
1809–12	– Lived in semi-retirement in Aix-en-Provence
1812	– Appointed governor of Illyrian Provinces
1814	– Plotted against Napoleon and supported restoration
1815	– Appointed Minister of Police by Louis XVIII
1816	– Denounced as a **regicide** and forced into exile

Joseph Fouché was one of the most ruthless and feared men of the Revolutionary and Napoleonic period and also one of its greatest survivors – a remarkable achievement given his passion for conspiracy and plotting against his superiors. During the Terror, he was a ruthless representative on mission sent to restore republican authority in the provinces. His advice to republicans on how to deal with the uncommitted: '... run them through with the republican weapon, the bayonet'.

While on missions, Fouché actively supported the policy of 'dechristianisation': church property – gold and silver – was to be systematically plundered and sent back to Paris, while cemeteries were to be stripped of religious emblems and their gates inscribed with the words 'Death is an eternal Slumber'.

Although a powerful and ruthless figure who spent many years at the centre of government, there were always question marks regarding his loyalty. His propensity to plot and conspire with the enemies of Napoleon and France led to his dismissal. Although he survived the fall of Napoleon and entered the service of the Bourbons, his past as a Jacobin regicide caught up with him and he spent the last years of his life to 1820 in permanent exile.

Gendarmes

The police were assisted in their normal duties such as the maintenance of law and order and crime prevention and detection by the well-organised body of **gendarmes**, of whom there were about 18,000 stationed throughout France in 1810. Gendarmes were a paramilitary force similar in organisation to the army in that they had uniforms and a distinct structure, yet they were quite separate from the military. Reports were submitted to Napoleon daily by Fouché on the work of his department. His agents were responsible for gathering vast amounts of intelligence about anyone and everyone who posed a potential threat to the state. The information collected in this way was collated and placed in dossiers that could be easily accessed through a filing system. Fouché's agents frequently uncovered sensitive personal details on those under surveillance. This information was sometimes used to blackmail these individuals and 'persuade' them to spy for Fouché.

Napoleon was very aware of the power that Fouché was amassing and took steps to limit this by acquiring information from other sources and relying less on his Minister of Police. He established a prefect of Police for Paris, who reported directly to him and who had a spy network of his own, operating independently of Fouché. Letters were opened, reports made, reputations destroyed and careers blighted as the result of information collected for Napoleon by these men – but not only by them. Provincial officials were expected to act as spies in the course of their work, and to relay their findings back to Paris.

Prefects

On 17 February 1800 a law was passed which reformed local government in France. The key position in this new structure was that of prefect. Each department would have a prefect (*préfets*). They and their assistants the sub-prefects (*sous-préfets*) of the **arrondissements** were the men responsible for managing local government throughout France. They acted as agents of the central government and were directly appointed by Napoleon and accountable solely to him. So, too, were the members of their advisory councils, and the mayors (*maires*) of the larger communes. Their direct accountability to Napoleon and the range of powers at their disposal placed them at the heart of the system of state control of the population. The other mayors and all the municipal councils were nominated by the prefect. The result was a highly centralised bureaucracy for the collection of taxes, the enforcement of conscription, the dissemination of propaganda, and the obtaining of information, operating through a body of well-trained and loyal administrators. The eminent British historian Richard Cobb described the whole structure as 'bureaucratic repression'.

The prefects, in particular, were expected to monitor closely public opinion in their areas and to report on any suspicious political activity. A system of house arrest was available through the prefects for anyone who did not warrant imprisonment but

Key terms

Gendarmes
A police force set up in 1790 and modelled on the cavalry attached to the royal family during the *ancien régime*.

Arrondissements
The sub-divisions making up each department.

Key question
Why was the prefect system such a powerful tool for maintaining control over the population?

Key date
Creation of the role of prefect: 17 February 1800

who was considered a danger to state security. The advice given by Lucien Bonaparte of what was expected of the prefects offers a valuable insight into their role.

Lucien Bonaparte's explanation to the prefects of their mission 1800

This post demands of you a wide range of duties, but it offers you great rewards in the future ... Your first task is to destroy irrevocably in your department, the influence of those events which for too long have dominated our minds. Do your utmost to bring hatred and passion to an end ... In your public decisions, be always the first magistrate of your department, never a man of the Revolution. Do not tolerate any public reference to the labels which still cling to the diverse political parties of the Revolution; merely consign them to the most deplorable chapter in the history of human folly ... apply yourself immediately to the **conscription draft** ... I give special priority to the collection of taxes: their prompt payment is now a sacred duty. Agriculture, trade, the industries and professions must resume their honoured status. Respect and honour our farmers ... Protect our trade ... Visit our manufacturers: bestow your highest compliments on those distinguished citizens engaged in them ... Encourage the new generations; fix your attention on public education, and the formation of Men, Citizens and Frenchmen.

Not very different were the obligations laid on senators when proceeding to their *senatoreries*. Napoleon wrote to them at length:

> Your most important duty will be to supply Us with trustworthy and positive information on any point which may interest the government, and to this end, you will send Us a direct report, once a week ... You will realise that complete secrecy must be observed as this is a confidential mission ... You will draw up detailed returns of all information about these persons [public officials, the clergy, teachers, men of importance, farmers, industrialists, criminals] basing your information upon facts and send the reports in to Us. You will observe the condition of the roads ... and investigate the state of public opinion on (i) the government, (ii) religion, (iii) conscription, (iv) direct and indirect taxation ...

Opposition

With such well-organised surveillance it is not surprising that the regime met with little serious political opposition. Any potential opposition leaders such as notables, intellectuals and members of the *bourgeoisie* were increasingly tempted into allying themselves with the government in the hope of rewards. The only means of opposition open to the ordinary people were resisting conscription, deserting once enlisted (despite the ferocious penalties for doing so) or joining one of the bands of **brigands**

Key terms

Conscription draft
All men who were eligible for compulsory military service.

Senatoreries
Estates of land awarded to members of the Senate.

Brigands
Gangs of outlaws roaming the countryside.

that operated on a grand scale in much of the French
countryside.

Conscription

Conscription had always been unpopular ever since it was
introduced in 1793, but recent research shows that, until the
massive **levies** of 1813, resistance to it was much weaker under
Napoleon than it had been under the Directory. Over 90 per cent
of the expected levies were raised without difficulty in the years
before 1808. It may have been partly due to better
administration, but, while Napoleon was winning victories and
casualties were low, resistance to conscription was not a serious
problem. Only when the military tide turned against him (from
1812) and the casualties mounted did resistance increase.

Levies
Soldiers raised by
conscription.

Key term

The *livret*

Ensuring that workers did not pose a threat to the regime was an
important role for the police. Urban workers, in particular the
sans-culottes, had been an active and militant feature of the great
upheavals of the early years of the Revolution between 1789 and
1793. Napoleon had directly witnessed popular power during the
journée of Vendémiaire (see pages 12–13), which he had helped to
suppress. He was thus aware of the power of ordinary people, and

Key question
What was the *livret*
and why was it
introduced?

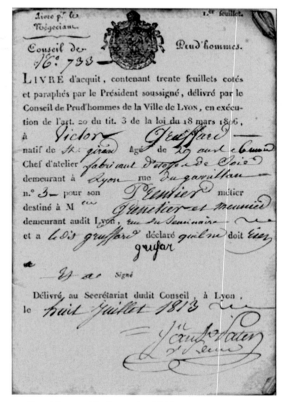

A page from a *livret* issued in Lyon in 1813.

Key terms

Guild system
The rigid control of entry into a range of professions and occupations in order to maintain high wages and prices.

Le Chapelier law
A law passed by the National Assembly in 1791 that banned strikes and made trade unions illegal.

Key date

Livret – a worker's passbook – was established:
1 December 1803

the potential threat they could pose to the state. When the *ancien régime* had been dismantled after 1789, one of the features abolished had been the **guild system**. This system had restricted workers by controlling entry into various trades. Following abolition, workers were free to follow any occupation of their choice. Workers' freedoms, however, did not last very long and they were once again reduced by the **Le Chapelier law**. Maintaining close control over workers was considered to be an important priority for the police.

In order to try and control the movement of workers, Napoleon reintroduced the *livret* on 1 December 1803. This had been one of the methods of controlling workers employed by the *ancien régime*. The *livret* was a passbook that every worker was expected to have, and to hand over to each new employer when he moved between jobs. The passbook also operated as a form of identity card since it contained the personal details of the holder and his profession, in addition to his employment record. Workers were unable to get other jobs without their *livrets* as this served as a clear indication that previous employers had released them and that their behaviour was good. If a worker wished to travel from one part of France to another he would be unable to do so without his *livret*. The movement of labour was, therefore, tightly controlled and those who did leave one employer for another were dependent on good references. A further restriction was that those workers who travelled from one department to another required official permission to do so.

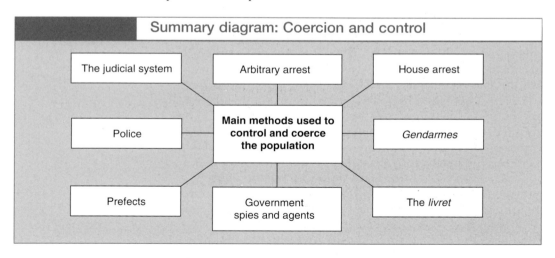

Summary diagram: Coercion and control

The judicial system — Arbitrary arrest — House arrest

Police — **Main methods used to control and coerce the population** — *Gendarmes*

Prefects — Government spies and agents — The *livret*

2 | Patronage and Bribery

The Legion of Honour

Key question
What was the Legion of Honour and how did it operate?

Many families had taken advantage of the large-scale redistribution of land which had taken place in the early 1790s. They had a vested interest in ensuring that they would not lose their property. Throughout his time in power, Napoleon was determined to favour property owners and would-be property owners. As a way of building up a strong body of personal support for himself and ensuring loyalty to his regime, particularly among the military, Napoleon dispensed a considerable amount of **patronage**. This took the form of gifts of money, land, titles, honours and government appointments. On 19 May 1802, he set up the Legion of Honour. This was divided into 15 cohorts (groups) each comprising 350 legionaries, 30 officers, 20 commandants and seven grand officers. Recipients received a distinctive decoration and a small annual award: 250 francs a year, rising to 5000 francs for grand officers.

In the 12 years following the establishment of the Legion of Honour, 38,000 awards (only 4000 of which went to civilians) were made. Between 1804 and 1808, new titles were created for the officials of the new imperial court. These ranged from 'grand dignitaries', such as the arch-chancellor, through 'grand officers', down to lesser dignitaries, such as the prefects of the palace. Some of these titles brought with them large estates, and, although these at first went only to members of the Bonaparte family, they were soon being bestowed on court officials and statesmen, as well as on the 26 outstanding generals who were created Marshals of France. The estates awarded to these generals were mostly in Poland, Germany and Italy. It was, therefore, probable that Napoleon's intention was to appeal to these men's self-interest, and use it to his own advantage. They knew that the only way of retaining their property was to remain loyal to Napoleon and ensure that he was able to maintain the Empire's frontiers.

Imperial nobility

On 1 March 1808 Napoleon went further and began the creation of a new imperial nobility. All 'grand dignitaries' became princes, **archbishops** became counts, mayors of large towns became barons, and members of the Legion of Honour were allowed to call themselves Chevaliers. These titles were awarded directly by the Emperor for state service, usually of a military kind. If the recipient possessed a large enough annual income – 200,000 francs in the case of a duke for instance – the titles could be made hereditary. Where worthy candidates for ennoblement had insufficient personal fortunes to support a title they were provided, like the generals, with estates in far-off parts of the Empire from which to raise the necessary revenue. In all, about 3500 titles were granted between 1808 and 1814.

One area in which civilians benefited was in the allocation of *senatoreries*. These were grants of large country estates to members of the Senate, together with a palatial residence and an annual income of 25,000 francs to support it. Included in the grant was appointment as *préfet* (prefect) not just of the usual *département* but of a whole region. Lesser individuals also benefited from Napoleon's personal gifts. For instance, more than 5000 presents of enough money to buy a house in Paris and to live there in comfort were made to army officers, government officials and minor members of the new nobility.

Key dates

Creation of the Legion of Honour: 19 May 1802

Creation of the new Imperial nobility: 1 March 1808

Key terms

Patronage
Using various means including bribery and rewards to gain support.

Archbishop
A senior figure in the church with authority over bishops.

Key question
What were the benefits of being a member of the imperial nobility?

Key term

Indoctrination
The process of imposing a set of beliefs and values on people.

However, Napoleon seems to have realised from the beginning that bribery as a means of control was unreliable, and was not on its own sufficient to maintain popular support even among the recipients. He believed that it would only work as part of a broader strategy, which embraced compulsion, intimidation and **indoctrination**. All of these became important features of Napoleon's policy for consolidating his power in France, and as such essential parts of his system of government.

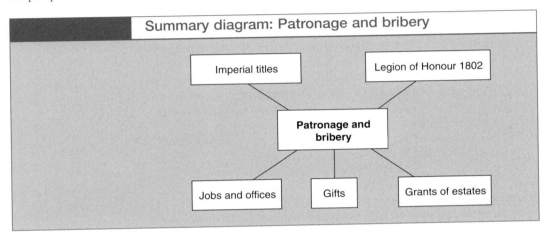

Summary diagram: Patronage and bribery

3 | Censorship and Propaganda

Censorship

Key question
What forms of censorship did Napoleon impose on France?

From an early stage in his military career, while campaigning in Italy, Napoleon had become very aware of the advantages to be gained in controlling the flow of information. In the numerous dispatches that he wrote and sent back to France while campaigning, he was particularly keen to enhance his own role in any of the battles he had taken part in. This early awareness of the benefits of **propaganda** was developed much more fully after he became First Consul and then Emperor. The benefits of propaganda, however, could only be fully realised if all other sources of information were controlled or closed to the population. Propaganda would always be more effective when used alongside **censorship**.

Key terms

Propaganda
Using the media to persuade the population to support the regime.

Censorship
The control or suppression by the state of media and culture considered critical.

The press was expected to act as the unquestioning mouthpiece of the government and to be the purveyor of official propaganda. Napoleon wrote

> The newspapers are always ready to seize on anything which might undermine public tranquillity ... Newspapers ... announce and prepare revolutions and in the end make them indispensable. With a smaller number of newspapers it is easier to supervise them and to direct them more firmly towards the strengthening of the constitutional regime ... I will never allow the newspapers to say or do anything against my interest.

Control of the press

What did Napoleon do to control the press in France?

- On 17 January 1800, he arbitrarily reduced the number of political journals published in Paris from 73 to 13 and forbade the production of any new ones. Only nine remained by the end of the year. In 1811, all except four of the Parisian papers had been suppressed and those that remained were made subject to police supervision.
- These survivors were kept short of reliable news and were forbidden to discuss controversial subjects. Topics such as the *coup* of Brumaire and the Revolutionary period, particularly the Vendée rebellion, were strictly off limits. Editors were forced to rely for news on the military bulletins or longer political articles published in **Le Moniteur**, the official government paper. Many of these were written by Napoleon himself or by his ministers.
- In 1809 censors were appointed to each newspaper.
- In 1811 provincial papers were reduced to one per department. Some departments had no newspaper at all.

Key date
Censorship of the press decreed: 17 January 1800

Key term
Le Moniteur
A popular newspaper founded in 1789. It became the official government newspaper in 1799.

Censorship of books and plays

It was not only newspapers that were censored. Up to 1810, reports on all books, plays, lectures and posters that appeared in Paris were sent daily to Napoleon. All publishers were required to forward two copies of every book, prior to publication, to police headquarters for inspection by the censors. In 1810, a regular system of censors was set up, more than half the printing presses in Paris were shut down, and publishers were forced to take out a license and to swear an oath of loyalty to the government. Booksellers were strictly controlled and severely punished, even with death, if found to be selling material considered subversive.

Authors were harassed and sometimes forced into exile if they criticised the government, however slightly, while dramatists were forbidden to mention any historical event that might, however indirectly, reflect adversely on the present regime. Many theatres were closed down. Others operated only under licence and were restricted to putting on a small repertory of officially sanctioned plays. One poet was consigned to detention in a mental asylum for writing: 'The great Napoleon is a great chameleon.' The same fate awaited any priest who criticised Napoleon from the pulpit.

Propaganda

The effectiveness of censorship in controlling the media was balanced by propaganda. Media output was closely manipulated by Napoleon to cast himself and his regime in the most favourable light. According the Geoffrey Ellis state propaganda had two main aims:

- a negative aim of stifling all opposition
- a positive aim of rousing morale among the 'citizen soldiers' and civilian subjects of the emperor by carefully co-ordinating celebrations of his military victories and imperial grandeur.

Key question
What were the main features of Napoleon's approach to propaganda?

Information

Napoleon sought to control the release of information. He had first adopted such an approach while commanding the Army of Italy in 1796. During this time he was deliberately constructing a heroic image of himself by carefully crafting his written dispatches. Information was released in two forms during this campaign – Orders of the Day and Bulletins. In general, Orders of the Day were issued to the soldiers under his command to raise morale. The Bulletins were designed to have much wider public appeal and were sent back to Paris where they were published in the government newspaper *Le Moniteur*. These accounts were invariably exaggerated and emphasised French victories and the role played in them by Napoleon. To 'lie like a bulletin', became a well-used phrase during the Empire and suggests a level of popular cynicism among certain sections of society, regarding Napoleon's propaganda.

Art

Italy also offered Napoleon an opportunity to win popular support by another means.

He was very aware that many of the élite of French society were also patrons of the visual arts. As Italy contained an enormous wealth of art, Napoleon ensured that any settlements he negotiated with defeated Italian states involved the transfer of paintings and sculptures to the **Louvre** in Paris. In 1803 the gallery which housed these works was renamed the *Musée Napoleon*. He hoped that the propaganda value of these transfers, which he arranged, would enhance his reputation and secure his place as a major benefactor of the arts. On a much more practical level, he fully grasped the propaganda value of visual images. During the Italian campaign, he either commissioned or allowed over 30 images of himself to be produced. Most of the prints based on these sold in large numbers to ordinary people and confirmed his status as the most popular general in France.

As Consul and then Emperor, Napoleon sought out and supported the leading French artists of the day. David, Ingres and Gros were all employed by him as state propagandists (see page 165). They frequently depicted him as a romantic hero-figure, or the embodiment of supreme imperial authority. Looking back to the imperial grandeur of ancient Rome, which in many ways he sought to emulate, Napoleon was often painted in a classical pose, complete with toga and laurel wreath. David, as 'painter to the government', was given the oversight of all paintings done in France, with particular reference to the suitability of the subject matter. It was David who painted the monumental official portrayal of Napoleon's coronation in **Notre Dame** (page 46). In contrast, the compassionate side of Napoleon's character was the theme of a painting by Gros of Napoleon visiting the plague victims at Jaffa.

Key terms

Louvre
The premier gallery and museum in Paris, on the site of a former royal fortress.

Notre Dame
The Catholic cathedral in Paris, located on an island in the river Seine.

Bonaparte Visiting the Victims of the Plague at Jaffa, 1804 by A.J. Gros.

Architecture

Many powerful leaders seek to leave their mark on the architecture of their capital and Napoleon was no exception. Two of the best examples in Paris of architecture initiated by Napoleon are among the city's most famous and best loved landmarks. The first, which was completed in 1810, is a 44-metre high column located in the centre of Place Vendôme to commemorate Napoleon's victory at Battle of Austerlitz in 1805 (see page 162). It was closely modelled on **Trajan's column** in ancient Rome. The central stone pillar was overlaid with a veneer of bas-relief bronze plates made from the 133 cannon captured at the battle. Figures on the plates were cast to glorify the achievements of the French army, exactly as the original had celebrated the Roman army. To complete the link with ancient Rome, a statue of Napoleon as Caesar was placed on top of the column. A much more dramatic addition to the Parisian skyline was the commission in 1806 by Napoleon of a monumental arch to celebrate the achievements of the French army. Although Napoleon would never see the completed Arc de Triomph, its site at the head of Paris' most famous boulevard, the Champs-Elysées, makes it the most prominent visible reminder of the Napoleonic era in Paris.

Trajan's column
Erected in 113AD to celebrate the victories of the Emperor Trajan and decorated with images of the Roman army.

Key term

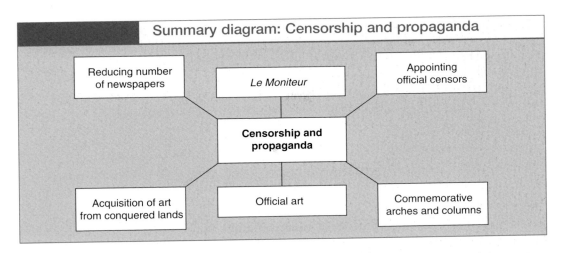

Summary diagram: Censorship and propaganda

- Reducing number of newspapers
- *Le Moniteur*
- Appointing official censors
- **Censorship and propaganda**
- Acquisition of art from conquered lands
- Official art
- Commemorative arches and columns

4 | The Key Debate

What sort of ruler was Napoleon, and how did his rule impact upon ordinary people? Was he a ruthless military dictator – a prototype for the fascist/communist dictators of the twentieth century – or merely a more refined model of the enlightened despots of the eighteenth century? A key issue is:

> What sort of ruler was Napoleon and how did his rule impact on France?

Richard Cobb

One of the most distinguished British historians of the French Revolution and the Napoleonic era was Professor Richard Cobb. He belongs to the 'history from below' tradition of studying the past, an approach characterised by detailed research of the impact of events upon the lives of ordinary people – as opposed to the study of 'great men' in history, or 'history from above'. One of Cobb's most important studies was an examination of crime and protest during the period 1789–1820. His study of aspects of French society covered poverty, conscription and famine, and their impact upon ordinary citizens. Against this background, Cobb had little doubt that Napoleon created 'France's most appalling regime', and that ordinary people played an important role in bringing it down.

Alfred Cobban

During the 1930s, Alfred Cobban published a study of *Dictatorship: Its History and Theory*. The timing was significant. War in Europe was looming and dictatorships were the dominant political systems in several European countries, most notably Germany, Italy and the Soviet Union. Cobban was emphatic in his belief that Napoleon was the greatest dictator in modern history. He rose to power via the army and was the architect of his own greatness. According to Cobban, Napoleon's ability alone held him on his throne, but he never made the mistake of over-

estimating the power of force in governing a country or of under-
estimating the power of opinion. To remain in power Napoleon
mobilised all factors that might support him – an obedient
church, rigid censorship and propaganda.

Jacques Bainville

Also writing in the 1930s was the French historian Jacques
Bainville. During that decade Bainville published a number of
influential works including *Napoléon* (Paris, 1931) and *Dictators*.
Bainville's assessment of Napoleon was that apart from glory and
art, it would probably have been better had he never lived. While
this would appear to be a damning judgement on the Emperor,
Bainville was careful to qualify his conclusion. He noted that
France in 1815 was smaller in terms of area than it had been in
1799, and the country's economy and society had suffered greatly
during the Empire. Yet Bainville considered Napoleon to be one
of the best examples of a dictator, and that dictatorship was not
necessarily a bad form of government. He admired the
authoritarianism that Napoleon displayed, but had reservations
about the impact of his rule.

Martyn Lyons

Martin Lyons supports the view that Napoleon was a dictator, but
highlights the distinctly personal aspects of his rule as opposed to
the coercive ones. Unlike the enlightened authoritarian rulers of
eighteenth-century Europe, Napoleon uniquely sought to consult
the people directly at various times. Lyons calls this 'dictatorship
by plebiscite'. He argues that Bonapartism 'rested on the
assumption that the leader himself embodied the nation and was
the living incarnation of popular sovereignty in action'. In the
system that he created parliaments elected by the people were of
limited importance. His rule was presidential in style in that it
created a strong executive that relegated parliamentary
government to a minor role. But the system, Lyons points out,
was supported by the 'coercive apparatus of the state', in
particular an active policing system and strict censorship.

Some key books in the debate

Jacques Bainville, *Napoléon* (Paris, 1931) and *Dictators* (London
1937).

Alfred Cobban, *Dictatorship: Its History and Theory* (Jonathan Cape,
1939).

Richard Cobb, *The Police and the People. French Popular Protest
1789–1820* (Oxford, 1970).

Martin Lyons, *Napoleon Bonaparte and the Legacy of the French
Revolution* (Palgrave Macmillan, 1994).

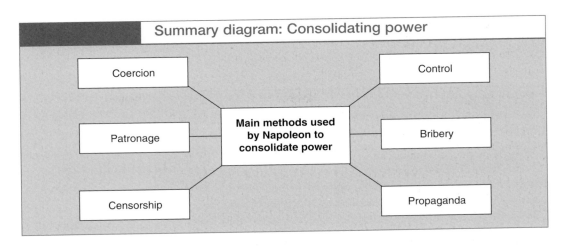

Summary diagram: Consolidating power

Coercion

Control

Main methods used by Napoleon to consolidate power

Patronage

Bribery

Censorship

Propaganda

Study Guide: AS Question

In the style of OCR A

To what extent was Napoleon a dictator?

Exam tips

The cross-references are intended to take you straight to the material that will help you to answer the question.

The command 'To what extent ...?' tells you to weigh up whether he was a dictator or not. Examiners will not be looking for one set answer, but you must address the question as set, which is about evaluating the nature of Napoleonic rule, which seemed to mix authoritarian features with apparent more liberal characteristics. If you want to score highly, you must assess both sides of the argument seriously, even if you are convinced that he definitely was or was not.

Evidence from his regime that might support the claim that he was a dictator could include:

- the increasingly authoritarian nature of the Constitutions (pages 44–5)
- the police state and restrictions on freedom (pages 64–5)
- the repression of opposition (page 62)
- the cult of personality surrounding Napoleon (page 164).

On the other hand, you must also need to consider evidence against, such as:

- the constitutions provided for assemblies and universal suffrage (page 40)
- ratification of changes by plebiscite (page 41)
- the Civil Code enshrined Revolutionary principles such as equality before law (page 51)
- the Concordat and Organic articles provided for religious tolerance (page 55).

You might also point out that some elements associated with dictatorship were relatively rare or not present in Napoleonic France, for example the use of arbitrary arrest, the direct involvement of the military in government.

You can argue the case either way, as long as you use evidence to support your claims. A strong answer will evaluate a range of factors that gives more or less equal discussion to both sides before reaching a judgement.

Study Guide: A2 Question

In the style of Edexcel

'A dictatorship dependent on coercion.' How far do you agree with this description of the regime established by Napoleon by 1804?

> ### Exam tips
>
> *The cross-references are intended to take you straight to the material that will help you to answer the question.*
>
> There are two elements to examine in this question: how far the regime was a dictatorship and, if so, how far it was dictatorship by coercion.
>
> In terms of 'dictatorship' you should examine the extent of Napoleon's control in 1799 and its growth in the period:
>
> - Consul for life (page 44)
> - the purging of the Tribunate and Legislative Assembly in 1802 (page 44)
> - becoming Emperor of the French (page 45)
> - the use of the powers of the prefects and the police (pages 64–5)
> - powers to control the press and the release of information (page 70)
> - powers to control the judicial system (page 51).
>
> How far does the use of plebiscites counter the charge of dictatorship, or was this 'dictatorship by plebiscite' which undermined the role of parliamentary government?
>
> You should also examine how far Napoleon's authority depended on coercion. You may consider that the exercise of patronage, bribery and the use of propaganda and the controls on the flow of information (pages 70–1) indicate a regime that primarily exercised control rather than coercion.

5 Napoleon and Europe: Conquest and Empire 1796–1807

POINTS TO CONSIDER

For many the most notable of Napoleon's achievements are his military conquests. These laid the basis of his empire in Europe and established his reputation as one of the greatest military commanders in history. The foundation of his empire was laid during the Italian campaign of 1796–7 and subsequently expanded and consolidated during the Consulate and then the Empire. The focus of this chapter will be on Napoleon's conflicts with European powers, which laid the basis for his empire, and the methods and tactics that he used to resolve them. A number of key areas will be examined. These are:

- Early campaigns in Italy and Egypt 1796–9
- Wars of the Consulate and early Empire 1799–1807
- Military and strategic developments
- Napoleon's leadership

Key dates

1796	March 2	Napoleon given command of the Army of Italy
1797	October 17	Treaty of Campo Formio
1798	May 19	Napoleon set out to invade Egypt
	August 1	Nelson destroyed the French fleet at Aboukir Bay
1799	August 23	Napoleon abandoned his army in Egypt and returned to France
1800	June 14	Battle of Marengo
1801	February 9	Peace of Luneville signed between France and Austria
1802	March 25	Peace of Amiens between France and Britain
1803	May	War resumed against Britain – now known as the Napoleonic War
1805	October 20	Austrian army defeated at Ulm
	October 21	Franco-Spanish fleet defeated by Nelson at Trafalgar
	December 2	Battle of Austerlitz
	December 26	Treaty of Pressburg

| 1806 | October 14 | Prussian forces defeated at the battles of Jena and Auerstädt |
| 1807 | July 7–9 | Treaty of Tilsit signed with Russia and Prussia |

1 | Early Campaigns in Italy and Egypt 1796–9

The Italian campaign 1796–7

Key question
What did Napoleon achieve during the Italian campaign of 1796–7?

It was the Italian campaigns of 1796–7, with a dozen victories in less than a year, which sealed Napoleon's reputation as a great military commander. This campaign also marked his emergence as a 'political general', a soldier not merely content to follow orders but to act independently in pursuit of his own goals as well as those of his country. A great deal has been written about the Italian campaign, by Napoleon himself and by others, some of it accurate, some of it a rather fanciful exaggeration of the facts. In many ways his time in Italy laid the foundation for the Napoleonic legend. The Italian campaign is notable for two significant developments in Napoleon's career:

- First, his gradual belief in his own sense of destiny – that greatness in some form awaited him.
- Second, his awareness of the value of propaganda in winning over not only those under his command but those who could be useful to him in future.

Key date
Napoleon given command of the Army of Italy: 2 March 1796

Napoleon was appointed commander of the Army of Italy on 2 March 1796. The often-repeated account of how a young, inexperienced general, who was a political appointee, dramatically won over to his side the sceptical veteran officers of the Army of Italy is a considerable exaggeration. Napoleon was already well known to the officers concerned, and they, far from deriding him, seem to have welcomed him on his arrival as the man most likely to lead them to victory.

When Napoleon arrived in Nice he assumed command of an army numbering nearly 63,000 men. Of these, only about 38,000 were fit or ready for active service. By all accounts the condition of the army was poor. Morale was low, the soldiers were badly clothed and fed, mainly because of corrupt administration. The troops had not been paid in months, the general level of hygiene among the lower ranks was poor and discipline was starting to break down. When Napoleon later reflected on his new command he was keen to emphasise its rather chaotic state, since it made his own role in reversing the situation all the more impressive. Yet despite its poor condition and the fact that it had not had much success since 1792, the majority of the army consisted of experienced and hardened campaigners, mostly volunteers who had joined in 1792, alongside a core of regular soldiers from the royal army. All it needed was inspirational leadership, and this Napoleon provided.

Shortly before the army left France for Italy, Napoleon addressed
his soldiers in person. There is no official record of his first
speech to his men, which was by all accounts a rousing piece of
oratory. Napoleon many years later produced a version of the
speech, while on board the **Bellerophon**. Most eyewitnesses, with
minor modifications, agree with the essential sentiments
expressed in his later version. In addressing his men he told
them:

> Soldiers! You are hungry and naked. The government owes you
> much. It can give you nothing. ... I want to lead you into the most
> fertile plains on earth. Rich provinces, great towns will be in your
> power: there you will find glory and riches.

Bellerophon
A British warship
on which Napoleon
was held while
awaiting transport
to St Helena in
1815.

Key term

The speech has been interpreted by many as a green light for the
army to loot and pillage its way across the north Italian plain.

The Italian campaign 1796–7.

French forces were certainly involved in this sort of activity, which was fairly typical of most armies at the time. In reality, given the uncertainty of regular wages from the state, the offer of plunder was considered an acceptable way of raising morale and restoring discipline.

Arrival in Italy

Within a month of his arrival in Italy, Napoleon had conquered and occupied Piedmont, and, at the beginning of May 1796, crossed the River Po into Lombardy in pursuit of the Austrian army. He seems to have regarded the subsequent Battle of Lodi and the entry into Milan as a psychological turning point in his career. Following these victories, which gave him a degree of confidence, Napoleon believed that he could 'perform great things, which hitherto had been only a fantastic dream'. Italy lay wide open to the plundering French soldiers as they marched

L'Imagerie Populaire by P.L. Duchartre and R. Saulmier shows Napoleon planting the French flag on the Lodi Bridge, 10 May 1796.

south, defeating four separate Austrian armies as they went. In February 1797, with the capture of Mantua, the French conquest of northern Italy was complete.

Napoleon next moved against Austria itself and a month later was only just over 60 miles from Vienna where, with his army exhausted and dangerously far from base, he offered the Austrians preliminary peace terms. While these terms were awaiting ratification, Napoleon completed his triumphant Italian campaign by occupying the Republic of Genoa (which adopted a French-style constitution and became the Ligurian Republic), by overrunning part of the Republic of Venice, and by concluding on his own initiative an agreement with the Pope. He then installed himself and his wife Josephine in near-royal splendour in a castle near Milan.

The Treaty of Camp Formio 1797

The Treaty of Campo Formio, negotiated by Napoleon, was signed on 17 October 1797. It brought to an end the war between France and Austria. The main terms of the treaty were:

- France was allowed to keep the Austrian Netherlands (modern-day Belgium).
- French gains in northern Italy, in what was once Lombardy, were consolidated into the newly formed Cisalpine Republic (Modena, Ferrara, Reggio, Bologna and the Romagna). This state became a French **puppet state**.
- The Ionian islands and the part of Dalmatia controlled by the Republic of Venice were given to France.
- Austria was allowed to retain control over Venice, but had to offer support to France in its efforts to gain the left bank of the Rhine in negotiations with the **Holy Roman Empire**.

The newly created Cisalpine Republic was given a system of government based on the French constitution of 1795 and its executive and legislative bodies were nominated by Napoleon himself. 'Only he can make peace, and he can do it on any terms he wants' was the comment of one Austrian envoy in Paris. It seemed a brilliant peace from the point of view of French national prestige and was received enthusiastically in Paris, where Napoleon was given a hero's welcome on his return in December 1797.

The significance of the Italian campaign for Napoleon

The Italian campaign transformed Napoleon from a minor general into the most famous soldier in the Republic. He had achieved what no one else had been able to do – end the war on mainland Europe. During the course of the campaign, he had wielded more real power than any other republican soldier. Napoleon had swept away old states and replaced them with new ones, and, on his own initiative, he had negotiated directly with the Austrians and the Pope. On occasions, he had ignored the views of the Directors. Their weakness and increasing reliance on

Key question
What were the main terms of the Treaty of Campo Formio?

Treaty of Campo Formio: 17 October 1797

Key date

Puppet state
A state directly under the control of another state.

Holy Roman Empire
A union of states of various sizes, mostly German speaking, which existed between 962 and 1806, whose rulers recognised the authority of an Emperor.

Key terms

Key question
What was the significance of the Italian campaign in Napoleon's career?

the army was further emphasised by the *coup* of Fructidor (see page 14).

In the mid-1790s, French government finances were in an increasingly parlous state. They were becoming increasingly dependent on the money Napoleon sent back from Italy. He imposed huge levies of cash on the defeated Italian states. Milan had to pay over 20 million francs to the French state in addition to important collections of art. Napoleon certainly delivered on his initial promise to his troops of 'glory and riches'. There was no longer any issue about lack of pay. The bond between the commander and his forces became extremely strong. In a revealing insight to a colleague in 1797 Napoleon confided: 'I have tasted authority and I will not give it up'. According to the historian Philip Dwyer, during the Italian campaign Napoleon '… had become confident, arrogant even, in the face of so many victories. He would gradually come to the realisation that he could exist, as a political entity, independently of the government in Paris'.

The Egyptian and Syrian campaign 1798–9

Key question
Why did Napoleon invade Egypt?

Key term

First Coalition
Had been in existence since 1793 when Britain joined the war against France.

The defeat of Austria effectively ended the **First Coalition**. Only Britain remained at war with France. Having secured victory in mainland Europe, the Directors hoped that Napoleon could complete the task by defeating Britain. He was appointed to command the newly formed 'Army of England'. When Napoleon reviewed the plans to defeat Britain, he concluded that French naval power was not strong enough to provide protection to any invasion force. The plan was shelved. He suggested an alternative plan. This involved attacking British commercial interests in the eastern Mediterranean by disrupting the trade route with India. The route passed through Egypt and along the Red Sea, both parts of the Ottoman Empire. Napoleon was also considering the possibility of using any gains made in Egypt to launch a direct assault on British interests in India. The need to keep this ambitious and potentially dangerous young general and his unemployed troops busy, and out of politics, was clearly a factor in the Directory agreeing to the proposal. Napoleon was appointed to command the newly formed Army of the Orient and to invade Egypt.

Egypt

Key date

Napoleon set out to invade Egypt: 19 May 1798

On the morning of 19 May 1798, a force of 38,000 men in 300 ships set out to invade Egypt. The Egyptian expedition was not only a military operation. It was also planned as a scientific and civilising mission – to the mysterious orient. The army was accompanied by 167 scientists, scholars and engineers who were to set up the Institute of Egypt in Cairo. The first task facing the invasion force was to avoid contact with the Royal Navy. Admiral Nelson had been sent to the Mediterranean to disrupt French plans. The French fleet successfully avoided the British, and even managed to capture Malta on route to Egypt. French forces landed in Egypt unopposed in July and soon captured the city of

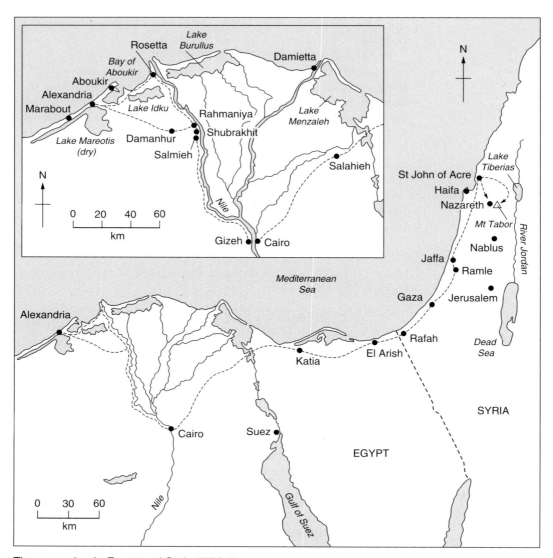

The campaign in Egypt and Syria 1798–9.

Alexandria. Following victory over Egyptian forces at the Battle of the Pyramids, Napoleon entered Cairo. His success was to some extent tarnished by news a few weeks later, that Nelson on 1 August 1798 had destroyed the French fleet at Aboukir Bay. The Army of the Orient was now cut off from France.

Key date

Nelson destroyed the French fleet at Aboukir Bay: 1 August 1798

Syria

Egypt was quickly occupied and French rule established. The decision to attack Syria was taken to try and force the Ottoman Empire out of the coalition with Britain. The campaign was not successful and proved to be one of Napoleon's first military setbacks. The town of Jaffa was captured after a short siege, following which French soldiers acting under Napoleon's orders massacred 3000 prisoners. The next French target was the fortress

Key question
Why did Napoleon abandon his army in Egypt?

Key date

Napoleon abandoned his army in Egypt and returned to France: 23 August 1799

Key question
What do the campaigns in Italy and Egypt reveal about Napoleon?

Key term

Blitzkrieg
A war of rapid movement where large numbers of forces are directed towards a very narrow front.

of St John of Acre. The French were drawn into an abortive, two-month siege, during which they lost half the army. With supplies running out and disease affecting his troops, Napoleon gave up the attempt to capture the fortress and returned to Egypt. Back in Cairo, he received news of French military defeats in Europe and an emerging political crisis in Paris. On 23 August 1799, amid great secrecy to avoid the British navy, Napoleon abandoned his army in Egypt and returned to France.

Conclusion

The campaigns in Italy and to a lesser extent in Egypt provide a useful insight into key aspects of Napoleon's career, military abilities and personality. These are:

- Militarily, they showed Napoleon at his best, and were a model for later *blitzkrieg* strategies that he used successfully until 1808 to defeat his enemies' old-fashioned and disunited armies.
- A number of the personality traits that later came to be associated with Napoleon became apparent during the course of these campaigns. Among these were great personal ambition, supreme self-confidence, determination, ruthlessness and supreme powers of leadership.
- He frequently exceeded his orders, particularly when negotiating peace terms with defeated enemies.
- He was guilty of unnecessary cruelty, as can be seen by his order of the cold-blooded murder of 3000 prisoners after the fall of Jaffa.
- His great awareness of the value of propaganda and self-promotion. The painting by Gros of Napoleon visiting the plague victims at Jaffa (see page 72) is a good example of this.

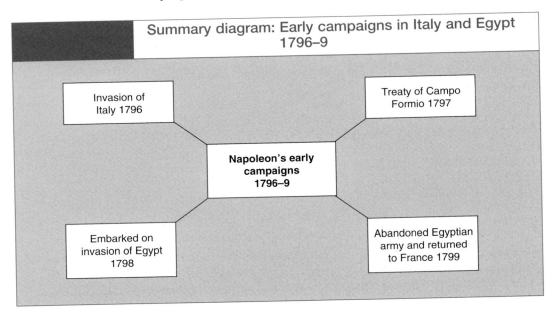

Summary diagram: Early campaigns in Italy and Egypt 1796–9

2 | Wars of the Consulate and Early Empire 1799–1807

Key question
What was the nature of the relationship between the members of the Second Coalition?

In the spring of 1799, the **Second Coalition** went to war with France. It was, in theory, a strong combination. In reality, however, it was nothing of the sort. It was not an overall coalition, rather a series of separate alliances, and even these links were not complete for there was no alliance between Britain and Austria. More importantly, there was no agreement on a unified military **strategy**, nor was there a commitment by the allies not to make a separate peace with France if it suited their individual interests to do so. Although Austrian and Russian forces expelled the French from Italy in the summer of 1799, they were unable to capitalise on their victories. News of these Italian defeats brought Napoleon hurrying back from Egypt and drew him into the plot which resulted in the *coup* of Brumaire (see pages 23–4). To the north of France the Anglo-Russian army which landed in Holland was defeated by the French. There followed recriminations between the Russian and British commanders, with each blaming the other for the defeat.

Tensions between the allies increased. Relations between Britain and Russia deteriorated further over the question of control over French-held Malta, which was being blockaded by Britain but promised to Russia in due course. At the same time, a rift developed between Austria and the other two powers. The Austrians were very suspicions of British intentions in the **Austrian Netherlands** and Russian ambitions in Italy. These differences exposed the much deeper divisions among the allies on the whole nature of the war against France. Russia for its part was unsympathetic to the British view, that the fight was one to destroy the Revolution totally. Austria favoured the eighteenth-century approach to war – have a limited conflict that would end in an exchange of territory, perhaps Belgium for Sardinia. The defeat of the Russian army by the French near Zurich in September 1799 led to the break-up of the Coalition, from which the **Tsar** withdrew in November of that year.

During the winter of 1799–1800, Napoleon, now First Consul, tried with some success to win Tsar Paul over to his side, while also attempting to make peace with Austria and Britain. As Britain and Austria could not agree between themselves what would be a fair settlement, it proved impossible to reach an agreement. The consequence of the stalled negotiations was Napoleon's decision that if France was to have peace he would have to impose it, but to do this he would have to defeat one of the allies first.

Key terms

Second Coalition
An anti-French coalition comprised of Britain, Russia, Austria and the Ottoman Empire.

Strategy
A plan of action designed to achieve the goal of victory in a war.

Austrian Netherlands
Modern-day Belgium which the Austrians had ruled since 1713.

Tsar
The Russian Emperor.

Napoleon's Second Italian Campaign 1800

Key question
What was the outcome of Napoleon's second Italian campaign?

The need to stabilise the military situation required an early victory and a quick peace. In order to strengthen his own position as First Consul, following the *coup* of November 1799, Napoleon once again turned his attention back to Italy. He embarked on a second Italian campaign aimed against Austria. With the bulk of

French forces, commanded by General Moreau, facing Austria along the Rhine, Napoleon planned for a short, rapid campaign in Italy. Relying on speed, his relatively small and ill-equipped force crossed the Alps, via the Great St Bernard pass, in May 1800 and descended onto the north Italian plain. This episode was the subject of one of Jacques-Louis David's most famous propaganda paintings of Napoleon (see the illustration on the front cover). Following a series of brilliant manoeuvres, he inflicted a decisive defeat on the Austrians at the Battle of Marengo on 14 June 1800. A further French victory at Hohenlinden in Bavaria six months later brought the war to an end. This was confirmed by the Treaty of Luneville, which was signed on 9 February 1801. The main terms of the treaty were:

Key dates

Battle of Marengo: 14 June 1800

Peace of Luneville signed between France and Austria: 9 February 1801

Peace of Amiens between France and Britain: 25 March 1802

- Austria fully recognised French control of Belgium, the left bank of the Rhine and the gains in Italy.
- Austria lost control of all northern Italy, except Venetia.
- The influence of Austria in Germany was reduced.

Key term

League of Armed Neutrality
An agreement by Russia, Sweden, Denmark and Prussia to prevent Britain trading with the Baltic.

Tsar Paul, irritated by Britain's refusal to give up Malta and its interference with neutral shipping, formed a **League of Armed Neutrality**. Its aim was to keep Britain out of the Baltic. Although the assassination of the Tsar in March 1801 and Nelson's bombardment of Copenhagen the following month brought the League to a speedy end, the new Tsar, Alexander I, despite being anti-French, showed no signs of wishing to form an Anglo-Russian alliance. With the collapse of the Second Coalition, Britain felt isolated and war weary. In these circumstances the British government felt it had little choice but to accept a peace settlement of some sort.

Key question
What was the significance of the Peace of Amiens?

The Peace of Amiens 1802

Preliminary discussions between Britain and France were started in October 1801 and finalised by the Peace of Amiens, 25 March 1802. Under the terms of the treaty:

- Napoleon agreed to withdraw from Naples and to guarantee the independence of Portugal and the Ionian Islands.
- Britain returned most of its colonial conquests with the exception of Ceylon (modern-day Sri Lanka) and Trinidad.
- Menorca was restored to Spain, Malta was evacuated, and Egypt restored to the Ottoman Empire.
- The British monarchy symbolically agreed to drop part of its title 'King of France', which came from the medieval period when Kings of England had also ruled France.

The terms of the Peace appeared more favourable to France than to Britain. Both sides were under no illusion that this was a permanent peace and viewed it more as a temporary truce before hostilities were resumed. Its significance was that it allowed both sides to regroup their armed forces and review their future strategies. The Peace of Amiens marked the end of the wars against Revolutionary France, which had started in 1792.

The start of the Napoleonic War 1803

The Treaty of Amiens was unpopular in Britain. Within a few months of its signing Napoleon intervened in the German states and Switzerland and was elected President of the new Italian Republic. In response, Britain refused to leave Malta and indicated its intention of retaining control over it. On 16 May 1803, after six months of deteriorating international relations, Britain declared war on France. There was, however, little that Britain, with a strong navy but a very small army, could do on its own to defeat France. In 1804, William Pitt, who had been Prime Minister since the resumption of hostilities, began the search for allies to join a Third Coalition. He announced his willingness to pay **subsidies** on an unprecedented scale to any ally willing to provide the troops needed to fight Napoleon on the continent, but neither Russia, Austria nor Prussia came forward. Austria and Russia were both anxious to see Napoleon defeated, but were not prepared to work together, as each still blamed the other for deserting the Second Coalition. In addition, Russia was not prepared to co-operate with Britain because the question of Malta was still unresolved.

Mastery on land lay with France, dominance at sea with Britain. Neither in itself was sufficient to provide victory for either side. Napoleon, who had rejected the possibility of invading Britain in 1798, decided to revive this strategy (see page 83). Plans were made towards the end of 1803 to assemble an invasion fleet and a vast army at Boulogne. These forces remained in the area for the next two years poised for an invasion of England. Success in this bold and ambitious plan depended on the French navy securing control of the English Channel long enough for the invasion fleet to transport the army over to England. While Napoleon was a brilliant commander of land forces, his grasp of naval warfare was far less assured. He had no understanding of the sea or its ways, nor of the importance of wind and weather in the deployment of sailing ships. Opposing him was his nemesis at Abakour Bay, Nelson – the greatest naval commander of the time.

The Battle of Trafalgar

The decision to launch the invasion was taken in 1805. A combined Franco-Spanish fleet was to escort the barges used to ferry the invasion army over to England. French commanders devised a plan to lure the Royal Navy away from the Channel. Nelson realised what the French were attempting and successfully engaged their fleet on 21 October 1805 at the Battle of Trafalgar just off the coast of south-west Spain. The combined Franco-Spanish fleet was destroyed and Napoleon was forced to abandon his plan to invade Britain. Even before this French disaster, Napoleon had gathered up his Army of England and marched south-east to the Danube to confront Austria, which declared war on France during the summer and had joined Britain in a Third Coalition.

Key question
Why did the war resume in 1803?

Key dates

War resumed against Britain – now known as the Napoleonic War: 16 May 1803

Franco-Spanish fleet defeated by Nelson at Trafalgar: 21 October 1805

Key term

Subsidies
Money paid by Britain to allies for funding their armies.

Key question
Why was the Battle of Trafalgar so important?

Key question
What do the campaigns of 1805–7 reveal about Napoleon?

Key dates

Austrian army defeated at Ulm: 20 October 1805

Battle of Austerlitz: 2 December 1805

Treaty of Pressburg: 26 December 1805

Prussian forces defeated at the battles of Jena and Auerstädt: 14 October 1806

Treaty of Tilsit signed with Russia and Prussia: 7–9 July 1807

Key term

Continental Blockade
An attempt to close all European ports to British ships.

The campaigns of 1805–7

The campaigns of 1805–7 that followed Napoleon's departure from Boulogne showed him at his military best, winning a series of crushing victories against the armies of Austria, Prussia and Russia. Austrian forces were decisively outmanoeuvred and forced to surrender at Ulm in October 1805. The French defeat of an Austro-Russian army at Austerlitz on 2 December caused Russia to retreat rapidly out of Napoleon's reach. Austria felt she had little option other than agree to peace and on 26 December 1805 signed the Treaty of Pressburg. The main terms of the treaty were:

- The recognition by Austria of French supremacy in northern Italy.
- Austria agreed that the German states of Baden, Bavaria and Württemberg were to be independent kingdoms.

Complicated negotiations between Napoleon and Prussia, involving Prussia's acquisition of Hanover in return for agreeing to enforce Napoleon's **Continental Blockade**, led to a breakdown of relations and then to war between the two countries. During a remarkable one-week campaign Napoleon destroyed Prussian military power at the battles of Jena and Auerstädt (14 October 1806). In February 1807 he marched through Poland to attack Russia, his only remaining continental enemy. At the bitterly fought Battle of Eylau each side inflicted heavy casualties on the other and neither was able to claim outright victory. By the summer, French forces gained the upper hand and inflicted a decisive defeat at Friedland in June. This convinced the Russians of the need to make peace. A settlement was agreed on 7 July 1807 at Tilsit, following a personal meeting between Napoleon and Tsar Alexander I. This took place initially on a raft in the middle of the River Niemen, which marked the Russian frontier. Two days later, the Prussians also agreed peace terms with Napoleon and these were formalised at a second treaty signed at Tilsit. The main terms agreed were:

- Alexander agreed to recognise French domination over western and central Europe.
- Russian territory in Poland was taken and created into the Grand Duchy of Warsaw.
- Almost half of Prussia's territory was taken and created into a new state – the Kingdom of Westphalia.
- Napoleon for his part agreed to recognise eastern Europe as a Russian sphere of influence.

Napoleon's domination of Europe 1807

Key question
What was the extent of Napoleon's domination over Europe by 1807?

In two years (1805–7) during a series of short, intensely fought, campaigns, Napoleon had in turn defeated three of his four opponents (Austria, Prussia and Russia). To deal with his only remaining opponent – Britain – he established, in November 1806, the Continental Blockade. Britain had taken no active part in the campaigns of 1805–7, merely restricting itself to supplying

The Plum-pudding in Danger, a caricature by James Gilray published 26 February 1805 showing the British Prime Minister William Pitt (left) and Napoleon (right) dividing up the world between them.

its allies with financial subsidies. Napoleon's achievements during this period were remarkable. These were:

- French domination in Germany as a result of the defeat of Austria and the abolition of the Holy Roman Empire.
- Confederation of the Rhine created as a French satellite state.
- Prussian power destroyed, and Prussian territory in Poland formed into the Grand Duchy of Warsaw.
- Prussia's lands in the west created into the new satellite kingdom of Westphalia.
- Napoleon crowned himself King of Italy, added Parma and Tuscany to the existing French possessions of Piedmont and Lombardy, and made Naples into a French satellite.
- Russia was forced to conclude peace in 1807, and Tsar Alexander compelled to make a formal alliance with France.

By the end of the year Napoleon controlled, directly or indirectly, the greater part of Europe. The 'Grand Empire' had come into being (see pages 103–10).

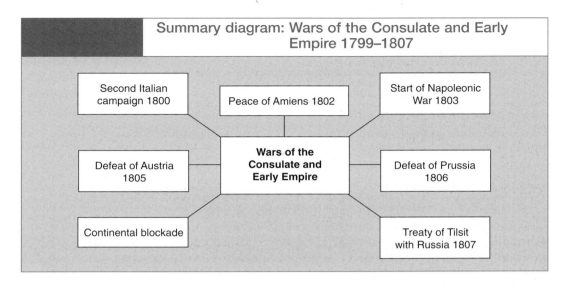

Summary diagram: Wars of the Consulate and Early Empire 1799–1807

- Second Italian campaign 1800
- Peace of Amiens 1802
- Start of Napoleonic War 1803
- Defeat of Austria 1805
- **Wars of the Consulate and Early Empire**
- Defeat of Prussia 1806
- Continental blockade
- Treaty of Tilsit with Russia 1807

3 | Military and Strategic Developments

The changing nature of war

Most wars in the eighteenth century were fought with more or less evenly matched armies. Many of these armies were made up of **mercenaries**. These armies were very similar to each other in training, equipment and structure. They tended to be quite small, containing sometimes as few as 30,000 men. The wars fought by these armies were normally undertaken with limited objectives such as the acquisition of a small province, more often than not to be eventually returned after use as a bargaining counter in maintaining the balance of power in the game of international diplomacy. While short wars tended to be the norm there were exceptions, such as the long wars fought over disputed successions (Spain 1700–13 and Austria 1740–8). Even in these wars the armies were comparatively small by later standards.

One of the greatest military theorists of the early nineteenth century was the Prussian von Clausewitz. His writings drew on his own direct experience of warfare as a soldier in the Revolutionary and Napoleonic wars. In his classic book *On War* (1832) he argued that 1793 marked a turning point in the organisation of armies and in the conduct of war in Europe. He considered that both were changed forever by the creation in that year by the French of the concept of the '**nation in arms**'. This was brought about by the decree of the *levée en masse* which transformed limited war into total war. According to Clausewitz:

> Perfected by Napoleon, military power based on the strength of the whole nation marched over Europe, smashing everything in pieces so surely and certainly, that where it only encountered the old-fashioned armies, the result was not doubtful for a moment.

The cry of *la patrie en danger* ('the nation in danger') had led in 1792 to the formation of a French national army consisting initially of 'patriotic volunteers'. Universal **conscription** had long been advocated by writers as different as **Guibert** and **Rousseau**. Both thought it the best way to raise a citizen army that would have wide support, and in 1793 conscription was introduced. A year later there were a million men under arms. (France had the advantage of having at that time the largest population in Europe, about 28 million, from which to draw recruits.) Although in practice the large majority of conscripts were from poor peasant families, in theory at least universal conscription brought together men from all classes of society in defence of *la patrie*.

Eighteenth-century generals tried to avoid battle, if at all possible, concentrating instead on sieges, or on manoeuvres to evade the enemy or to gain a tactical advantage. The nature of warfare during the Revolutionary and Napoleonic period changed these methods and approaches. The *élan* of the Revolutionary armies was something alien to established military practice. The men fighting in the new French armies were not there as mercenaries, nor as men impressed against their will, but as citizens honourably defending *their* revolution against its threatened destruction by outside forces. Instead of avoiding battle they actively sought it. Often ill-disciplined and ill-equipped, they relied on shock tactics and the momentum of the bayonet charge to bring them success, especially in their early encounters.

The year 1793 was a watershed in other ways than the introduction of conscription – it marked the first *amalgame*, the merging of remnants of the old army with the new. The introduction of veteran soldiers into the new army did much to bring order into its early chaotic organisation without destroying its verve, and formed it into a fighting force that Napoleon used as the basis of his *Grande Armée*. Napoleon, therefore, inherited significant developments that had been introduced by the Republic, and which he subsequently built upon.

The development of the *Grande Armée*

Napoleon took the opportunity during the four years of comparative peace between 1801 and 1805 to reorganise the French armies. He introduced a structure that would be adopted by all European forces for the next century and a half. According to the military historian Michael Howard this, '… made possible almost unlimited decentralisation under a single command'. This new structure was based on the ideas of Guibert, whose work was probably the most important influence on Napoleon's military development. The whole army was divided into corps of about 25,000–30,000 men each composed of two or three divisions, infantry and cavalry; some of the cavalry were kept separate, as were the reserve artillery and several élite groups, the most important of which was the **Imperial Guard**. Each corps was commanded by a **Marshal** who was directly responsible to Napoleon, the commanding general of the army.

Key figures

Comte de Guibert 1743–90
French general and military writer, author of the influential *General Essay on Tactics* 1770.

Jean-Jacques Rousseau 1712–78
Leading philosopher whose ideas influenced Napoleon.

Key terms

Élan
Enthusiasm and passionate commitment for the republican cause.

Grande Armée
The name used by Napoleon for his army in 1805.

Key questions
How did Napoleon change the structure of the French army? What was the aim of this new structure?

Key terms

Imperial Guard
The most élite regiment in the French army.

Marshal
The highest rank in the French army. Napoleon promoted 26 generals to Marshal of the Empire.

The aim of the new structure was to allow unity of command under Napoleon, while providing the various corps commanders with a measure of flexibility and autonomy if required. This could be achieved by:

- Giving each corps a particular role on a campaign march, but also allowing for this to be quickly changed if circumstances made it necessary.
- Allowing regiments to be transferred from one corps to another if required.
- The deployment of infantry or cavalry detachments away from the core of the army as **skirmishers** or moved round as protective screens to shield the movements of the rest of the troops.

Such movement was designed to create uncertainty, and leave the enemy confused as to what was happening. In battle as well as on the march, flexibility was the key. Once enemy forces had been detected, the goal was to manoeuvre in such a way that would lure them into taking up an unfavourable position, and then tempt them into committing their whole force, including reserves, into an all-out attack.

Napoleon would at this point order his own reserves to launch a surprise counter-attack on the enemy's rear and/or flank. In the decisive French charges and relentless pursuit that followed, heavy casualties would be inflicted on the fleeing enemy. These casualties sometimes, as at Marengo, Ulm, Austerlitz and Jena, numbered three times as many as those suffered by the French. This strategy was not new, it had been proposed many years earlier by Guibert, but this does not diminish the brilliance of Napoleon's early victories. To win them, he took what had been only a military theory and successfully put it into practice. As Napoleon himself said, 'everything is in the execution'.

The development of winning tactics

For some time before the Revolution, military thinkers had argued about what were the best **tactics** to use when deploying the main part of the army, the infantry, on the march and in battle. Should they be in line or column? The column, a long file of soldiers moving slowly along a single road, was the traditional marching formation, but was extremely vulnerable to enemy attack and almost powerless to take offensive action in an emergency. The line abreast was the equally traditional battle formation, three more or less stationary ranks of musketeers firing continuously to order. Well-trained, disciplined troops could be very effective in this formation against infantry or cavalry, but were always vulnerable to concentrated artillery fire.

In 1791 a compromise was reached between the 'column or line' schools of thought, and embodied in a new drill manual. This allowed the commander to choose whatever combination of line and column seemed best to him at the time, in what came to be called '**mixed order**'. It was a development of this 'mixed order' that Napoleon most frequently employed in battle: the

Key terms

Skirmishers
Small groups of soldiers operating independently, fighting minor engagements and living off the land.

Tactics
The methods used by generals and commanders to conduct battles.

Mixed order
Placing troops in a combination of lines and columns.

Key question
What was Napoleon's approach to deploying troops in battle?

infantry in a concentrated but mobile formation made up of both line and column, moving around the battlefield as required, firing at will, followed by with a massed bayonet charge when needed, and supported by the cavalry.

Tactics in the campaigns of 1805–7

During a campaign Napoleon dispersed his forces into self-contained groups. These advanced simultaneously at a distance of perhaps as much as a mile from each other along several roads, in effect forming a series of columns in line abreast. This allowed for mutual support and reinforcement in case of attack and at the same time simplified the **requisitioning** of supplies from the countryside through which the army was passing. Following Guibert's guidance once again, Napoleon ensured that the army should travel light and therefore speedily, covering an average of 12–15 miles a day and living off the land instead of relying on slow supply wagons or on supply depots requiring careful advance preparation. The army on the march was, thus, well spread out and extremely mobile, easily able to move into a loose net-like formation to trap enemy forces manoeuvring in a traditional compact group. They could then be rounded up, and forced to fight at a disadvantage. Campaigning for Napoleon was, until 1807, a successful blend of mobility, speed and surprise, which brought rich rewards. Not until the enemy learnt how to counter his strategies did the situation change.

Like all Revolutionary generals, Napoleon was committed to the idea of the offensive and to the importance of forcing the enemy to give battle, but only when that enemy had been out-manoeuvred. While he was able to maintain the surprise element, Napoleon won every encounter. At Ulm in 1805 the Austrians, remaining stationary, were surrounded. At the twin battles of Jena–Auerstädt in 1806, the Prussians, while on the move, were surrounded, as the French attacked and the battle began. It was an example of the inability of an army using old-fashioned methods to meet Napoleon on equal terms. The Prussians, still operating in accordance with the teachings of **Frederick the Great** (most of their generals had learnt their craft in his campaigns), were organised in slow and unwieldy line-formation. Restricted in their movement, they were annihilated, losing 45,000 men and all their artillery.

Impact of Napoleon's methods

While Napoleon's army remained a national one – the French nation in arms – fighting offensive wars and pursuing a policy of mobility and surprise against the old-fashioned, semi-static armies of the *ancien régime*, he was very successful. In fact Napoleon was so successful in his early campaigns that his victories changed the pattern of war. These changes were:

- Instead of taking land in the eighteenth-century manner from states in decline (as Poland had been partitioned by its

Key question
How did the new methods used by Napoleon affect the campaigns of 1805–7?

Key term

Requisitioning
The forcible purchase of food and other supplies for the army from the civilian population.

Key figure

Frederick the Great 1712–86
Prussian ruler from 1740 to 1786, who created one of the most formidable armies in Europe.

Key question
How did Napoleon change the pattern of war?

neighbours shortly before the Revolution) he took – and kept – territory belonging to the strong (e.g. Austria and Prussia).

- His victories were so complete that diplomats were not required for peace negotiations – he could, and did, dictate his own terms on the defeated.
- From 1805 onwards, he developed the use of war as *une bonne affaire* (a good thing) financially. Peace treaties imposed on defeated countries not only provided for the free quartering of Napoleon's troops on their territory, but included the payment of massive indemnities – Prussia was forced to find 311 million francs after its defeat at Jena in 1806. War had become self-financing and supported the French treasury. It would continue to be so for Napoleon, as long as he went on winning.

Weapons and training in the *Grande Armée*
Weapons

Key question
In what ways was Napoleon a conservative military thinker?

Key term

Musket
A smooth-bored, muzzle-loading flintlock rifle, firing a single lead bullet and fitted with a bayonet.

While armies and their deployment under Napoleon might have changed, weaponry did not begin to do so significantly until the middle of the nineteenth century, when industrial technology caught up with military theory. All Napoleon's campaigns were conducted using the weapons of the *ancien régime*. The **musket** was still the standard infantry soldier's weapon. Its fire-power was limited, its rate of fire slow and its accuracy poor, except at close range. The artillery was equally inaccurate and slow, with a range of about half a mile. It took a skilled gun crew to be able to fire a round a minute, even with the new, lighter cannon introduced into France in the 1770s. By training, Napoleon was an artillery officer and he did make full use of horse artillery. This gave much greater mobility to the guns, and allowed commanders to concentrate artillery fire in a barrage. The aim was to open up gaps in the enemy's front line for infantry or cavalry to attack. These tactics, which Napoleon made good use of, especially after 1806 as armies grew larger, were not, however, his innovations – he had learnt them during his training at artillery school.

In some ways Napoleon was surprisingly conservative in his military thinking and could be unreceptive to developments in weaponry and military technology. He ignored new inventions brought to his attention, such as 'a water wagon driven by fire' (submarine), 'rockets' (incendiaries), the telegraph (a mechanical semaphore system) and the percussion charge (a replacement for the flintlock). He seems to have known about but to have ignored also the cheap Prussian innovation of a sharp knife attached to a musket that could be used by the infantry to open the cartridges so saving time by cutting out the need to bite and thus allowing rapid fire. He disbanded as unnecessary the small corps of (ground-anchored) observation balloons used for reconnaissance; but he reintroduced, for use by the heavy cavalry, the helmet and breastplate, already obsolete in the time of Louis XIV.

Training

Training for new recruits was very basic and continued to follow the programme, intended to combine enthusiasm with discipline, laid down for the Revolutionary armies in the early 1790s. A week in the home base was followed by a hardening-off march of 50 or 60 days to the front, practising drill and gaining experience by following the example of seasoned veterans along the way. Most practical training was still provided, especially in battle, by veteran soldiers in the tradition of the *amalgame* of 1793. In 1805, for instance, half the total strength of the army had fought under Napoleon at Marengo (1800) and a quarter had served in the Revolutionary wars; most of the officers and non-commissioned officers were experienced campaigners, although a high proportion of the ordinary soldiers were raw conscripts. The army consisted, therefore, of a mixture of old and young, experience and inexperience, combined under one command.

Key question
How were French soldiers trained?

The size of Napoleon's *Grande Armée* has been disputed at length by military historians. For the years before 1805, estimates vary from about 300,000 to 600,000. It is now thought, based on the known average figure of 73,000 men enrolled each year in France, that in 1805–6 Napoleon's army numbered between 500,000 and 600,000. In addition he had other troops to call on, the auxiliary levies provided by the satellite states, which by 1807 represented about a third of the total strength of his armed forces.

Napoleon's strategic planning

It used to be stated that Napoleon planned his campaigns and battles well ahead and in meticulous detail, and that his victories came from following his plans minutely; but military historians are now much less certain that this was so. There is some evidence on this point from Napoleon himself, when, in 1804 he declared:

Key question
What was Napoleon's approach to military planning?

> Military science consists in calculating all the chances accurately in the first place and then giving accident, almost mathematically, its place in one's calculations. It is upon this point that one must not deceive oneself and that a fraction more or less may change everything. Now the apportioning of accident and science cannot get into any head, except that of a genius ... Accident, luck, chance, whatever you choose to call it – a mystery to ordinary minds – becomes a reality to superior minds.

Some years later he wrote to his brother Joseph that 'in war nothing is achieved except by calculation. Everything that is not soundly planned in its detail yields no result.'

Recent reassessments of Napoleon's military career suggest that:

- While he always formulated a general plan, whether for a whole campaign or a particular battle – 'my great talent, the one that distinguishes me the most, is to see the *whole* picture distinctly'

– he was basically an opportunist, prepared to adjust his plans according to changing circumstances and to take advantage of enemy errors or weakness.

- He could improvise brilliantly in the heat of battle and frequently did so, abandoning his original plan without hesitation.
- He was, however, unwilling to take others into his confidence. This habit of keeping his ideas to himself resulted in a weakness of the command structure, which was to have serious results in later years.

In the same way, the view that Napoleon was forever moving his troops from one place to another, making in the process lightning marches across Europe, has been discredited. Such marches, like the famous one from the Channel coast to the Danube in 1805, were the exception. When he needed to, Napoleon could organise the rapid movement of large numbers of men over wide areas to converge on his chosen target, but normally his marches were shorter, slower and less dramatic.

'A grand strategy'

Key question
Did Napoleon have a grand strategy?

Whether he had 'a grand strategy' in the sense of a broad, overall design is difficult to say. The only consistent theme running through the years from 1800 to 1815 was his hatred of Britain. Following the defeat of his invasion plan at Trafalgar in 1805, Napoleon did adopt another strategy to try to defeat Britain. His alternative plan was to turn the weapon of its own industrial and commercial superiority against Britain by attempting to destabilise the British economy. He therefore concentrated from 1805 onwards on dealing with his enemies on land, while keeping up the campaign against Britain by means of the Continental Blockade. This strategy envisaged undermining British trade, particularly in manufactured goods, by denying it access to lucrative European markets. The Continental Blockade had an important consequence for the war since it meant the need for further conquests to try to ensure that mainland Europe was closed to British exports.

Napoleon's generalship: an assessment

Key question
Was Napoleon a great general?

Modern historians no longer accept unquestioningly that Napoleon was a great general. R.S. Alexander believes that: 'His record was far from uniformly brilliant; it was marred by major defeats.' The main points raised by those who question his abilities as a general are:

- He was not an innovator, made no significant contribution to tactics, introduced no new weapons, was not open to new ideas, and his contribution to strategy was not original.
- The armies he commanded were those created during the Revolution by the *levée en masse*, many years before he came to power.
- He introduced no new training methods, underestimated supply problems, and made other errors of judgement, often

because of his ignorance of climatic and geographical conditions. This led to avoidable losses in Egypt and in **Saint-Domingue** from heat and fever, and on other occasions, as when crossing the Oder in 1806, from cold, snow and mud.

- Sometimes out of sheer obstinacy, as at Boulogne in 1805, he refused advice from those who knew better than to underestimate, as he did, the dangers to his ships from tide and weather.
- His lack of interest in the provision of maps covering the terrain over which he was to march, his often inadequate reconnaissance, and his failure to appreciate the difference between foraging in the prosperous and well-populated west of Europe and in the bare lands further east, caused his men unnecessary hardship.
- Napoleon may have declared that the men's health was of paramount importance to him, but the sick and wounded on campaign were left to die and army medical services were reduced to save money.

Key terms

Saint-Domingue
An important French colony in the Caribbean.

Homme de guerre
Literally man of war, a reference to Napoleon as a military figure.

Despite these well-founded criticisms, however, Napoleon was nevertheless a great general who achieved great conquests in a relatively short space of time. According to the military historian Charles Esdaille, a key factor in the dramatic improvement of French military fortunes after 1800 was 'the irreplaceable genius of Napoleon himself'. Wellington thought that he was 'a great *homme de guerre*, possibly the greatest who ever appeared at the head of a French army'. Furthermore, Napoleon was not merely an inspired military leader: he also knew how to exploit his victories, to extract the maximum advantage from those he defeated. As Martin Lyons points out, French domination relied on diplomatic success as well as military achievements, and the great achievement of French diplomacy was to keep the coalition powers divided.

His military reputation rests largely on the successes of his early campaigns in Italy and to a degree Egypt, and on those of 1805–6, when he was still young and energetic, full of enthusiasm and, it seemed, invincible. His methods, if not exactly new in theory, were new in practice and he used them well. They were a break with eighteenth-century tradition, and confusing to the opposition. Given his hold over his men and the incapacity of his enemies to match him and his army, his victories multiplied rapidly. If his career had finished in, say, 1807, it would have been one of undisputed military glory, justifying his admirers' plaudits. But it did not finish then, and the failures and defeats of the later years, the blunders and ill-judged decisions of the later campaigns, in Spain, in Russia, even at Waterloo, must be taken into account in painting the overall picture of Napoleon as a military leader.

The weakness of Napoleon's enemies: allied disunity

Britain, Russia, Austria and later Prussia formed a series of anti-French coalitions with each other, but these were continually undermined by their mutual suspicions and jealousy (see Table 3, below). Only Britain remained opposed to France for the whole period. The other three powers were tempted away from time to time by Napoleon's offers of territory, for as well as making use of the opportunity to profit from quarrels among the allies, Napoleon's foreign policy was based on '**divide and rule**'. His normal strategy was to keep at least one of these major powers as an ally while he dealt with the others.

Key term

Divide and rule
The attempt to ensure that potential enemies were kept apart.

Table 3: Anti-French coalitions 1793–1815

Number	Year of formation	Member countries in anti-French coalitions
First	1793	Britain, Holland (1794), Prussia (1795), Spain (1795), Austria (1797)
Second	1799	Britain (1802), Russia (1799), Austria (1801), Ottoman Empire (1801)
Third	1805	Britain (1805), Austria (1805), Russia, Sweden
Fourth	1806	Britain, Prussia (1806), Russia (1807) Sweden (1809)
Fifth	1809	Britain and Portugal (since 1808), Austria
Sixth	1813	Britain, Russia and Sweden, Portugal, Prussia and Austria

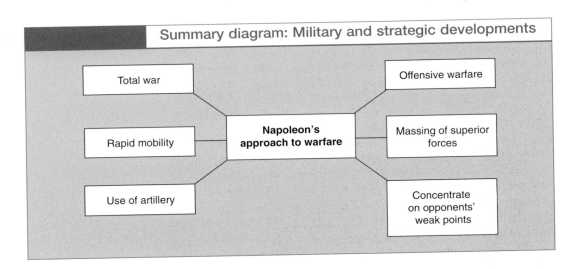

Summary diagram: Military and strategic developments

4 | Napoleon's Leadership

Key question
What were
Napoleon's qualities
of leadership?

As head of state and head of the army Napoleon was a great organiser. He devoted a great deal of time to government business even while campaigning. Napoleon possessed enormous self-belief. In 1804 he wrote: 'I am destined to change the face of the world ... and this confidence gives me the means of success.' According to the French historian François Furet, Napoleon's 'most important secret was his genius for action and tireless energy, which he threw into dominating the world.' Despite a reputation for aloofness, when he wished to charm he could quickly win over anyone met, however initially hostile he might be. When necessary he could be ruthless in pursuit of his objectives, as with the murder of the Duc d'Enghien (page 45).

His contemporaries had no doubt about the charismatic quality of his leadership. His great adversary Wellington said of him that the moral effect of his presence in the field was worth an additional 40,000 men to the French army. This he ascribed partly to Napoleon's dual position, as both head of state and commander-in-chief, that gave him unparalleled control over events, but also to his great personal popularity with the army. The British newspaper *The Times*, which was not sympathetic to Napoleon, in its obituary notice of July 1821, remarked that 'He had the art, in an eminent degree, of inciting the emulation and gaining the affections of his troops'.

By the use of theatrical and emotional language in his Bulletins and Orders of the Day, Napoleon formed a special bond between himself and the army. He played on the ideas of military glory, of patriotism and of comradeship, while at the same time giving the impression that he had a deep paternal concern for his men. To this they responded with real devotion. In a Bulletin from 1805, during the campaign against Austria, he wrote: 'The Emperor is among you. He sets the example; he is on horseback day and night; he is amongst his troops, wherever his presence is necessary'. Later in the same campaign he set out to rally the men by allying himself with them: 'Whatever the obstacles we meet we shall overcome them, and we shall not rest until we have planted our banners on the territory of the enemy'. When the campaign was over, he skilfully combined praise and promises. 'Soldiers! I am very pleased with you. Today at Austerlitz you have proved that you have the courage which I knew you had ... I shall lead you back to France and there I shall do all I can to take care of your interests.' Sometimes he played on their self-interest with promises of material reward in the form of loot. As he said, 'The most important quality in a general is to know the character of his soldiers and to gain their confidence. The military are a **Freemasonry**, and I am their Grand Master.'

So great was Napoleon's charisma, even in the dark days of 1812, that a sergeant in the Imperial Guard, describing the chaos and suffering of the retreat from Moscow by the remnants of the *Grande Armée*, noted the impact of the Emperor's presence:

Freemasonry
A secretive organisation that looks after the interests of its members.

Key term

They walked – on frozen feet, leaning on sticks – silently, without complaining, men of all the nations making up our army, covered with cloaks and coats all torn and burnt, wrapped in bits of cloth, in sheepskins, in anything to keep out the cold, holding themselves as ready as they could for any possible struggle with the enemy ... The Emperor in our midst – on foot, his baton in his hand ... he so great, who had made us all so proud of him, inspired us by his glance in this hour of misfortune with confidence and courage, and would find resource to save us yet. There he was – always the great genius; however miserable we might be, with him we were always sure of victory in the end.

Despite his great powers of leadership, both military and political, his hold over his empire and his country did not last very long. He was ultimately overwhelmed by forces he could not control and decisions he should not have made. These will be considered in the next two chapters.

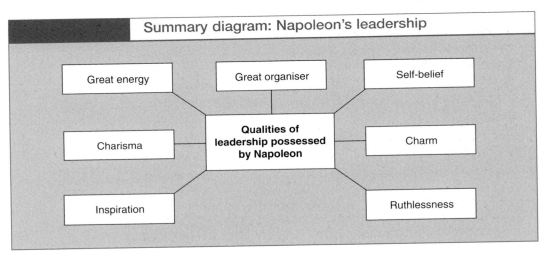

Summary diagram: Napoleon's leadership

Great energy

Great organiser

Self-belief

Charisma

Qualities of leadership possessed by Napoleon

Charm

Inspiration

Ruthlessness

Some key books in the debate
Michael Broers, *Europe Under Napoleon 1799–1815* (Arnold, 1996).
David G. Chandler, *The Campaigns of Napoleon* (Weidenfeld & Nicolson, 1993).
Philip Dwyer, *Napoleon: The Path to Power 1769–1799* (London, 2007).
Charles Esdaile, *Napoleon and the Transformation of Europe* (London, 2003).

Study Guide: AS Question

In the style of OCR

To what extent was Napoleon's generalship the main reason for his military success in Europe to 1807?

Exam tips

The cross-references are intended to take you straight to the material that will help you to answer the question.

'To what extent …?' at the start of the question tells you to assess the relative importance of causal factors that explain military success. One cause is given (Napoleon's generalship) and you must weigh up the importance of that against other reasons, even if you are going to reject it in favour of something else that you believe to have been more important. There is no 'right' answer and a strong essay will sort out the causes into a clear rank order of importance.

You may want to start with the given factor: his generalship. In assessing its importance, you might discuss issues such as:

- he knew how to motivate his men (page 80)
- the quality of the senior officers he chose
- the quality of his planning, strategy and tactics on campaign (page 94).

You might want a round this off with a *short* section considering his military genius.

Against that, there are various alternative causes of his military success that could be brought into your evaluation, for example:

- Napoleon inherited a well-organised and modern mass army of high-quality and battle-experienced men
- his enemies were weak, divided and poorly led, and often used out-of-date tactics (page 86).

Note the end date, so do not wander off-message with examples from later battles.

6 The Napoleonic Empire 1804–10

POINTS TO CONSIDER

Creating the Napoleonic Empire is considered to be one of Napoleon's most notable achievements. The empire that he constructed through conquest, along with the system of client and puppet states, was the largest in Europe since Roman times. He adopted a variety of approaches to governing the various territories that were directly or indirectly under his control. The reaction of the peoples he came into contact with varied enormously. While some welcomed French rule, others were passionate in their rejection of it. In many parts of Europe, he stirred the flames of nationalism. This chapter will address a number of issues:

- The composition of the Napoleonic Empire
- Napoleon's treatment of conquered territory
- The creation of the Napoleonic Empire
- Napoleon and nationalism
- Napoleon's expectations from the Empire

Key dates

1804	May 18	Napoleon proclaimed hereditary Emperor of the French
1805	May 26	Napoleon crowned King of Italy
1806	August 6	Dissolution of the Holy Roman Empire
	October 14	Battle of Jena
	November 21	Berlin decree established Continental Blockade
1813	October 16–19	Battle of Leipzig

1 | The Composition of the Napoleonic Empire

Key question
How was the Napoleonic Empire structured?

The Empire came into existence on 18 May 1804, when Napoleon was proclaimed hereditary Emperor of the French. His coronation six months later at Notre Dame in the presence of the Pope provided him with the blessing of the Catholic Church. In reality the Empire had begun long before 1804, with the Revolutionary conquests and those of the Consulate (see pages 79–82). During both of these regimes, the frontiers of the *ancien régime* had been expanded up to and beyond France's

Key date
Napoleon proclaimed hereditary Emperor of the French: 18 May 1804

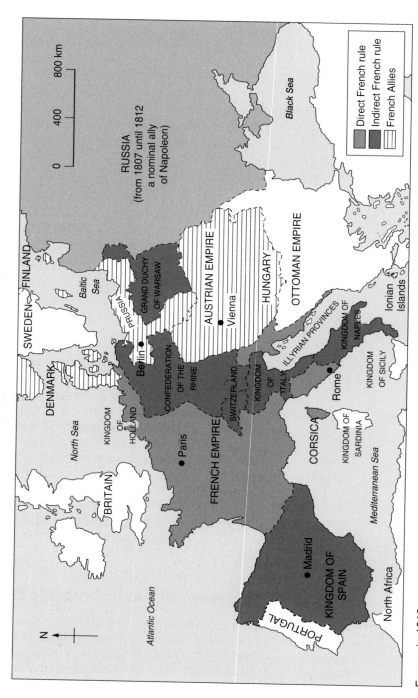

Europe in 1810.

natural frontiers. The momentum of expansion followed closely the pace of military conquest.

The 'Empire' is often referred to as if it were a single entity embracing all French-controlled Europe. It was, however, a more complicated arrangement than that. The French Empire, properly speaking, was:

- The *pays réunis* – territory that was directly ruled from Paris. This comprised France of the natural frontiers (with its borders at the Rhine, Alps and Pyrenees) plus the annexed territories of Piedmont, Parma, Tuscany, the Papal States, the Illyrian Provinces and, after 1810, Holland (see the map on page 104).
- The *pays conquis* – a semicircle of nominally independent satellite states ruled by Frenchmen, usually close relatives of Napoleon. These formed a buffer zone protecting the borders of the French Empire from attack.

The satellite states, combined with the French Empire proper, formed the Grand Empire. In the west, the satellites included at various times Switzerland, the kingdoms of Spain, Naples and Italy; Napoleon's Germanic Confederation of the Rhine (of which the Kingdom of Westphalia formed part); and, until 1810, Holland. In eastern Europe, there was the Grand Duchy of Warsaw which had been created out of conquered Polish lands as a barrier to Russian expansion into central Europe.

Table 4: Territories of the Empire – the *pays réunis* 1804–14

Date	Territory
1804	108 Departments
Territories annexed:	
1805	Ligurian Republic
1808	Parma and Kingdom of Etruria (Grand Duchy of Tuscany created for Napoleon's sister Elise 1809)
1809	Papal States (the part not already included 1808 in satellite Kingdom of Italy)
	Rome named 'second city of Empire', 1810
1809	Illyrian Provinces
1810	Kingdom of Holland annexed (Napoleon considered Louis to be too lenient with the Dutch to remain king of a satellite Holland)
1811	The Hansa towns of Hamburg, Bremen and Lübeck, and Duchy of Oldenburg

In addition to the *pays réunis* and the *pays conquis* there was a third group. This was the *pays alliés*, a small group of allied states. The states in the Confederation of the Rhine were ruled by their native sovereigns but owed their allegiance to Napoleon. Included in these states was Saxony, whose king was given oversight of the Grand Duchy of Warsaw. Of the great continental powers, Austria, Prussia and Russia were each, from time to time, brought by military or diplomatic pressures into Napoleon's direct sphere of influence. Each in turn became his ally, though not always willingly and only for a limited period. Even the outlying Baltic powers came under Napoleon's control when he involved them in operating the Continental system. The most powerful of these was Sweden, much weakened by the loss of its province, Finland, to

Russia. In 1810, Sweden was forced to accept a Napoleonic marshal as heir to the throne. Only the Ottoman Empire and Britain remained permanently outside Napoleon's control.

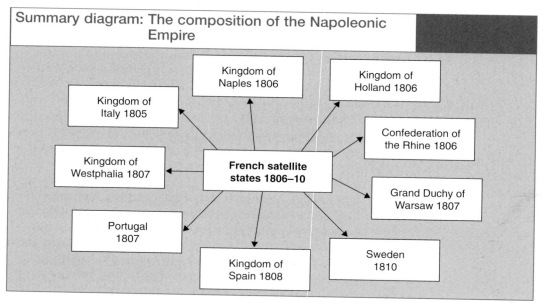

Summary diagram: The composition of the Napoleonic Empire

2 | Napoleon's Treatment of Conquered Territory

The states which made up the Grand Empire can be divided into one of two categories:

- lands **annexed** directly to France
- satellite states under French control but enjoying a measure of independence.

How France treated the territories it controlled depended largely on which category it belonged to. The extent of Napoleon's influence varied too, depending on the length of time a particular country remained under his authority. By far the greatest impact was felt in those annexed territories that were closest to France itself and that had been subject to its laws and influence the longest.

The annexed territories

Among the annexed territories that had been under French control for the greatest period of time were Nice, Savoy, Belgium and the German lands west of the Rhine. They had been annexed before 1799, and had been quickly incorporated into the French administrative system. They were divided into departments for civil affairs and for military divisions for the purpose of recruiting soldiers to the army. By the time of Brumaire, other changes were imposed on these territories, the most important being:

- the abolition of feudalism, particularly the payment of **feudal dues**
- the confiscation and sale of property and lands belonging to the nobility or church.

Key questions
How did France treat its different territories? What changes were imposed on the annexed territories?

Annexed
Taken over by a foreign power as of right.

Feudal dues
Either financial or work obligations imposed on the peasantry by landowners.

Key terms

In 1802, Piedmont, which had been under French occupation since 1796, was formally annexed, to be followed in 1805 by the Ligurian Republic. All these states which were ruled from Paris came to be regarded as territorial extensions of the **'old France'**, and an integral part of the new Napoleonic France. As such all the national institutions flourished there:

- the Concordat
- the Civil Code
- the Imperial University
- the judicial process of civil and criminal courts
- the taxation system.

Key terms

'Old France'
The France of the pre-Revolutionary period.

Freehold property
Property fully owned by an individual.

Land tenure
The various legal ways in which land can be held.

Research on the impact of French rule in these annexed territories has concentrated not so much on the legal, economic and administrative changes introduced there, as on looking at the evidence for an underlying social and economic continuity from pre- to post-Napoleonic times. In Piedmont, where the feudal system was in decline before the French conquests of 1796–7 and **freehold property** was already a common form of **land tenure**, it is now thought that the introduction of French law made little real impact and simply gave legal recognition to an existing situation. In the economically developed lands on the west bank of the Rhine the *bourgeoisie* adapted to the new methods, while at the same time retaining old ones. At first they fell in with the wishes of their French rulers and, after 1815, with those of their new masters, the Prussians. They managed also to defend and maintain their pre-Napoleonic social status, their old trade privileges, local customs and commercial interests.

German and Italian territories that were annexed in the period 1806–9 were subject to French law and influence for a much shorter time. As a result, the effects of the changes introduced by Napoleon do not appear to have been as profound or long-lasting as elsewhere. Indeed, there is some suggestion that the social structure in these territories did not differ much from that of the old regimes.

The satellite states

Key question
What advice and guidance did Napoleon give to the rulers of the satellite states?

The satellite states were nominally independent, but in reality had little freedom of action. From the beginning, their rulers were strictly supervised and tutored by Napoleon in the way they should approach their tasks. Napoleon's stepson, Eugène de Beauharnais, was told by the Emperor:

> By entrusting you with the government of Our Kingdom of Italy we have given you proof of the respect which your conduct has inspired in Us. But you are still at an age [23] when one does not realise the perversity of men's hearts: I cannot therefore recommend too strongly caution and watchfulness … let no one have your complete confidence and never tell anyone what you think … If you ever find yourself speaking … from the heart, say to yourself 'I have made a mistake' and don't do it again. The less you talk the better … learn to listen and remember that silence is often

as effective as a display of knowledge: however much people flatter you, they all know your limitations ... So long as a prince holds his tongue, his power is incalculable.

When the new Kingdom of Westphalia was established in 1807, Napoleon wrote a letter to his brother Jerome suggesting some approaches to governing his new subjects and the benefits of French rule. Jerome was urged to:

• be a constitutional King and observe the constitution faithfully
• win the confidence and the affection of the people
• promote men of talent even if they lacked noble rank
• abolish all kinds of servitude
• provide the benefits of the *Code Napoléon*, public trials and the introduction of juries
• ensure the subjects enjoy a degree of liberty, equality and prosperity.

He concluded his advice by noting that: 'Such a method of government will prove a more powerful barrier separating you from Prussia than the Elbe, the fortresses and the protection of France.'

There were many occasions when Napoleon wrote to his brothers expressing his fervent desire for the well-being of the imperial subjects. In a letter to Joseph he stated: 'The aim of your administration is the happiness of My Italian peoples ... count yourself a failure unless the Italians believe you love them.' While the sentiment expressed was commendable, it was in effect rather meaningless. Napoleon was not concerned with fostering the simple happiness of the common people, nor, despite his assertions, with encouraging the spread of liberty and equality by actively ending feudalism throughout the Empire.

While it appeared that feudalism as a legal status had been abolished in the satellite states, in actuality it survived in many areas in its old form of noble privileges, feudal dues, **serfdom** and even labour services. The traditional view that Napoleon abolished feudalism in the territories he conquered needs to be modified. At best, his achievements in this direction seem to have been patchy and largely restricted to those countries he first annexed. Continental research on the subject indicates that part of Napoleon's reforms remained more theoretical than actual, and that, in effect, he settled for a pragmatic compromise with the traditional feudal structures of the satellite states. It now seems likely that the pre-Napoleonic noble or *bourgeois* classes continued to survive in sufficient numbers for the social structure to remain largely unchanged in much of French-occupied Italy, Germany and Poland. This is possibly one reason why the Empire collapsed so quickly in 1814, and why the allies met with little opposition in restoring the old dynasties and regimes at the **Vienna Congress**. The old social structure had largely survived the Napoleonic era and its representatives were once again ready to re-emerge and resume their dominant role in society.

Key terms

Serfdom
A system where the population is tied to the land and not free to leave the control of their feudal lord.

Vienna Congress
A meeting of the great powers (1814–15) to agree a settlement in Europe after Napoleon's defeat.

Summary diagram: Napoleon's treatment of conquered territory

3 | The Creation of the Napoleonic Empire

Key question
Why was the Napoleonic Empire created?

Napoleon's own explanation for the need to expand his territories was:

- to protect the territory of Revolutionary France from attack by the 'old monarchies' of Europe
- to export the Civil Code, the Concordat and other benefits of Napoleonic rule to the oppressed peoples of neighbouring states
- to provide oppressed peoples with liberty, equality and prosperity
- to end of the old regimes in Europe
- to provide guarantees to citizens everywhere in the Empire against arbitrary government action.

Napoleon's justifications for his imperial expansion contain some praiseworthy sentiments. In private, however, Napoleon expressed some rather different hopes for the Empire. One illustration of this relates to the reasons why the Kings of the satellite states should establish the Civil Code. The expectation expressed in public was that it would benefit the people. In private, he wrote that it must be established because 'it will fortify your power, since by it all **entails** are cancelled and there will no longer be any great estates except those you create yourselves. This is the motive which has led me to recommend a civil code and its establishment everywhere.'

Key term

Entail
The procedure to control the inheritance of property by ensuring that it passed down the owner's line of descendants.

Why did Napoleon create his empire?

Key question
What explanations are given of why Napoleon created his empire?

What drove Napoleon to create the Empire has been the source of some debate among historians. Geoffrey Ellis believes that Napoleon's conquests offered him opportunities to exploit the territories not only to secure his military domination but also to reorganise civil life in the annexed lands. His imperial vision became a natural extension of his personal dynastic ambition. Napoleon believed that 'what was good for Napoleon must be good for France, and so in turn good for the conquered Europe as a whole'.

As so often, when dealing with Napoleon, his own views serve only to confuse the situation. It is difficult to determine from the evidence available, much of which is contradictory, which of his actions were preplanned and which were spontaneous; which reflected his real policies and which were pragmatic compromises. As he himself said, 'I would often have been hard put to it to be able to assert with any degree of truth what was my whole and real intention.' It is probable that no single interpretation provides a clear insight of what Napoleon's guiding principles were, but among those generally given considerations are:

- overweening ambition
- personal glory
- the pursuit of power for its own sake.

On reflection, these now appear over-simplified explanations for an individual with such a complex personality. There may also have been other motives, forming a much more diverse pattern. Two motives which appear have a measure of consistency are;

- his preoccupation with the idea of a universal empire
- his desire to encourage nationalism in the countries of the Empire.

Universal empire

In 1812, one of his advisers dared mention to Napoleon that 'the Great Powers are becoming afraid of a universal monarchy. Your dynasty is already spreading everywhere, and other dynasties fear to see it established in their own countries.' However, Napoleon was not annoyed but pleased with the information. A universal monarchy was the first step towards achieving his long-held dream of a universal empire made up of French-controlled vassal states. Metternich, the Austrian Chancellor, certainly thought this dream was the basis of Napoleon's ambition:

> Napoleon's system of conquests was unique. The object of universal domination to which he aspired was not the concentration of an enormous region in the immediate hands of the government, but the establishing of a central supremacy over the states of Europe, after the ideal of the Empire of **Charlemagne**.

Support for Metternich's view can be found in Napoleon's quite extraordinary correspondence with the Pope between 1806 and 1808 that reveals his obsession with Charlemagne. The Holy Roman Emperor (one of the titles of the Austrian Emperor), and who was still widely regarded as Charlemagne's titular successor, had been dispossessed by Napoleon at the Treaty of Pressburg. In his own mind at least, he appears to have assumed this role when he crowned himself King of Italy at Milan on 26 May 1805:

Key question
What inspired Napoleon to create a universal empire?

Charlemagne 742–814
King of the Franks who created an empire covering much of western and central Europe.

Key figure

Napoleon crowned King of Italy: 26 May 1805

Key date

> As far as the Pope is concerned, I *am* Charlemagne. Like Charlemagne, I join the crown of France with the iron crown of Lombardy, My Empire, like Charlemagne's, marches with the east. I therefore expect the Pope to accommodate his conduct to my requirements. If he behaves well [i.e. implements the Continental Blockade] I shall make no outward changes – if not, I shall reduce him to the status of a Bishop of Rome.

It became clear to Napoleon by 1808 that he was not going to secure an agreement with the Pope. Napoleon, as the new Charlemagne, then assumed the right to

Key term

The Donation
Charlemagne's gift of Rome and most of Italy to the Pope.

- quash **the Donation**
- imprison the Pope and
- annex the Papal States to the Kingdom of Italy.

At the height of his power (1810–11), Napoleon's Empire with its satellite, family-ruled kingdoms exceeded the limits of Charlemagne's Empire. The title, King of Rome, granted to his son, was formerly borne by the Habsburg heirs to the Holy Roman Empire. This served to underline Napoleon's imperial power and dynastic legitimacy. It is possible that it was at this point that Napoleon began to regard the Empire of Charlemagne as merely a first stage in his ambitions, and to look to founding a new Roman Empire as his future goal. His known admiration for Caesar as well as Charlemagne, his interest in the East and his decision to make Rome the second city of his empire, suggest that this may have been a possibility. There is, however, no hard evidence to substantiate the theory.

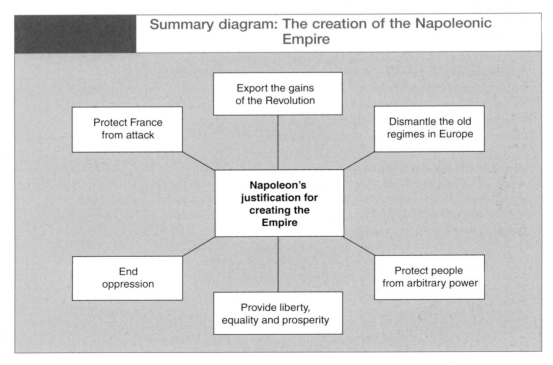

Summary diagram: The creation of the Napoleonic Empire

4 | Napoleon and Nationalism

The whole question of Napoleon's relationship with **nationalism** is a complicated one. As a young man, he had experienced and sympathised with the rise of nationalist sentiments in France during the Revolution. He spoke later about the 'great people' and their right to nationhood; but what was right for his own people was not, in his opinion, the automatic right of others. It was 'France first and always', and the Empire must serve the interests of France. Napoleon did not fully appreciate that sweeping away the old ruling dynasties of Europe and replacing them with an unwelcome foreign government would create, especially in Germany, the very thing he was trying to avoid, the growth of nationalist aspirations.

After his final defeat in 1815, Napoleon was exiled to the small island of St Helena in the south Atlantic. While under the custody of the British he reflected on his reign. In the memoirs that he dictated while on St Helena, Napoleon spoke about the hopes he once had of fulfilling the national aspirations of his subject peoples. But these hopes, he pointed out, had been crushed by the behaviour of the 'old monarchies', which had prevented him from realising them. Given time and peace, he told **Las Cases**, on St Helena, he would have been successful in a programme of national unification:

> One of my grandest ideas was *l'agglomération*; the concentration of peoples geographically united, but separated by revolutions and political action. There are scattered over Europe more than 30 million French, 15 million Spanish, 15 million Italians and 30 million Germans. My intention was to make each of these peoples into a separate national state. As regards the 15 million Italians, *l'agglomération* had already gone far; it needed only time to mature; every day ripened that unity of principles and legislation, of thought and of feeling, which is the sure and infallible cement of human societies. The annexation of Piedmont and Parma were only temporary expedients; the single aim was to guide, guarantee and hasten the national education of the Italian people.

At one time these declarations were taken at their face value. Now they are considered as a product of Napoleon's desire to recast his image after 1815 in a more favourable **liberal** light. Whatever he may have said after 1815, while in power he had not tolerated nationalist ambitions among his subject peoples – or their rulers. After 1806, his policies became much more ruthless and he became **despotic** in his dealings with his imperial subjects. He increasingly assumed the guise of a dictator who alone knew what was best for the Empire, as the following examples illustrate:

> … my Italian subjects know me too well to forget that there is more in my little finger than in all their heads put together. In Paris, where people are more enlightened than in Italy, they hold their tongues and bow to the judgement of a man who has proved that he sees

Key question
What was Napoleon's attitude towards nationalism?

Key terms

Nationalism
Close identification by a group of people with the language, history, traditions and culture of a territory.

l'Agglomération
Bringing together people who share the same language, culture and traditions.

Liberal
Toleration of the rights and views of others, including individual freedom and equality.

Despotic
The abuse and misuse of power by a ruler.

Key figure

Emmanuel, Comte de Las Cases 1766–1842
Author of *Memorial of St Helena* (1823), based on lengthy conversations with Napoleon.

further and more clearly than they do. I am surprised that in Italy they are less obliging. (1806)

I understand Italian affairs better than anyone else. (1810)

When, in 1810, Holland was annexed to France, Napoleon wrote:

I shall do what suits the interests of my Empire. I did not take over the government of Holland in order to consult the common people of Amsterdam or to do what they want. The French nation has been wise enough to rely upon my judgement. My hope is that the Dutch will come to have the same opinion of me.

The Dutch, however, had a very different opinion of their new political masters. Charles Lebrun, the official appointed as Governor-General of the annexed Dutch territories, informed Napoleon in 1811:

I told Your Majesty that tranquillity reigns here. I did not say that there is general contentment ... I hope that the enemy will not appear, but should that happen I doubt very much that we could count on the help of the Dutch.

As events in Spain showed (see page 124), he completely misjudged the situation. Napoleon expected to impose French rule there with little or no difficulty:

Some agitations may take place, but the good lesson which has just been given the city of Madrid [the massacre carried out by Murat in May 1808] will naturally soon settle affairs ... The Spaniards are like other people and are not a class apart; they will be happy to accept the imperial institutions.

The belief that Napoleon was a reformer who consciously rationalised and systematised the conquered territories, socially, legally and economically, and so began the process of 'modernisation' in Germany and Italy, has now been revised. It remains true, however, that by 1811, geographically speaking, he had simplified the map of Europe by amalgamating and rearranging small states into larger blocks. But this was done without regard to national considerations. The new blocks were simply constructed as convenient administrative units for the Grand Empire.

Napoleon and the emergence of nationalism in selected states

Key question
In what way did Napoleon contribute to the emergence of nationalism?

Even before the French Revolution, a number of philosophers and writers had identified nationalism as an important new force in contemporary politics. As the German philosopher Von Herder (1744–1803) wrote:

Nothing seems more contradictory to the true end of governments than the endless expansion of states, the wild confusion of races and nations under one **sceptre**. An empire made up of a hundred peoples and one hundred and twenty provinces which have been forced together is a monstrosity not a state body.

The success of the Revolution in establishing, during the 1790s, a spirit of French unity and national solidarity encouraged nationalist aspirations elsewhere in Europe, where new importance was being attached to local customs and traditional culture, to a shared national language and beliefs. Napoleonic **imperialism** gave a further impetus to nationalist developments by provoking a spirit of resistance to foreign, that is French, rule and to the military and financial burdens that accompanied it. Nowhere was this process more marked than in Germany.

Napoleon's universal empire, by its very nature, ran counter to the principle of nationality. How, therefore, did Napoleon came to be so firmly associated with paving the way for national unity among the peoples of the Empire? That belief was based largely on Napoleon's own words about wanting to 'unify each of these peoples'. These views are now considered to be an illustration of Napoleon's attempt to rewrite history. Yet while he took no positive steps to encourage nationalism, the effect of his military actions and annexations *was* to arouse nationalist ambitions in Germany and, to a lesser extent, in Italy, Poland and Spain.

Germany

At the end of the eighteenth century Germany was enjoying a great cultural **renaissance** in which music, philosophy and literature all played a part. The playwright Schiller defined the current mood in 1802, 'The greatness of Germany consists in its culture and the character of the nation, which are independent of its political fate.' The catastrophic defeat of Prussia on 14 October 1806 at the Battle of Jena changed the whole situation. Prussia's subsequent recovery and growth in national confidence are attributable to the following factors, all of which were the unintended consequence of Napoleon's policies:

- the adoption of French ideas by Prussia at the same time as it reacted against French domination
- the defeat of Austria and the dissolution the Holy Roman Empire on 6 August 1806, which was an unintended bonus since it weakened the political influence of the powerful Habsburg Empire
- the reduction of Habsburg power, which encouraged Prussian ideas of leading a future united all-German state
- the adoption of military and administrative reforms.

By modelling reforms along French lines, Prussia created a national army, a strong central government and a new education system. The aim was to stimulate in the people a common spirit of patriotic devotion to the cause of *German* nationalism. The Battle of Leipzig, 16–19 October 1813, which drove out the French and destroyed the Confederation of the Rhine, became a central event in German nationalist mythology.

Key terms

Sceptre
A symbolic rod held by a monarch to represent authority.

Imperialism
The process of creating an empire.

Renaissance
Renewed interest in learning and the arts.

Key question
How did Napoleon contribute to the emergence of German nationalism?

Key dates

Dissolution of the Holy Roman Empire: 6 August 1806

Battle of Jena: 14 October 1806

Battle of Leipzig: 16–19 October 1813

Italy

Key question
How strong was
nationalism in Italy?

In Italy, the situation was different. There was no notion of a *Volk* as there was in Germany. Italian sentiment, too, was less generally anti-French than elsewhere. Indeed, the urban middle class actively welcomed the reduction of Catholic power brought about by Napoleon's confrontation with the Pope. During **the Hundred Days** campaign, the flamboyant Murat, Napoleon's brother-in-law and King of Naples, issued a proclamation. He declared war on Austria and called on all Italians to fight for national unity and independence. Initially his campaign was successful when he marched north and captured Rome and Bologna, but soon afterwards he was defeated by an Austrian army, and was later shot. The idea that Napoleon paved the way for Italian unification, and that his rule was central in the history of the *Risorgimento*, is only indirectly true. Italian national aspirations did not gain ground until well *after* 1815, as a political reaction to the unwelcome restoration of most of the old ruling families and the old regimes.

Poland

Key question
What did Napoleon
do to foster Polish
nationalism?

Napoleon's role in the growth of Polish nationalism was a little unusual. Poland had for centuries been an independent state, yet between 1772 and 1795 it had been partitioned between its much more powerful neighbours, Russia, Austria and Prussia. Under Napoleon, it was given a partial lease of life when he created the satellite Grand Duchy of Warsaw in 1807. The new state was also given a constitution, which was welcomed by the Poles with great enthusiasm as a step towards the full reinstatement of their country. Napoleon, however, ignored Polish nationalist ambitions and used the Duchy simply as a recruiting ground for his army and a pawn in his dealings with Russia. In 1812, when he needed troops for the Russian campaign, Napoleon made some rather vague promises of future independence for the Poles in return for 98,000 men. The men were found but the promises were never fulfilled.

Nevertheless, the Poles continued to support Napoleon to the bitter end, and for their pains lost everything. At the Congress of Vienna, Poland was again divided among its powerful neighbours. Yet Polish nationalism was far from extinguished and survived, stimulated by romantic traditions of military glory gained by its soldiers as a part of Napoleon's *Grande Armée* on battlefields all over Europe. These heroics sustained the Poles well into the twentieth century, during which time Napoleon, who treated them so cynically, continued to appear in art and literature as the focus for their dreams of national independence.

Key terms

Volk
People bound
together by a
common heritage
and shared
language.

The Hundred Days
Napoleon's
campaign in 1815
to try to regain the
throne.

Risorgimento
Mid-nineteenth-
century movement
to create a unified
Italian state.

Spain

Key question
What influence did
Napoleon have on the
emergence of
Spanish nationalism?

Spain is usually included in the list of countries where Napoleon's action is claimed to have had some influence on the development of nationalism. While Napoleon's treatment of the Spanish did undoubtedly provoke a widespread popular response against him, it does not appear to have marked the emergence of nationalism in the country (for events in Spain, see pages 124–9). The population, both rich and poor, were temporarily united by hatred of the French invaders and by the savagery of the fighting. Once their actions helped to expel the French, the country resumed its rather corrupt and ineffective government.

Summary

Within the Napoleonic Empire, nationalism was largely the prerogative of the intellectual middle classes. Very rarely did it filter down to the great mass of the people, who had enough to do to keep themselves and their families alive without worrying about political ideas. It would be wrong, therefore, to consider the predominantly peasant armies of the allies as fighting a war of 'national' liberation in 1813 as some historians have claimed. At the so-called '**Battle of the Nations**' they fought out of traditional loyalty to the *ancien régime* and to drive away the French, not for reasons of national pride.

Napoleon's vision of a united Europe is for many an attractive proposition and in contemporary European politics appears to be slowly coming to fruition. Yet this is not a vision shared by all of Europe's citizens. In '**perfidious Albion**' – as Napoleon liked to describe Britain – opponents of further European integration still regard him as an 'ogre' and invoke his name in a pejorative way. The following is one expression of this view: 'Napoleon tried to submerge Britain in a single European state and he obviously wanted to abolish the pound' (the *Guardian*, 7 October 1999).

Key question
How important was nationalism within the Napoleonic Empire?

Battle of the Nations
Another name for the Battle of Leipzig – a large battle involving over 500,000 troops.

Perfidious Albion
A phrase coined during the French Revolution to describe the untrustworthiness of the British.

Key terms

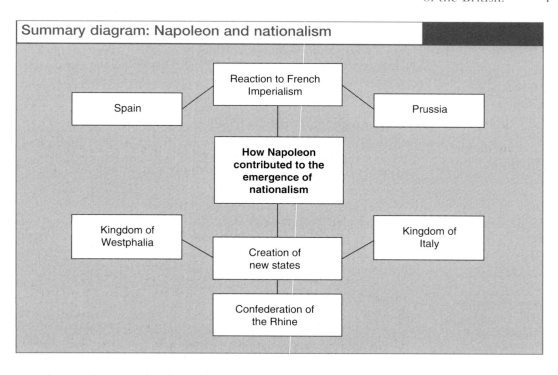

Summary diagram: Napoleon and nationalism

- Spain
- Reaction to French Imperialism
- Prussia
- **How Napoleon contributed to the emergence of nationalism**
- Kingdom of Westphalia
- Creation of new states
- Kingdom of Italy
- Confederation of the Rhine

Key question
What did Napoleon want from his empire?

5 | Napoleon's Expectations from the Empire

Financial and military needs

Between 1807 and 1813, French military expenditure soared from 462 million francs to 817 million francs. To a considerable degree, Napoleon's imperialism was paid for by his defeated enemies. As the historian Paul Kennedy noted: 'War, to put it bluntly, would support war.' After its defeat at Jena in 1806, Prussia had to pay France 311 million francs, roughly equivalent to half the French government's ordinary revenue. Napoleon's approach to the territories he had conquered had important differences:

- The annexed territories were treated as if they were part of France and enjoyed the same rights, and were subject to the same social and legal obligations, as well as the provision of conscripts and the payment of taxes.
- The position of the satellite states was very different. They were never allowed to forget that they existed solely to serve the interests of France.

The satellite states not only formed a strategically important buffer zone to protect French borders, but fulfilled a number of other valuable functions in the Napoleonic Empire. They were first and foremost military vassal states and Napoleon's relationship with them was rather like that of a medieval 'warrior overlord', extracting the maximum advantage from them for the minimum return. They provided about a third of the total strength of the *Grande Armée*, in the form of auxiliary troops, and were used to support and provision the regular army. This was a continuation of the Revolutionary tradition that French armies should '**live off the land**' wherever they were garrisoned outside France. In addition, as the price of defeat, they had to pay substantial **tribute monies** that were used to finance Napoleon's future campaigns.

A striking example of Napoleon's treatment of a satellite state is the Kingdom of Italy. The military and financial demands made on it in the interests of France ruined its economy. From 1806 onwards, its six million inhabitants had to pay an annual tribute of £1.5 million to the French treasury, as well as making substantial cash contributions towards building ships for the French navy. When the supply of currency ran out and the **Viceroy** protested that it was impossible for the kingdom, now heavily in debt, to continue supporting 100,000 French troops on its soil or to find any more ready money, Napoleon responded not with help but by adding to the Kingdom of Italy's obligations the outstanding debts of the Papal States, and by demanding a year later an extra £1.5 million towards the cost of the campaign in Russia.

The Kingdom was also forced to recruit and maintain an army of 55,000 men for French service outside Italy. When conscription was introduced, the effect on the population of Rome was dramatic. The population fell from 136,268 in 1809 to 112,648 in

Key terms

Live off the land
The expectation that an army would supply itself from the area in which it was located.

Tribute monies
Financial contributions to the French state.

Viceroy
Napoleon's direct representative in Italy.

1814 largely as a direct result of young men trying to avoid being called up. In addition to all this, the working of the Continental Blockade (see pages 119–20) placed a severe strain on the commercial life of the country and destroyed its silk industry. The story in other satellite states was not dissimilar.

Dynastic and social needs

As well as their military and financial uses, the satellite states provided for Napoleon's dynastic and social needs. The distribution of crowns among Bonaparte relatives served two purposes for Napoleon. It enabled him to fulfil his clan loyalties to his brothers and sisters, with the expectation that in return they would remain loyal to him and so secure his hold over the Empire. Also, with such a large number of Bonaparte sovereigns available, he could expect in due course to arrange useful marriage alliances with older royal houses and give his successors the dynastic respectability the family presently lacked (see the family tree on page 177).

When the imperial nobility was created it became necessary to endow the nobles with lands and revenues. The completeness of the Revolutionary land settlement left Napoleon with no available land in France for rewarding military or civilian personnel with *dotations*. The satellite states were exploited to provide the necessary land. Poland, in particular, was despoiled in this way, to the grave detriment of its economy. Even before the formal creation of the Grand Duchy of Warsaw, major endowments of land were made to 26 French marshals and generals. These gifts alone were on a scale that deprived the Duchy treasury of a fifth of its potential revenue from the former royal lands. The loss of income from further enormous land-grabs, added to other financial demands, ended by bankrupting the Duchy.

Napoleon considered it to be an utmost priority of the rulers of the satellite states to put the interests of France above all else. In a typical outburst he scolded his brother Louis, King of Holland, for not doing this:

> I myself drew up the constitution which was to provide the basis of your Majesty's throne on which I placed you. I hoped that developing in close proximity to France, Holland would possess that affection for France which the French nation has the right to expect of its children, and even more so of its princes. I hoped that, raised in my political principles, you would feel that Holland, which has been conquered by my subjects, only owes its independence to their generosity; that Holland lacking allies and an army could be, and would deserve to be, conquered on the day it sets itself in opposition to France … I have sufficient grievances against Holland to declare war on her.

In 1806 in another letter he spelled out just as clearly to Joseph, the King of Naples, the need to give priority to French interests and to instil fear in order to govern effectively and maintain the stability of the Empire:

Key question
What were the dynastic and social contributions of the satellite states?

Dotations
Lavish gifts of land which accompanied the titles awarded by Napoleon.

Key term

I see that you promise in one of your proclamations not to impose any war taxation and that you forbid Our soldiers to demand full board from their hosts … these measures are too narrowly conceived. You do not win people to your side by cajoling them … Levy a contribution of 30 millions from the kingdom of Naples … it would be ridiculous if the conquest of Naples did not bring comfort and well-being to My army … If you do not make yourself feared from the beginning you are bound to get into trouble … your proclamations do not make it clear enough who is master. You will gain nothing by too many caresses … if they [the people] detect they have no master over them, they will turn to rebellion and mutiny.

In no context was the subservient position of the satellite states made more obvious than in connection with the operation of the Continental Blockade.

Enforcing the Continental Blockade

Key question
What impact did the Continental Blockade have on the territories of the Empire?

Key date
Berlin decree established Continental Blockade: 21 November 1806

Historians are divided in their views on whether the annexed lands benefited or not from Napoleon's control over their affairs. Michael Broers, for instance, considers that the experience of what he calls the Outer Empire (Spain and the Illyrian provinces) was 'truly a short sharp shock'. On the other hand, some consider it to have brought valuable material advantages. One of these advantages may well have followed the Berlin decree, which was issued on 21 November 1806 and brought the Continental Blockade into operation. The Continental Blockade (also known as the Continental system) had two main purposes:

• to protect domestic markets from foreign competition
• bring about the defeat of Britain by closing all continental markets to British trade and so bring about the collapse of its economy.

Theoretically, home markets included those of the annexed territories. Industry in Belgium, such as textiles and manufacturing, generally benefited from access to the large imperial domestic market now that cheaper British goods were unavailable. The experience of Piedmont, however, was very different. It was greatly discriminated against, as was the Kingdom of Italy in the matter of exporting silk. In order to increase production by the silk manufacturers of Lyon, Piedmont was prohibited from providing silk for manufacture anywhere else. As far as many satellite states were concerned, the Blockade operated entirely to their disadvantage. Against them one-sided preferential tariffs and equally one-sided trade restrictions were imposed.

The imperial decrees of 1806 and 1810, for instance, abolished the traditional trading links between the Kingdom of Italy and its neighbours. All export trade had to be with France only; at the same time, Italy was 'reserved' as a market (more accurately a dumping ground) for French goods of all kinds at high prices. Eugene de Beauharnais, Viceroy of the Kingdom of Italy, was told that his country would be annexed if it exported silk anywhere except to France:

> It is no use for Italy to make plans that leave French prosperity out of account. Above all she must be careful not to give France any reason for annexing her; for if it paid France to do this, who could stop her? So make this your motto too: France first [*la France avant tout*].

Louis, King of Holland, received a warning about his slackness in enforcing the Blockade:

> … the independence of Holland can continue only so long as it is not incompatible with the interests of France … Unless care is taken to avoid thwarting the system of trade [the Continental Blockade] laid down by France, Holland may lose her independence.

Apart from its impact on the manufacturing industries, Napoleon's economic policy also had a damaging effect on farming communities in the satellite states. This was especially so in the good years when France produced enough food of its own and prohibited local producers from exporting their surplus foodstuffs. This resulted in severely depressed agricultural prices in much of the Empire, which in turn led to a lower standard of living for those who could no longer afford the inflated prices demanded for imported French goods, the only ones available for purchase.

Napoleon's imperial policies were not altruistic. He had no intention of exporting the benefits of the Revolution to the rest of Europe, nor of fostering happiness among his peoples, nor of developing national unity in Germany, Italy or elsewhere. Martin Lyons suggests that 'Napoleon's priority was imperial conquest …' And while there is more than an element of truth in this, it is perhaps not the entire picture. According to R.S. Alexander, he was more than just a conqueror: 'He had a plan for an integrated Europe with centralised control, and it was because he thought in terms of the Empire as a whole that he so often clashed with his satellite rulers.' His own views, written while in exile, only serve to cloud the issue since he indicated he was planning on doing much more, but was prevented by the actions of the various coalitions.

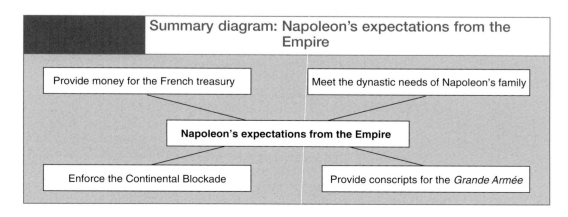

Summary diagram: Napoleon's expectations from the Empire

Provide money for the French treasury

Meet the dynastic needs of Napoleon's family

Napoleon's expectations from the Empire

Enforce the Continental Blockade

Provide conscripts for the *Grande Armée*

Study Guide: AS Question

In the style of OCR

How far do you agree that the main impact of Napoleon's treatment of the conquered territories and satellite states was to stir up resentment and opposition?

Exam tips

The cross-references are intended to take you straight to the material that will help you answer to the question.

The instruction 'How far …?' tells you that your task is to weigh up the impact of Napoleonic rule outside France. There will be no 'right' answer and your mark will depend on the quality and breadth of your assessment as you weigh both sides. In support of the contention, you might consider:

- the opposition in Spain to the attempt to impose French rule (pages 124–5)
- the taking up of arms at different times and then together by 'allies' like Austria, Russia and Prussia
- the stirrings of German nationalism in opposition to the French (page 114)
- peasant resentment at conscription and taxation (page 65)
- resentment and opposition to the impact of the Continental system (pages 119–20).

For balance, you must consider the fact that in some areas and among some groups, French rule/influence was welcomed, for example:

- Enthusiasm among the Poles, early Italian nationalists, early German nationalists, allies like Bavaria (page 115).
- Those who benefited from changes introduced by the French such as the *Code Napoléon* (page 106), the attacks on aristocratic and church privileges (page 107), and the end of the Holy Roman Empire (page 114). These might generally be the middle classes, but the abolition of serfdom had a much wider impact.

Stronger answers will go further and point out that the answer depends on which part of Europe you examine and the relative strength of French influence/control. Then back that up with evidence so an argument is made rather than assertions merely given.

7 Napoleon and Europe: Decline and Fall c1810–15

POINTS TO CONSIDER

Napoleon's ascendancy over Europe in territorial terms was at its height in 1810. From this position of dominance his empire started to collapse in rather spectacular fashion over the next five years, following which he was driven into exile. His continuing struggle with Britain led him to make a number of, what in hindsight appear to be, ill-judged decisions, that paved the way to his eventual defeat. Of these decisions the first to have a significant impact on his downfall had been taken before 1810 and related to his policy towards Spain. The aim of this chapter is to explore how and why the Napoleonic Empire and era were brought to an end. There are a number of themes that will help you to understand this:

- Prelude to defeat 1807–12
- The final campaigns 1813–15
- Factors explaining Napoleon's decline and fall

Key dates

1807	November 23	Milan Decree
	November 30	Capture of Lisbon by General Junot
	December 17	Milan Decree
1808	May 2–3	Uprising in Madrid against French occupation
1809	July 2–4	Battle of Wagram
1810	January 12	Napoleon divorced Josephine
1812	June 22	Napoleon invaded Russia
	September 7	Battle of Borodino
	September 14	Napoleon entered Moscow
	October 19	Start of the retreat from Moscow
	October 22–23	The Malet conspiracy
1813	March 16	Prussia declared war on France
	August 12	Austria declared war on France
	October 16–19	Battle of the Nations
1814	March 31	Allied forces entered Paris
	April 6	Napoleon abdicated
	May 30	First Treaty of Paris
1815	March 1	Napoleon landed in France – start of the Hundred Days

June 18	Battle of Waterloo
June 22	Napoleon abdicated for a second time
October 17	Napoleon landed on St Helena

Key question
Why was 1807 such an important year for Napoleon?

1 | Prelude to Defeat 1807–12

Although the frontiers of 1807 were not those of the Empire at its greatest extent, the year marked an important point in Napoleon's career. He had defeated his three most powerful mainland enemies and set in motion the Continental Blockade, which he hoped would bring about the collapse of Britain. The map of Europe had been redrawn with the creation of the new states of Westphalia and the Duchy of Warsaw and new treaties made with Prussia and Russia (see the map on page 104). In November 1807 Russia declared war on its former ally, Britain, thereby removing, in the short term, the prospect of another anti-French coalition. The following year his desire to bring about the defeat of Britain took him back to Italy. Napoleon invaded and occupied the Papal States in an attempt to force the Pope to impose the Continental Blockade. As he noted:

> His Holiness is sovereign of Rome, but I am the Emperor. My enemies must be his enemies. When Charlemagne made the popes **temporal sovereigns** he meant them to remain vassals of the [Holy Roman] Empire; nowadays far from regarding themselves as vassals of the Empire, they refuse to belong to it at all … In the circumstances the only possible course was to occupy Rome with troops … and to reduce the popes to their proper rank …

Key term

Temporal sovereigns
Those who exercise political power over an area as opposed to spiritual power.

The acquisition of the Papal States consolidated Napoleon's hold over Italy, all of which, apart from the island of Sicily, was now under French control. Although the Empire would continue to expand until 1810, the seeds of its ultimate downfall were sown in 1808. Napoleon made two great mistakes, the consequences of which would prove to be disastrous. These were:

- the occupation of Spain in 1808
- the invasion of Russia in 1812.

Both decisions were partly motivated, as had been the invasion of the Papal States, by the need to enforce the Continental Blockade against Britain. As long as British sea-power remained pre-eminent in Europe Napoleon had little chance of defeating Britain by direct military means. The best he could hope for was to use his land-based power, and control of Europe's coastline, as an economic weapon to prevent British trade entering the continent. His plan was to ensure that the whole of the European coastline, from the Mediterranean to the White Sea, was closed to British trade. To make the blockade, which had been decreed in 1806, more effective Napoleon proposed modifying it. He issued two decrees from Milan on 23 November and 17 December 1807, which extended the Continental Blockade to include **neutral countries**.

The 'Spanish ulcer': the Peninsular War 1808–14

The **Iberian peninsula** in which the war was fought consisted of two countries, Spain and Portugal. While Spain and its **Bourbon monarchy** had a rather strained relationship with France, Portugal was a neutral state, although by inclination, pro-British. Following Portugal's refusal to join the Continental Blockade, Napoleon sent an army into Spain with orders to invade Portugal and seize control of its ports. Lisbon was captured on 30 November 1807, but the royal family, court and most of the government evaded capture and fled the country. The defeat of Portugal was the prelude to the Peninsular War, a war which would prove to be disastrous for Napoleon for the following reasons:

- About half of all French soldiers who fought in the campaign were lost.
- It failed totally in its primary objective, of enforcing the Continental Blockade.
- Despite overrunning Portugal in 1807 Napoleon was unable to ensure that the Blockade was enforced along its coastline. The value of British exports entering Europe through Portuguese ports actually doubled between 1808 and 1809.

Franco-Spanish relations between 1799 and 1807 were for the most part strained. Napoleon informed Spain that its position was simply that of a French ally whose duty was to supply men and money as and when required. Spain was a country with a large yet rather unstable empire in central and south America, ruled by a weak monarchy and a corrupt administration. The wealth of the country was largely in the hands of the Catholic Church and the aristocracy. Napoleon believed that Spain could be bound more closely to France without too much difficulty if the grip of these two institutions was loosened. But as the historian Felix Markham notes, 'Napoleon's initial and persistent error was in assuming that there was a substantial middle class in Spain which would welcome enlightened reform on the French model.' This proved to be a very costly assumption. In 1808 Napoleon summoned the Spanish King and his heir to the south of France. The Spanish King was deposed and replaced by Napoleon's brother Joseph. Napoleon felt that he would be able to control his brother much more effectively than he had been able to do with the King of Spain.

As King of Naples, Joseph had been a popular ruler. When he arrived in Spain he was bitterly disappointed with his reception. He wrote that: 'Not a single Spaniard is on my side.' Napoleon sent one of his most trusted marshals, Murat, with an army to occupy Madrid and impose French rule. The Spanish capital erupted in revolt on 2–3 May 1808, against the French occupation. Murat responded with great ferocity and 100

Key question
Why did the Napoleon become involved in the Iberian peninsula?

Key dates

Milan Decrees: 23 November and 17 December 1807

Capture of Lisbon by General Junot: 30 November 1807

Uprising in Madrid against French occupation: 2–3 May 1808

Key terms

Neutral country
One which takes no side in a conflict.

Iberian peninsula
The area encompassing Spain and Portugal.

Bourbon monarchy
The Spanish royal family, closely related to the deposed French royal family.

The Shootings of May Third 1808 by Francisco Goya.

Key terms

Juntas
Local resistance
committees.

Guerrilla fighters
Irregular soldiers
who draw supplies
and support from
the local
population.

Spaniards were executed in retaliation for the killing of 31
Frenchmen. The scene was immortalised by the Spanish artist
Francisco Goya's horrific painting, and helped to rouse the whole
population to patriotic anger against the French occupying forces.

The reaction of many of the population was to set up *Juntas*
which were co-ordinated by the clergy and members of the
nobility. Their aim was to raise *guerrilla* **fighters** and regular
soldiers to fight the French occupiers. A small and comparatively
inexperienced French army was defeated at Baylen by a force of
Spanish regular troops in July 1808. Encouraged by news of
resistance to the French occupation and responding to a Spanish
request for help, Britain sent an expeditionary force to the
peninsula. It landed in August 1808 and was able to drive the
French out of Portugal.

With the military situation deteriorating in both Spain and
Portugal, Napoleon decided to assume personal control of
operations in the peninsula. He arrived in the autumn of 1808,
with his 270,000 strong Army of Spain, and soon reversed the
tide of defeat. British forces were forced to give up the territory
they held, and were evacuated from Corunna by the Royal Navy.

The nature of the Peninsular War

Key question
How was the
Peninsular War
fought?

The war in the Iberian Peninsula was brutal and savage, with
atrocities were committed by both sides. Wounded soldiers were
particularly vulnerable and were frequently mutilated and their
remains hung from trees (see the image on page 126). The
conflict was characterised by the emergence of what became well

established in the nineteenth and twentieth centuries (particularly in relation to liberation struggles), namely *guerrilla* warfare. In 1812, it was estimated that there were between 33,000 and 50,000 Spanish irregular forces engaged in the campaign against Napoleon. They were able to tie down a much larger French force, which confronted by irregular forces, never quite knew where the next attack was coming from. The arrival of a British force under the command of **Sir Arthur Wellesley** (the future Duke of Wellington) in Portugal in 1808 had a profound impact on the nature of the struggle in a number of ways:

- As the British army was comparatively small, made up of only 35,000 men and lacking both artillery and cavalry, it relied heavily on *guerrilla* forces.
- Wellesley proved to be a formidable opponent, and, although a cautious commander, he was able to exploit French weaknesses regarding lack of supplies, while at the same time fully exploiting British naval supremacy to resupply and reinforce his own forces.

Main events of the Peninsular War

News of Austria's mobilisation at the beginning of 1809 prompted Napoleon to leave Spain after barely two months. Following his departure, the British army returned to Portugal and were once again able to expel French forces. When they entered Spain, however, they were less successful. After the bloody and inconclusive Battle of **Talavera** (July 1808) the Anglo-Spanish army decided not to advance further into Spain. In 1810 Masséna launched an invasion of Portugal to force out the British and enforce the Continental Blockade. Wellington, the British commander, withdrew to defend Lisbon, where he constructed a powerful defensive line across the peninsula on which Lisbon was built. Secure behind the **lines of Torres Vedras** and supplied by

Key figure

Arthur Wellesley 1769–1852 Duke of Wellington, leading British soldier during Napoleonic War. Played a key role in winning Peninsular War and Battle of Waterloo. Prime Minister 1828–30.

Key question
What factors contributed to Napoleon's defeat in the Peninsular War?

Key terms

Talavera Following this battle, Wellesley was created Viscount Wellington.

Lines of Torres Vedras A system of carefully constructed defensive fortifications protecting Lisbon.

The Disasters of War: Heroic feat! Against the dead! created by Francisco Goya in the period 1810–14. Goya was the first modern artist to use the power of visual images to depict the horrific reality of war and to bring this to a large audience.

Profile: André Masséna, Prince D'Essling 1758–1817

1758 – Born in Nice, the son of a shopkeeper of Jewish ancestry

1771 – Went to sea as a cabin boy, travelled around Mediterranean and visited French Guiana in South America

1775 – Enlisted in the French army as a private and rose to rank of warrant officer by time he left in 1789

1791 – Rejoined army as an officer, promoted to Colonel the following year

1792 – Sent to Italy where he soon distinguished himself

– Promoted first to rank of Brigadier-General (August), then General (December)

1796 – During the French campaign in Italy acted as one of Napoleon's main subordinates, took part in battles of Arcole and Rivoli

1799 – Appointed to command an army in Switzerland where his victory over the Russians forced them to withdraw from the Second Coalition

1800 – Returned to Italy where he was besieged in Genoa by the Austrians; the delay his holding out caused allowed Napoleon to defeat them

– Given command of the Army of Italy but forced to resign some months later after accusations of poor administration and financial irregularities among his junior officers

1804 – Recalled from his enforced retirement, promoted to rank of Marshall of France. Captured Verona and helped to defeat Austrian forces in northern Italy

1809 – Played a key role in helping to defeat Austria during the Fifth Coalition, given title Prince d'Essling by Napoleon in 1810

1810 – Led invasion of Portugal during Peninsular War; allies retreated back to lines of Torres Vedras; he failed to dislodge them

1811 – Forced back to Spain and relieved of his command

1815 – During Hundred Days campaign refused to give his support to Napoleon

André Masséna was one of Napoleon's most brilliant commanders. He fought against some of the ablest generals of the time including Marshal Suvorov (Russia), Archduke Charles (Austria) and the Duke of Wellington (Britain). Only Wellington, during the Peninsular War, managed to defeat him. Napoleon referred to Masséna as, 'the greatest name of my military Empire'.

He came from a very humble background, and joined the army as an ordinary soldier. His ability, courage and sheer determination saw him promoted through the ranks to attain the highest position in the French military – Marshal. Masséna's vast experience, with service over a period of 35 years, gave him a unique insight into every level of the army. According to the historian Donald Howard, 'if it were not for Masséna and the marshals who served their apprenticeship under him, it is quite probable that there would have been no Napoleonic Empire'.

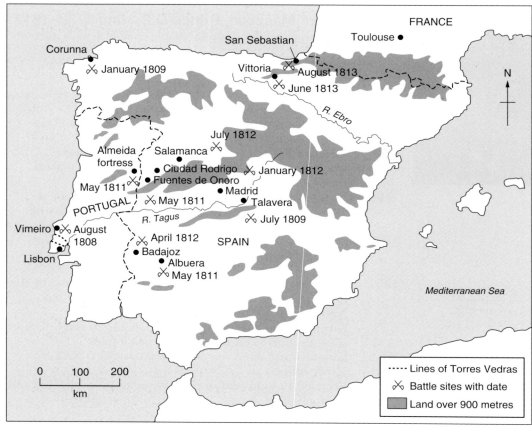

The main locations and battles of the Peninsular War.

the navy, Wellington prepared for a lengthy siege by the French. Masséna was unable to dislodge the British and suffered 25,000 casualties in the process. In March 1811, he withdrew his forces back into Spain. As Wellington shrewdly observed that same year, there were 353,000 French troops in Spain and yet they had no authority beyond the spot where they stood.

The British and their allies were content to disrupt French forces without confronting them in major battles. After France's military disasters in Russia, Wellington decided it was opportune to move on to the offensive. In 1812 he captured Ciudad Rodrigo and Badajoz. Following the defeat of Marmont at Salamanca he captured Madrid. Northern Spain was liberated in 1813 following his victory at Vittoria. The liberation of the Iberian peninsula was finally achieved when French forces were driven back across the Pyrenees and defeated at Toulouse in 1814.

Why did Napoleon lose the Peninsular War?

The war in Spain and Portugal was never popular in France. France's defeat in the Iberian peninsula was due to a number of factors:

- The nature of the war fought in Spain and Portugal did not suit the French army. Both countries were poor and barren and

there was little opportunity for French soldiers to live off the land. French supply lines were lengthy and were constantly disrupted by *guerrilla* forces.
- Napoleon did not grasp that the *guerrilla* war constantly diluted the strength of his armies as they struggled to protect their supply lines and bases.
- The decision by Britain to commit forces to mainland Europe proved to be crucial.
- Napoleon's decision to leave Spain at the beginning of 1809 was an error. Without his inspirational leadership, and with no other supreme commander, the war was left in the hands of mutually hostile generals.
- The Royal Navy was able to supply food and equipment, and transport troops, without interference to Spain and Portugal. This was a major factor in enabling the British army to remain in the Peninsula and was particularly important during the siege of Lisbon.
- The brilliance of Wellington as a commander.

Consequences of losing the Peninsular War

The fiercely fought campaign in the Iberian Peninsula had a number of significant consequences for Napoleon and France. These were:

Key question
What impact did the loss of the Peninsular War have on Napoleon?

- The long drawn-out nature of the campaign, often against *guerrilla* forces, eroded French military prestige. Maintaining garrisons in Spain proved to be both expensive and a significant drain on French military resources. As the war evolved it became increasingly demoralising, the conflict meriting the apt term the '**Spanish ulcer**'.
- In addition to weakening France, the Peninsular War relieved the pressure on Britain. The economic damage to the British economy from the Continental Blockade was eased. Access to Spanish markets in Europe and South America helped to boost British exports to £48 million in 1810 (from £38 million in 1808).
- As French forces suffered a growing number of defeats, other countries were encouraged to renew their efforts to resist Napoleon.
- Large numbers of ordinary Spanish people rose in revolt against French rule.
- The Franco-Spanish attack on Portugal prompted Britain to commit military forces to defend its ally.
- Napoleon's inability to resolve the situation cast doubts on his military and political judgement.

Key term

Spanish ulcer
An ulcer is a wound that weakens the victim but is rarely fatal.

Over the course of the Peninsular War, Britain proved to be a tenacious and formidable opponent. In assessing the significance of the war in Spain and Portugal, the historian Paul Kennedy concludes: 'the security of the British Isles and its relative prosperity on the one hand, and the overstretched and increasingly grasping nature of French rule on the other, at last interacted to bring down Napoleon's empire'.

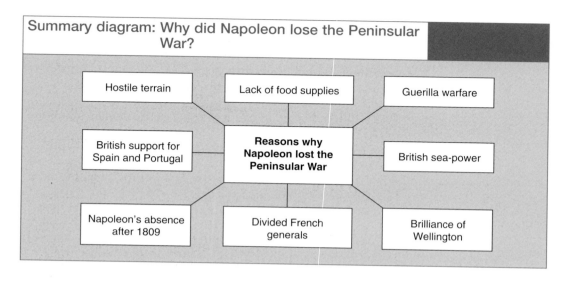

Summary diagram: Why did Napoleon lose the Peninsular War?

Reasons why Napoleon lost the Peninsular War

- Hostile terrain
- Lack of food supplies
- Guerilla warfare
- British support for Spain and Portugal
- British sea-power
- Napoleon's absence after 1809
- Divided French generals
- Brilliance of Wellington

War with Austria 1809

News of widespread Spanish resistance to French occupation spurred Austria into opting for another struggle against Napoleon. When the Emperor reached Paris from Spain in January 1809, he faced the reality of fighting a war on two fronts. With many of his best soldiers tied down in the Iberian peninsula he had to raise a new army. The quality of this force was not as good as the army that had defeated Austria four years previously. In contrast, opposing Napoleon was a reformed and rejuvenated Austrian army led by an outstanding commander, the Archduke Charles. Wellington thought the Archduke the best general of the age and said of him: 'He knows more about it than all of us put together.' Austria took the initiative and invaded Bavaria in southern Germany.

Leaving Paris on 14 April, Napoleon headed for central Europe and the Danube valley. He caught up with the Austrians at Eckmüll and inflicted a crushing defeat on their forces. They were expelled from Bavaria, and on 12 May Napoleon occupied Vienna. Following the Battle of Eckmüll, the Archduke withdrew and waited for an opportunity to counter-arrack. This came when Napoleon left Vienna. After a ferocious artillery barrage the Archduke attacked the French near the villages of Aspern and Esseling. In the subsequent two-day battle (known as the Battle of Aspern) each side lost 20,000 men, killed, wounded or missing, before the French withdrew on to a large island in the middle of the Danube. This was the first significant military defeat of Napoleon's career. With honours even, a third encounter took place during 2–4 July 1809 at Wagram. Once again the casualties on both sides were enormous, over 30,000 from each army. The battle ended in an Austrian retreat and a request for an armistice. It was the last of Napoleon's great victories. In October the Treaty of Schönbrunn was signed. It was a peace dictated in typical Napoleonic style. The main terms of the treaty were:

Key question
Why and with what consequences did Austria go to war with France in 1809?

Battle of Wagram: 2–4 July 1809

Key date

- Austria lost the Illyrian provinces on the Adriatic coast, with their population of 3.5 million.
- The Austrian army was reduced to 150,000 men.
- An indemnity of 85 million francs had to be paid to France.
- Austria agreed to join the Continental Blockade.

When the Austrian Emperor complained about the severity of the terms, Napoleon merely replied that if Austria had kept the peace made in 1801 at Lunéville, 'both countries might have been spared many sufferings' (see page 87).

Dynastic concerns

Key question
Why did Napoleon divorce Josephine?

Key date

Napoleon divorced Josephine:
12 January 1810

The lack of a male heir to secure the succession to the Empire was a serious concern for Napoleon. After eight years of marriage to Josephine they still had no children. The Empress was now 46 and was considered to be past child-bearing age. He believed that the only solution to his problem was to divorce his wife and remarry someone much younger. Napoleon informed his wife of his decision towards the end of 1809 and they were divorced on 12 January 1810. He immediately set about searching for a suitable bride. After proposals for marriage with the Tsar's sister fell through, the Austrian Emperor offered his 18-year-old daughter, Marie-Louise, as a replacement. In March 1810, before the bride left for France, a proxy marriage took place in Vienna at which the bridegroom was represented by Napoleon's recent enemy, Archduke Charles. The marriage was designed to seal a

Marie-Louise (1791–1847) and the King of Rome (1811–32), a painting by Baron François Pascal Simon Gérard.

new alliance with Austria, but when the new Empress arrived in Paris she received only a lukewarm welcome. It was reported that the crowd that saw her arrive 'had been attracted only out of simple curiosity and showed neither enthusiasm nor joy'. She was, after all, the niece of Marie-Antoinette. A diplomatic consequence of the marriage was the end of the alliance with Russia, which was suspicious of the powerful Franco-Austrian block being established in central Europe.

The invasion of Russia 1812

The Franco-Russian *rapprochement* made at Tilsit in 1807 was not easy to maintain and both sides felt uncomfortable about the relationship. There were a number of issues that caused friction between the two countries and led to a resumption of hostilities. The main factors that led to conflict were:

Key question
Why did Napoleon invade Russia in 1812?

- Mutual distrust of each other's hostile expansionist aims in the Baltic, central Europe and the Balkans.
- Napoleon's refusal to support the Tsar's ambitions to seize Constantinople (Istanbul) – he had similar aspirations of his own.
- The Austrian marriage annoyed the Tsar, as did Napoleon's annexation of the North German coastal state of Oldenburg. The Tsar's sister was married to the ruler of the Duchy of Oldenburg and its independence had been guaranteed at Tilsit.
- Alexander attacked Sweden with French encouragement, but then without French agreement seized and annexed Swedish Finland.
- There were arguments over the future of the Grand Duchy of Warsaw.
- The main disagreement arose over the Tsar's virtual withdrawal from the Continental Blockade. On the last day of 1810, he introduced a new trade tariff that discriminated against France and favoured of Britain.

Napoleon determined on war to restore his dominance over the Tsar and to reinforce the Continental Blockade. The army Napoleon gathered to invade Russia was the largest he ever assembled. It was also one of the most cosmopolitan forces created since the time of the **crusades** in the twelfth century. The *Grande Armée* of 600,000 consisted of Germans, Swiss, Spanish, Portuguese, Italians, Poles and Lithuanians. Only about 270,000 of the total were Frenchmen. Michael Broers argues that whereas Napoleon had clear political reasons for invading Russia, he had never before gone to war with such ill-defined military goals. 'In truth, the defined objectives of the campaign of 1812 did not extend much beyond catching a Russian army and defeating it in the field.' Napoleon had never before commanded such a large force, over such a vast area. Just before leaving Paris in 1812 to join the *Grande Armée*, he described the campaign he was about to launch as, '... the greatest and most difficult enterprise that I have ever attempted.' Over the course of the campaign he was uncharacteristically indecisive at critical moments.

Crusades
Attempts by Christian countries in western Europe to free the holy places in Palestine from Muslim control.

Key term

Events of the Russian campaign 1812

Key question
How did the Russians react to the French invasion?

Key dates
Napoleon launched an invasion of Russia: 22 June 1812

Battle of Borodino: 7 September 1812

Key terms

Scorched earth
The destruction of food supplies and shelter to deny the invaders any support or help as they advanced.

Cossacks
Fierce Russian mounted soldiers from the southern region of the Ukraine.

On 22 June 1812, without any declaration of war, Napoleon crossed the River Niemen onto Russian territory. He was unable to use his usual strategy of luring the enemy towards him and forcing a decisive battle early in the campaign. The much smaller Russian armies refused to engage the French, preferring to retreat before them, destroying food supplies as they went. Napoleon was, therefore, drawn ever deeper into Russia, extending his supply lines and increasing the difficulties for his large, slow-moving force of catching up with the enemy. Medical supplies and food were short, and disease struck down 60,000 men even before the campaign had properly begun. The Russian army's **scorched earth** tactic meant that Napoleon found it difficult to feed his men – they were unable to live off the country – and over 1000 cavalry horses died from eating unripe corn in the fields.

By the time Napoleon reached Vitebsk, his army was demoralised. It had already suffered the same number of casualties, either from disease or by being picked off by skirmishing **Cossacks**, as would be expected from large battles. By mid-August the central army group commanded by Napoleon had lost nearly 100,000 men. Pressing on to Smolensk, they found the city had already been destroyed by the retreating Russians and that no food or shelter was available there. The recently appointed Russian commander, the one-eyed Kutusov, urged on by the Tsar, now decided to stand and fight, and waited with an army of about 120,000 west of Moscow near the village of Borodino. There, on 7 September 1812, in a day-long battle of great ferocity both sides suffered heavy casualties. After a prolonged artillery duel and fierce fighting the French lost 30,000

The Burning of Moscow 1812. A contemporary caricature of 1812 showing Napoleon viewing the city of Moscow which had been set on fire by the retreating Russian forces.

men, and Kutusov's army 50,000. The next day, the Russians began an orderly withdrawal, enabling Napoleon to claim victory. In his Order of the Day Napoleon, parodying Henry V at Agincourt, declared: 'Let them say this of you: He was present at this great battle under the walls of Moscow.' In reality the walls of Moscow were still 60 miles away.

On 14 September 1812 Napoleon's advance guard rode into a largely deserted Moscow. The rest of the army followed, 'all clapping their hands and shouting, Moscow, Moscow'. Two days later, two-thirds of the city was in ruins, burnt down by fires started on the orders of the Russian governor to destroy food and ammunition supplies. The Tsar refused to negotiate despite the loss of Moscow. Another Tilsit was impossible to contemplate in the patriotic fervour of the moment.

The unusually mild autumn tempted Napoleon to linger in Moscow for over a month. He ignored the warnings of bad weather to come, and only the eventual realisation that the *Grande Armée* would starve to death if he stayed longer in the ruined and empty city caused him to order a withdrawal. Laden with loot and slowed down by their wounded, the army began the retreat on 19 October 1812. Napoleon ordered them to take a route to the south of the one by which they had come, in the hope that there he would find in an unravaged countryside food and shelter for his army, which now numbered only 107,000. The Russian army, however, soon pushed the French north again and back onto their original route. This forced them to march over the battlefield of Borodino, still strewn with the stripped and decaying bodies of 30,000 of their own dead.

Key dates

Napoleon entered Moscow:
14 September 1812

Start of the retreat from Moscow:
19 October 1812

The retreat from Moscow 1812

The retreat from Moscow was one of the great military disasters of modern European history. An indication of what it was like is given in the memoirs of a French *émigré*, General Comte de Rochechouart, who was serving with the Russian Imperial Guard, in 1812:

Key question
What were conditions like during the retreat from Moscow?

> Nothing in the world more saddening, more distressing. One saw heaped bodies of men, women and children: soldiers of all arms, all nations, choked by the fugitives or hit by Russian grapeshot; horses, carriages, guns, ammunition wagons, abandoned carts. One cannot imagine a more terrifying sight than the appearance of the two broken bridges, and the river frozen right to the bottom. Immense riches lay scattered on this shore of death. Peasants and Cossacks prowled around these piles of dead, removing whatever was most valuable … Both sides of the road were piled with the dead in all positions, or with men dying of cold, hunger, exhaustion, their uniforms in tatters, and beseeching us to take them prisoner. However much we might have wished to help, unfortunately we could do nothing.

By the time Napoleon reached Smolensk in mid-November, there were only 50,000 left in the *Grande Armée* itself. Sickness and

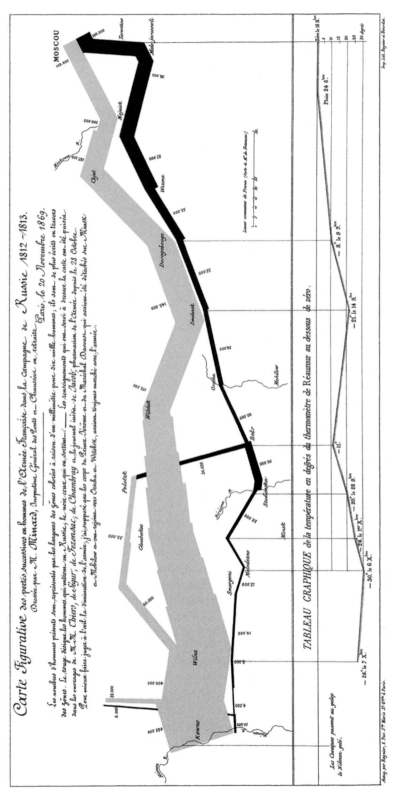

Charles Minard's 1869 chart showing losses of men and temperatures during the invasion of Russia in 1812. The thick grey line on the left represents the *Grande Armée* as it crossed the Niemen on the way to Moscow. Notice how the line gets thinner. What caused this? The journey of the army as it returns from Moscow is shown by the black line from right to left in the diagram. This black line steadily gets much narrower. The temperature chart on the lower part of the diagram records the severity of the Russian winter, which falls to –30°C.

skirmishers, famine and exhaustion had taken their toll, and the winter had only just begun to bite. In snow and intense cold, the army, now further depleted, left Smolensk and marched west. The Russians reached the River Beresina (a tributary of the Niemen) before the French, and demolished the bridges. Thus prevented from escaping, Napoleon's army faced destruction. That anything of the *Grande Armée* survived was due to Napoleon's discovery of a ford and the building of two temporary bridges across the river. In the panic to reach safety, after these temporary bridges were destroyed to prevent a Russian pursuit, many were drowned in the freezing water. Of the 40,000 men of the *Grande Armée* who got safely across the bridges some 25,000 survived to reach Germany at the end of the year.

Reasons for Napoleon's defeat in 1812

Despite the version of events put out by Napoleon in his famous 29th Bulletin, that it was the snow and ice, the intense cold and the frostbite that destroyed the *Grande Armée*, this was not so. The army, together with its auxiliaries, was destroyed long before winter arrived in the first days of November. Twice as many men (35,000) were lost on the retreat in a week of fair weather in late October as were lost in a week of snow and ice on the road from Smolensk to the Beresina in mid-November. Even more instructive is the fact that 350,000 (more than half the total French forces) died *before* they reached Moscow.

There were a number of reasons why Napoleon and the *Grande Armée* failed so catastrophically in Russia. These are:

Key question
Why was Napoleon defeated in Russia?

- Bad management and poor supply arrangements. There was no fodder for the horses, nor **frost nails** for their shoes, and no bandages for the wounded. Many supplies proved inadequate or non-existent.
- Lack of local knowledge, and over-confidence. The maps which the army had were inadequate, covering little more than a few miles inside the Russian border. Napoleon significantly underestimated the task confronting him. He allowed himself nine weeks to defeat Russia and return in triumph to Germany.
- His army had only summer clothing and enough food for three weeks (he intended to be comfortably ensconced in Moscow as Emperor of the East by then).
- There was unusual confusion in the French army command. General Caulincourt wrote after leaving Moscow, 'Never was a retreat worse planned, or carried out with less discipline; never did convoys march so badly … To lack of forethought we owed a great part of our disaster.'

Frost nail
A nail with a sharp head driven into the hoof of a horse to prevent it slipping in icy conditions.

Key term

The fragility of the imperial government was exposed by the Malet conspiracy of 22–3 October 1812, when a plot by a former general almost succeeded in persuading some key officials that the Emperor was dead and a provisional government needed to be formed. But the ruse failed to convince everyone and the plotters were arrested and summarily executed.

The Malet conspiracy: 22–23 October 1812

Key date

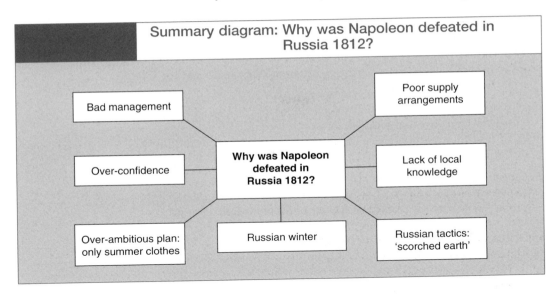

Summary diagram: Why was Napoleon defeated in Russia 1812?

2 | The Final Campaigns 1813–15

The allies united: the Sixth Coalition 1813–15

Key question
How did the great powers respond to Napoleon's defeat in Russia?

The failure of his Russian campaign and the destruction of the *Grande Armée* encouraged a general diplomatic realignment among the European powers. This began in February 1813 with the signing of an anti-French alliance by Russia and Prussia. Tsar Alexander now saw himself as the saviour of Europe from French domination. Under his leadership, a Sixth Coalition was formed, consisting initially of Russia, Prussia and Britain. It was still not a full alliance, being based only on separate bilateral treaties between Britain and Russia and Britain and Prussia. With the destruction of the *Grande Armée* which had invaded Russia, Napoleon set about raising a new army. Through conscription and mobilisation, he amassed an army of 170,000 men to meet the threat from Alexander and his Prussian ally. On 16 March 1813 Prussia declared war on France.

Key date
Prussia declared war on France: 16 March 1813

The military campaign that followed was short and intense, consisting of two important battles. These were fought at Lützen (2 May) and Bautzen (20 May). Although Napoleon was victorious in both, he was unable to inflict a decisive defeat on his enemies. Both sides suffered heavy casualties. In addition to fighting in central Europe, Napoleon was still involved in the Peninsular War. The continuing prospect of fighting a war on two fronts, with reduced resources, led him to accept an Austrian proposal for an **armistice** which was agreed on 4 June.

Austria's attitude towards the Sixth Coalition was initially one of hesitant suspicion. There were two reasons for this:

Key terms

Armistice
Cessation of hostilities usually preceding a peace treaty.

Chancellor
Head of the Austrian government.

- The **Chancellor**, Metternich, distrusted Russo-Prussian ambitions towards the small German states who traditionally looked to Austria for protection.
- Napoleon's marriage to Marie-Louise had left Austria in an awkward position as a nominal ally of France.

Peace negotiations

Over the course of lengthy meetings with Russian and Prussian negotiators in Dresden, Metternich drew up a peace proposal for Napoleon. Under the terms of the agreement Napoleon had to:

Key question
Why did the peace negotiations fail?

- return the Illyrian provinces to Austria
- give up the Grand Duchy of Warsaw
- withdraw from Germany and Italy
- recognise the independence of the states of the Confederation of the Rhine.

Negotiations for a general peace treaty came to nothing. Napoleon would make no concessions, and would surrender no territory. He seems to have feared that a negotiated settlement would mean the end of his power, as he was not one of the hereditary sovereigns of Europe. They, he said, could lose 20 battles and keep their thrones; he, as an upstart soldier, could not. 'My domination will not survive the day when I cease to be strong and therefore feared.' War, rather than diplomacy, had always been his preference, and characteristically he chose to stake his all on military victory to settle the issue of his future.

Resumption of hostilities: the war of the Sixth Coalition

The collapse of the negotiations brought the armistice to an end and led to a resumption of the war. On 12 August 1813, Austria declared war on France. It was the first occasion on which *all* the great powers, Britain, Russia, Prussia and Austria, were at war with Napoleon at the same time, although there was still no single alliance binding them together. Following a succession of relatively minor engagements, the decisive conflict in the war took place at Leipzig between 16 and 19 October 1813. In one of the largest and bloodiest battles of the Napoleonic era, the 177,000 strong *Grande Armée* was opposed by 250,000 allied troops. Over the course of the three-day 'Battle of the Nations', the allies won a decisive but expensive victory. Outnumbered, Napoleon was heavily defeated and forced back to the Rhine. With his influence in Germany gone, the Grand Empire start to unravel quickly:

Key question
What was the consequence of Napoleon's defeat by the allies?

Key dates

Austria declared war on France: 12 August 1813

Battle of the Nations: 16–19 October 1813

- Baden, Bavaria, Württemberg and the other states of the Confederation went over to the allies.
- Jerome was driven out of Westphalia.
- Saxony was occupied by Prussia.
- The Grand Duchy of Warsaw was occupied by Russia.
- A popular revolt in Amsterdam drove the French out of Holland.
- The Illyrian Provinces were abandoned.

News from Napoleon's other front in Spain was equally gloomy. Wellington and his allies had expelled the French from the Iberian peninsula and were poised to cross the Pyrenees into France. Only Belgium, Switzerland and Italy constituted the once mighty Grand Empire.

Key question
How did Napoleon react to the offer of a cease-fire by the allies?

The victory of the allies 1814

For the first time since 1792, France was facing invasion by the rulers of old Europe. Reports made by commissioners sent round the provinces by Napoleon showed that public morale was very low. There was very little popular support in France for continuing the war. The reasons for this were:

- The financial situation was desperate, with little money to fund a new campaign.
- After 20 years of almost continuous warfare the burden of conscription had become intolerable.

Against a background of discontent and opposition, Napoleon set to work to try and raise yet another army. The people wanted peace; Napoleon wanted victory.

Napoleon's only hope was that Austria, Prussia and Russia would quarrel over the future of Germany and Poland and that the coalition would collapse as a result. This was averted when intense diplomatic pressure by the British government in February 1814 led the allies to offer Napoleon a ceasefire, the Treaty of Chaumont. The treaty called on Napoleon to give up all his conquests, and restore France to its pre-Revolutionary 1791 borders. In addition, the allies agreed to convert their coalition into a formal Quadruple Alliance, which committed each of the four powers not to conclude a separate peace but to fight on until Napoleon was defeated. They would then remain in alliance for 20 years while political and territorial plans, outlined in the treaty, were put into effect in a post-Napoleonic Europe. At long last, the allies had come together in a properly united alliance of powers legally bound to each other in a common purpose. Napoleon rejected the allied terms, effectively ending any chance of a negotiated settlement. According to the military historian Correlli Barnett: 'Bonaparte's decision to fight in 1814 instead of making peace marks the supreme example of his irresponsibility as a national leader.'

Key question
What circumstances contributed to bring about Napoleon's first abdication?

Napoleon's first abdication 1814

During the campaign of 1814, Napoleon displayed all his outstanding powers of leadership. Winning five battles in three weeks, he shook the confidence of the allies. In many ways, the victories were too late as he was faced by a determined and numerically superior opposition. Moreover, there was no real mood in France to continue the war. The French state was starting to crumble. When Marshal Marmont surrendered Paris to the allies and led his troops over to their side, the war was in effect over. On 31 March 1814 the allies entered Paris along with the newly restored Bourbon King, Louis XVIII. The Senate proclaimed Napoleon deposed on 2 April. Napoleon's obstinacy had lost him everything. He agreed to abdicate on 6 April 1814:

Key dates

Allied forces entered Paris: 31 March 1814

Napoleon abdicated: 6 April 1814

> Since the allied powers have proclaimed the Emperor Napoleon to be the sole obstacle to the re-establishment of peace in Europe, the Emperor Napoleon, faithful to his oath, states that he is ready

to relinquish the throne, to leave France and even to give up his life for the good of his country.

In a bout of depression Napoleon attempted to take his own life. He took a potion of poison prepared during the retreat from Moscow. Napoleon had kept the poison but it had lost its potency and, when swallowed, all it induced was a severe bout of vomiting. He recovered and was reconciled to his fate, which was settled by the Treaty of Fontainbleau. Through the mediation of Tsar Alexander I, Napoleon was granted the sovereignty of Elba, a small island off the north-west Italian coast (see the map on page 4), and a pension. He reached the island on 4 May 1814.

The Hundred Days campaign 1815

Following Napoleon's abdication, and the restoration of the monarchy, discussions took place to determine a peace settlement with France. These were agreed at the first Treaty of Paris on 30 May 1814. The terms were very lenient:

- France was restored to its frontiers of 1792.
- A number of French colonies that had been captured were restored.
- There was to be no indemnity or army of occupation.
- Looted art treasures did not have to be returned.

The wider issue of producing a territorial settlement in Europe was not as easily achieved. When the great powers met in the Congress of Vienna in the autumn of 1814 there were real tensions, mostly over the redrawing of the map of Europe, and especially the future of Poland. The Tsar wanted all of Poland with compensation for Prussia. Matters became so acrimonious that Britain and Austria, encouraged by the restored Bourbon government of France, made a secret alliance against Prussia and Russia. Napoleon followed the negotiations in Vienna carefully and aware of the deep divisions among the allies, sensed an opportunity to recover his throne. Devastated at having been exiled without his wife and son, he was also angry that the pension promised him by the allies had not been paid.

Sensing an opportunity to split the allies and recover his throne, Napoleon escaped exile on Elba and landed in southern France on 1 March 1815. This marked the start of the 'Hundred Days' campaign. This proved to be Napoleon's last dramatic gamble to recover his throne. He proclaimed: 'The eagle will fly from steeple to steeple until it reaches the towers of Notre Dame.' Napoleon offered to negotiate separately with Austria and Britain, in order to break up the alliance. Both rejected his offer, declared him an outlaw and aligned themselves with Prussia and Russia against him.

The Battle of Waterloo 1815

As Napoleon marched north to Paris, many of his former soldiers and generals rejoined him. The recently restored Bourbon monarchy fled from the city. Napoleon realised that he would

Key question
Why did Napoleon decide to return to France and seize power?

Key dates

First Treaty of Paris: 30 May 1814

Napoleon landed in France – start of the Hundred Days: 1 March 1815

Key question
Why was the Battle of Waterloo so decisive?

Key terms

Acte Additionnel
A supplement to Napoleon's previous constitution, granting some liberal reforms such as freedom of the press.

Regency
A period when the authority of a child ruler is exercised by an adult until he or she comes of age.

Key dates

Battle of Waterloo: 18 June 1815

Napoleon abdicated for a second time: 22 June 1815

Napoleon landed on St Helena: 17 October 1815

need to make political concessions and offer some liberal guarantees. He did this through the *Acte Additionnel*, which was drafted by one of his most persistent critics, the liberal-minded Benjamin Constant. Constant agreed to serve Napoleon and the *Acte* was approved by a plebiscite, albeit with a very low turnout of only 20 per cent of the electorate. Napoleon raised an army of 125,000 men. He realised that a quick victory over the allies was needed in order to unite France behind him and to reassert his authority over the country. His immediate targets were the two allied armies in Belgium under Wellington and the Prussian General, Blucher, before they could combine with significant numbers of Austrian and Russian forces heading towards France. Napoleon issued what was to be his last Order of the Day on 14 June 1815: 'Soldiers … the allies have begun the most unjust of aggressions. Let us march to meet them … for every Frenchman with a heart, the moment has come to conquer or perish.'

On 18 June 1815 one of the decisive battles in modern European history was fought near the Belgian village of Waterloo. Napoleon had a slight numerical advantage over Wellington, 72,000 men to 68,000. The outcome of this evenly balanced struggle was ultimately determined in favour of the allies by the arrival of the Prussians. As Wellington said the next day 'it was a damned close thing – the nearest run thing you ever saw in your life'. Napoleon's defeat at Waterloo, in effect, marked the end of the Napoleonic era and extinguished any realistic attempt he might have had of retaining his throne.

Napoleon's second abdiction 1815

Key question
Why did Napoleon abdicate for a second time in 1815?

Following his defeat, an undaunted Napoleon at once began planning a new campaign. There was very little enthusiasm among the French army or the French population for continuing the war. Without political or popular support, Napoleon had no option but to agree to demands for his second abdication. His proposal that a **Regency** should be set up for Napoleon II, his young son, was ignored. On 8 July, Louis XVIII made his second entry into Paris. After Napoleon's final abdication on 22 June 1815 and subsequent exile, the second Treaty of Paris (November 1815) reduced the frontiers of France still further, to those of 1790. The First Empire was ended. Napoleon's fate was to be exiled to the tiny island of St Helena, one of the most remote parts of the British Empire. He arrived on the island on 17 October 1815 and remained there until his death on 5 May 1821.

The end of the Napoleonic Empire

Key question
What arrangements were made by the Great Powers to contain France within its borders?

There remained the problem of the territories of the French Empire and of the satellite states. Each of the allies had different views on what should be done and great power unity was constantly threatened by suspicion and disagreement. After lengthy deliberations at the Congress of Vienna, a treaty was signed on 9 June 1815. It was accepted by all the allies that France needed to be contained within its revised frontiers, and that this could be best done by surrounding it with a ring of

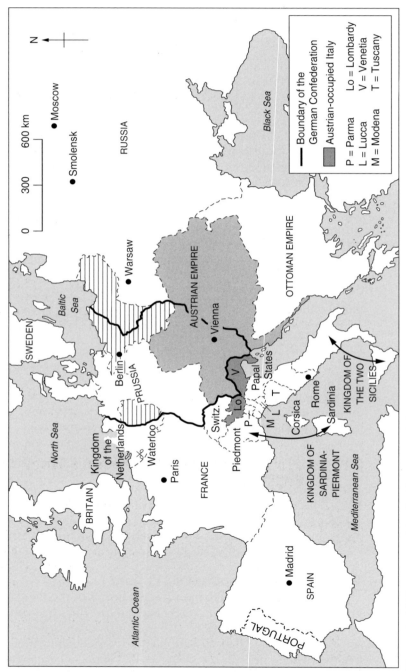

Europe in 1815, as agreed by the Congress of Vienna.

buffer states – not the weak and feeble neighbours who had collapsed in 1792–3, but strong, potentially hostile states which would prevent any future French aggression. The following changes were made:

- Austrian influence was restored in northern Italy (in Lombardy and Venice).
- A newly strengthened kingdom of Sardinia-Piedmont (including Nice, Genoa and Savoy) guarded the south-east frontier with France.
- To the north, Belgium was united with an independent Holland behind a fortified frontier.
- In the east, Switzerland's guaranteed independence barred the way, as did the Rhineland, now a part of Prussia.

In this way the frontiers that France had threatened most often during the seventeenth and eighteenth centuries were blocked off.
As far as the former satellite states were concerned the settlement agreed was generally, though not completely a conservative one. The following decisions were agreed:

- In Italy, Naples was returned to Bourbon rule and the other states were restored to their pre-1796 boundaries and mostly to their former ruling families.
- The Papal States were returned to the Pope.
- In Germany, Napoleon's suppression of a large number of minor German states was confirmed and 41 (later reduced to 38) sovereign states were brought together in a new German Confederation, whose borders were not dissimilar to those of the old Holy Roman Empire.
- Russia acquired most of Poland.
- Spain was returned to Bourbon rule.

The map of Europe once again looked much the same as it had done in the eighteenth century, before the French wars. Geographically, Napoleonic Europe had disappeared.

3 | Factors in Explaining Napoleon's Decline and Fall 1808–15

The changing nature of the *Grande Armée* and warfare

Key question
How did the *Grande Armée* change after 1807?

There were changes in the military organisation and methods of warfare of both Napoleon and his enemies after 1807. In that year the *Grande Armée* was still strong enough to defeat all who stood in its way, Austrians, Prussians or Russians. Yet in a number of ways it was undergoing change:

- It had lost many of its experienced and disciplined troops and, although new recruits were available to fill the gaps, they went into battle untrained and often unreliable.
- The French army had been created as a national army, but, by 1807, its character had changed. It had become increasingly cosmopolitan. Two-thirds of the men were either non-French

troops from the annexed territories or foreign auxiliaries from the satellite states of the Grand Empire.

- Napoleon's earlier tactics of attack by mixed columns of infantry and skirmishers were no longer so successful. This was because high casualty levels resulted in poor quality replacement conscripts who were unable to deploy these tactics.
- After 1807, Napoleon, like his predecessors, resorted to crude attack columns, lines of infantry thrown at enemy lines with little concern for casualty rates. His tactical options were increasingly limited and he began to rely much more on sustained artillery barrages.
- As Napoleon's armies became larger – over 600,000 crossed the Niemen into Russia with him in 1812 – they were more difficult to manoeuvre and to supply.

His later campaigns had, therefore, to depend much less on the surprise elements of speed and mobility than before, and his battles to rely much more on the sheer brute force of artillery barrages or the weight of numbers storming the enemy lines in a massed charge of cavalry or infantry. His later victories were much costlier in men than the earlier ones. For example, 30,000 were lost at Wagram in 1809 compared with the 8000 lost at Austerlitz in 1805. French losses overall in the Austrian campaign of 1809 were almost equal to those of the enemy.

Military improvements among the allies

For as long as the rest of Europe continued to employ old-fashioned methods Napoleon's new-style armies had been invincible. This situation did not last. His enemies learnt to play Napoleon at his own game. They made a number of important changes to enable them to defeat Napoleon:

Key question
What did Napoleon's enemies do to improve their armies?

- Copying Napoleon's tactics, his enemies became more flexible in their approach and developed their artillery to match his.
- They increased the size of their armies to equal or exceed his.
- Prussia and Austria, after their disastrous defeats, replaced their old foreign mercenary armies with new national ones, designed to have a new structure, armaments and equipment in accordance with the new methods of warfare.
- New methods were adopted to pin Napoleon down to a more defensive style of warfare, by denying him the opportunity to force an early and potentially decisive battle.
- Greater co-operation among the allies enabled them to field a combined force of superior manpower to Napoleon.

The Peninsular War and invasion of Russia

To some extent, Napoleon contributed to his own downfall by the disastrous 'mistakes' of the Spanish and Russian campaigns. These were embarked upon by Napoleon through his determination to force both countries to implement the

Key question
How did the campaigns in Spain and Russia weaken Napoleon?

Continental Blockade against Britain. In both Spain and Russia he failed to grasp the following factors:

- He grossly underestimated the sheer size of the country he was hoping to conquer, and was ill-informed about both the terrain and the climate he would encounter.
- Accustomed to allowing his armies to 'live off the land' in countries they were campaigning in, he wrongly expected they could do so in Spain and Russia. In Spain *guerrilla* fighters, and in Russia scorched earth policies, produced unexpected difficulties for the French troops to supply themselves with food.

The impacts of both these campaigns on the French army and economy were enormous in the following ways:

- The 'Spanish ulcer' eventually cost Napoleon about 300,000 men and 3000 million francs in gold, and brought the first serious defeats for his armies.
- In Russia, matters were even worse: over 500,000 men dead, missing or taken prisoner, and 200,000 trained horses and 1000 guns lost – all in the course of a campaign lasting only six months.
- This enormous loss of experienced officers and men weakened the French army, especially the cavalry, for future campaigns, leaving it over-dependent on new levies of raw recruits.
- The disasters of 1812 and the defeats in the Peninsular War shattered Napoleon's reputation for military invincibility, and encouraged his enemies to renew their efforts to defeat him.

Qualities of leadership

Key question
How did Napoleon's leadership contribute to his downfall?

It was a weakness in Napoleon's command structure that he did not take his senior officers into his confidence when on campaign, nor allow them any independence of action. He retained all power and all decision making in his own hands. It was an entirely personal leadership. In the early campaigns, when his army was still quite small, this did not matter a great deal; but as armies became larger – already in 1806 Napoleon was at the head of an army at Jena of about 165,000 men – personal control over the entire field of operations became more difficult to achieve. Even then, Napoleon did not establish a permanent staff to share the command. He continued to tell his marshals what to do, and they continued to do it. As one of them remarked, 'the Emperor needs neither advice nor plans of campaign … our duty is just to obey'. The consequence of such an approach was seen in Spain. After Napoleon left in 1809, his senior staff proved quite unable to cope.

By 1814, Napoleon's early self-confidence and determination had degenerated into supreme egoism, obstinacy and an unwillingness to face facts – a fatal combination for a commander about to meet for the first time a united enemy able to deploy a numerically superior combined force. The wars had become a case of France against the rest, with the result that Napoleon was faced with odds that even he could not prevail against. As Charles Esdaile concludes, the major European powers decided to fight fire with fire by reforming their armies: 'France was confronted with new "nations-in-arms" at a time when, thanks to Napoleon, she had ceased to be one herself.'

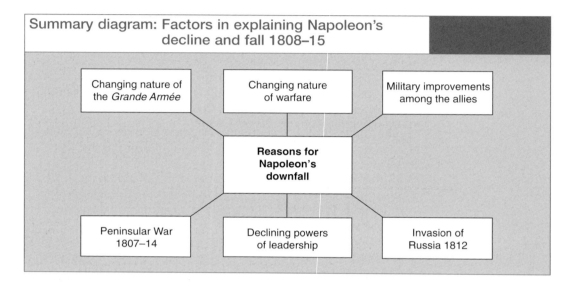

Summary diagram: Factors in explaining Napoleon's decline and fall 1808–15

4 | The Key Debate

Since the end of the Second World War, a dominant theme in European affairs has been the slow and steady progress made towards greater integration between the various countries. In 2009 there were 27 member countries in European Union plus other applicants waiting in the wings. Napoleon claimed while in exile he had intended to create a united Europe where all the people were bound together, '… everyone who travelled would have everywhere found himself in one common country'. Were these musings from exile merely empty rhetoric or was there some substance to them? A question that has been considered by many historians is:

> Was Napoleon's relationship with Europe that of conqueror or unifier?

Paul W. Schroeder

In his book *The Transformation of European Politics 1763–1848*, Schroeder seeks to place the Napoleonic era within a wider context of developments that were occurring in Europe between roughly the mid-eighteenth and the mid-nineteenth centuries. Schroeder is very critical of Napoleon's rule, particularly his incessant obsession with war and the acquisition of land through conquest. His firm belief is that the Empire was very much 'colonial in nature' and was designed to subjugate the territories to French interests. According to Schroeder Napoleon's colonial system was never intended as a first step towards creating some sort of federal or integrated Europe. Napoleon, he argued, conquered simply for the sake of conquering and his colonial system had 'no underlying purpose at all'.

Charles Esdaile

Esdaile has produced a number of works devoted to the military aspects of Napoleon's rule. To an extent he echoes Schroeder's evaluation by arguing that the Napoleonic Empire was 'bent on nothing more than exploitation'. When confronted by a country which possessed 'unbridled militarism' and the resources to support this in creating 'a colonial Empire in Europe', the other European powers resisted force with force. Esdaile argues that despite Napoleon's views produced in exile, it would be unwise to take the emperor's claims at face value. All that can be said for certain of his dreams of creating a new European order is, '… they were never realised'.

Clive Emsley

Emsley in his book *Napoleon* (2003), points out that at the Congress of Vienna, while the overwhelming aim of the victorious allies was to prevent a resurgent France from once again threatening the peace of Europe, not all of the changes made during the Empire were dismantled. He notes that there was no attempt to re-establish the hundreds of tiny states that had existed in Germany in 1789, and that the Napoleonic reorganisation was maintained to a degree. There was also a measure of continuity with the Napoleonic era into the post-1815 period in Italy and Poland, where many of the administrative and legal reforms introduced during the Empire were retained. Emsley argues that it is possible to assert that Napoleon, 'aspired to creating a pacific and pacified, united states of Europe, though it seems extremely doubtful that he ever possessed a considered plan as such'.

R.S. Alexander

According to Alexander when history is viewed from the perspective of the other great European powers then Napoleon does clearly appear to be a Conqueror. This is particularly the case when the plight of less powerful people in European and non-European states is examined. Yet, Alexander argues, it is hard to see in Napoleon nothing but the Conqueror. There was a system at the heart of the Empire that went well beyond despoliation. The issue is, did this make Napoleon a unifier, at least in intention? The answer according to Alexander is that alongside 'France first' came the introduction of the Napoleonic model, with his aspiration that in the long run it would improve the lives of the majority. The Napoleonic model did prove to be a catalyst for the emergence of the modern state in much of Europe, which to some extent has brought unity through 'a shared perception of common interest'.

Some key books in the debate

R.S. Alexander, *Napoleon* (London, 2001).

Clive Emsley, *Napoleon* (London, 2003).

Charles Esdaile, *The French Wars 1792–1816* (Routledge, 2001).

'The British Army and the Guerrilla War in Spain' in *The Road to Waterloo* (Alan Sutton, 1990).

Charles Esdaile, *The Peninsular War* (Penguin, 2002).

Charles Esdaile, *Napoleon's Wars* (Penguin, 2007).

Paul W. Schroeder, *The Transformation of European Politics 1763–1848* (Oxford, 1994).

Study Guide: AS Question

In the style of OCR

To what extent was defeat in Russia the main reason for Napoleon's downfall?

Exam tips

The cross-references are intended to take you straight to the material that will help you answer to the question.

Here your task is to evaluate the reasons for Napoleon's downfall. One causal factor is given to you and your answer must examine that factor seriously, even if you want to dismiss it as being far less important than another. Your essay must also decide between the causes that you consider if you are to give a judgement that addresses 'To what extent …?'

You may want to start by assessing the role of defeat in Russia in bringing Napoleon down (page 137). Come to a clear judgement on this. Then consider and weigh up various alternative reasons, for example the Continental system (page 119) and the Peninsular War (page 129), the consistent opposition of Britain (page 99), the formation of the Sixth Coalition (page 137), the campaign of 1814 (page 139).

Strong answers will show how these elements were not a series of separate factors but were inter-related. Successful answers will also distinguish between different types of contribution to his downfall: long-term reasons (for example the Continental system), short-term reasons (for example the role of the Prussians at Waterloo). As you develop your answer, provide mini-conclusions along the way that assess the situation at the end of each section. Do not leave everything to one conclusion at the end. The examiner should be able to see how your argument is developing.

Study Guide: A2 Question

In the style of Edexcel

How far do you agree with the view that the Peninsular War played the prime role in Napoleon's downfall?

Explain your answer, using Sources 1, 2 and 3 and your own knowledge of the issues related to this controversy.

Source 1

From: A. Matthews, Revolution and Reaction Europe 1789–1849, *published 2001.*

The Peninsular War is important in explaining Napoleon's eventual defeat for several reasons. First the defeat of a small French army at Baylen was significant because it punctured the image of French invincibility. Secondly, Spanish resistance encouraged the Austrians to take up arms in 1809, causing Napoleon to leave Spain at a crucial moment. Thirdly, the Spanish and Portuguese resistance provided the British with a continental theatre of operations against France. The constant *guerrilla* attacks and lack of a decisive victory sapped French morale, required the maintenance of a force of over 200,000 men in the peninsula which strained French resources and increased the levels of conscription and taxation at home. This served to undermine French support for Napoleon. The need to maintain forces in Spain meant that there were fewer for operations elsewhere and that, in 1809 and 1812, Napoleon was fighting on two fronts. Taken together, these reasons help explain Napoleon's own admission about its prime role in his downfall.

Source 2

From D.M.G. Sutherland, France 1789–1815: Revolution and Counterrevolution, *published 1985.*

With the tribute from the conquered territories lost, France was [in 1814] expected to finance the war entirely from her own resources at a time when large sectors of the economy were unable to do so … It is no wonder that, as political control slackened, the country underwent a fiscal rebellion. Nor was there time to raise, equip and train a new army. At the end of January 1814, only 63,000 of the levy of 300,000 had been enrolled. Nor were there any weapons since many of the arsenals in Germany had been cut off by the allied advance. Altogether it was estimated that 700,000 muskets had been lost in the previous two years. … That he would not have time to reconstitute and train his armies ought to have been clear to Napoleon once the allies decided on a winter campaign.

Source 3

From this book.

By 1814, Napoleon's early self-confidence and determination had degenerated into supreme egoism, obstinacy and an unwillingness to face facts – a fatal combination for a commander about to meet for the first time a united enemy able to deploy a numerically superior combined force. The wars had become a case of France against the rest; with the result that

Napoleon was faced with odds that even he could not prevail against. As Charles Esdaile concludes, the major European powers decided to fight fire with fire by reforming their armies: 'France was confronted with new "nations-in-arms" at a time when, thanks to Napoleon, she had ceased to be one herself.'

Exam tips

The cross-references are intended to take you straight to the material that will help you to answer the question.

This question provides you with sources that relate to the reasons for Napoleon's downfall. You should use them, together with your own knowledge, to discuss the statement. It is important that you treat questions of this type differently from the way you would plan an essay answer. If you ignore the sources, you will lose more than half the marks available. The sources raise issues for you. Make sure you have identified all these issues, and then add in your own knowledge – both to make more of the issues in the sources (add depth to the coverage) and to add new points (extend the range covered).

The sources explore different factors each of which played a part in Napoleon's downfall:

- Source 1 emphasises the Peninsular campaign.
- Source 2 emphasises the weakness of Napoleon's army, economic weakness and disaffection in France.
- Source 3 emphasises the overwhelming odds that Napoleon faced in 1814.

Your answer will be stronger, however, if you cross-refer between the sources rather than treating them singly. The final references in Source 2 relate to decisions made by the allies; you should use this in combination with Source 3 and your own knowledge to discuss the allied strength in 1814, and the reasons for that (page 139). There are references in Source 1 to the morale-sapping drain on French resources, which you can use in combination with Source 2 and your own knowledge to show that the position of the French domestic economy and the erosion of support for the war was a significant factor (page 139). You should use your own knowledge also to explore:

- Napoleon's declining powers of leadership (page 145). Note the reference in Source 3 to 'unwillingness to face facts' and the comment in Source 2 'ought to have been clear'.
- The significance of Napoleon's mistakes and misjudgements in the Russian campaign (page 137).
- The significance of the British naval blockade (page 129).

The effects of the Peninsular campaign could be viewed as having been responsible for the lingering death of the Napoleonic Empire, but other factors played their part. Were they rather like a bout of pneumonia carrying off a weakened patient? Could the 'patient' have made a recovery had these other factors not intervened? But was the role of the Peninsular War of prime significance in creating the 'patient's' vulnerability? You should consider the weight of evidence in the sources and from your reading and then present a clearly stated judgement on whether you assign the prime role to the Peninsular War or to other explanations.

8 Napoleon: Impact and Legacy

POINTS TO CONSIDER

Napoleon's remarkable life continues to fascinate and enthral each new generation. Leaving one island in 1778 to embark on a career which would change the map of Europe, he died on another island in 1821 in lonely exile, reflecting on past glories and lost opportunities. On St Helena, while in the custody of the British, he produced his version of the past, an attempt to rewrite history. This led to the growth of the Napoleonic legend. This chapter will focus on three broad themes relating to Napoleon's career. They are:

- Napoleon and the Revolution
- The impact and legacy of Napoleon's rule on France
- The Napoleonic legend

Key dates

1792	November 19	Decree of Fraternity
1806	November 21	Berlin Decree launched the Continental Blockade
1815	October 17	Arrival of Napoleon on St Helena
1821	May 5	Death of Napoleon
1823		Publication of Las Cases' *Mémoriale de Sainte-Hélène*
1832	July 22	Death of Napoleon's son
1840	December 15	Napoleon's remains were buried in Paris
1848	December 10	Louis Napoleon elected President of the Second Republic
1851	December 2	Louis Napoleon seized power and later declared himself Napoleon III. Start of the Second Empire

1 | Napoleon and the Revolution

Napoleon's relationship with the Revolution was a changing one. It altered with the passage of time and according to circumstances. On a number of occasions in the early part of his career, he claimed to be a 'son of the Revolution', the staunch upholder of its principles and the inheritor of its teachings on

Key question
In what sense was Napoleon heir to the French Revolution?'

liberty and equality. The proclamation of 15 December 1799, outlining the new Constitution, announced firmly that 'the Revolution has been stabilised on the principles which began it'. In 1800, with rather less Revolutionary zeal and a more pragmatic approach, he told the Council of State:

> We have finished the romance of the Revolution. Now we must begin its history, looking only for what is real and possible in the application of its principles and not what is speculative and hypothetical. To pursue a different course today would be to philosophise, not govern.

After becoming Emperor, he frequently promised that 'the French Revolution need fear nothing, since the throne of the Bourbons is occupied by a soldier', and at the end of 1812 he was still talking of his 'firm resolve to make the most of all that the Revolution had produced which was great and good'. However, his support for revolutions in general had waned. He began to see himself as a personal peacemaker between revolutionaries and royalists.

> The greatest *seigneurs* [landowners] of the old regime now dine with former revolutionaries. My government has brought about this fusion.

In exile on St Helena, however, he sought in the *Mémoriale* to justify his actions and policies and to reinvent himself as the great defender of the Revolution and guardian of its achievements, the 'prince of liberal opinions':

> I closed the gulf of anarchy and cleared away the chaos. I purified the Revolution, dignified nations and established kings. I excited every kind of emulation, rewarded every kind of merit, and extended the limits of glory.

When the Revolution began in 1789, Napoleon was a 20-year-old army officer. He was immediately caught up in the excitement and became an ardent patriot, although his enthusiasm was temporarily dampened in August 1792 after witnessing the storming of the Tuileries, and the massacre that followed. Much later, he expressed the view that a revolution, however justified, 'is one of the greatest evils by which mankind can be visited' because of the violence and suffering it brings in its train, but he was able to console himself by reaffirming his belief that 'The Emperor has healed the wounds which the Revolution inflicted.'

Revolutionary ideals in practice

Napoleon insisted that he maintained the principles and preserved the positive gains of the Revolution; but how far did his domestic policies actually accord with his declared revolutionary ideals? The phrase most commonly linked with the French Revolution is 'Liberty, Equality and Fraternity'. How did Napoleon's policies measure up to these three Revolutionary ideals?

Key question
Did Napoleon preserve or destroy the Revolution?

Key question
How much liberty was
there in Napoleonic
France?

Liberty

During the Hundred Days, Napoleon, in the course of a long conversation with Benjamin Constant, the liberal thinker who had been one of his most persistent critics, defended his past illiberal actions on the grounds of political necessity. 'I am not an enemy of liberty', he said, '[but] I set it aside when it obstructed my way.' And set it aside he did, restricting liberty of action and freedom of expression, moulding thought and belief, and imposing absolute political authority. This was achieved in a number of ways:

- through his law codes, particularly the Criminal and Penal Codes, which were much closer to the practices of the *ancien régime* than to those of the Revolution
- the use of censorship and propaganda, the practice of indoctrination in the *lycées* and via the imperial catechism
- the activities of the spy network and of the police.

These all played a part in the establishment and maintenance of the Napoleonic state – at the expense of liberty. In 1814, when Napoleon was facing the Allied invasion of France – the first time foreign troops had been on French soil since 1792 – his advisers begged him to call on the memories of those Revolutionary days and rally the people to the country's defence. 'How can I', said Napoleon, 'when I myself have destroyed the Revolution?'

Key question
How much of the
equality established
by the Revolution did
Napoleon retain?

Equality

The Revolution abolished a range of special privileges enjoyed by numerous groups and individuals and institutions. In place of privilege, the Revolution set out to embed the principle of equality in French society and the French state. Among the special privileges which were abolished were:

- all feudal rights and dues
- the tax exemptions of the church and the nobility
- the privileged estates themselves – the nobility was abolished in 1790
- the dominant role of the Catholic Church within the state
- royalty
- inequality before the law.

The abolition by the Revolution of feudal dues and services was confirmed by Napoleon, and equality before the law was more or less preserved in his Civil Code. The rights to the ownership of property in general, and to the continued enjoyment of *biens nationaux* acquired during the Revolution in particular, were also safeguarded. However, the Napoleonic era broke with the gains made during the Revolution in the following ways:

- The creation of the Legion of Honour and the new imperial nobility marked a clear break by Napoleon with the Revolution (see page 67). The creation of an élite was considered contrary to the idea of equality. According to Napoleon: 'I instituted the new nobility ... to satisfy the people, as the greatest part of those I ennobled sprang from them – every private soldier had a right to expect he could earn the title of duke.' This claim, on close examination, carries little conviction. Of the 3200 imperial titles he created (the majority between 1808 and 1811), only of 20 per cent were common people ennobled for military service, 22 per cent came from the old nobility, but the overwhelming majority – 58 per cent – came from the ranks of the *bourgeoisie*. The historian Jean Tulard considered that the formation of a new imperial nobility in 1808 was a decisive turning point, which marked the beginning of the end of the Napoleonic Empire since it represented a violation of the egalitarian principles of the Revolution.

- In the army, promotion for a conscripted peasant was difficult, and the chances of reaching any rank higher than that of lieutenant were extremely remote. Men like Ney, Murat, and Masséna (see the profile on page 127), who rose to be marshals, were the exceptions. While a number of Napoleon's generals were from military families of noble origin, the majority came from the *bourgeoisie*. Despite the saying attributed to Napoleon that every soldier carried a field-marshal's baton in his knapsack, no private soldier ever found one there.

- Taxation was another area of inequality. The Directory had revived the pre-Revolutionary practice of levying indirect taxes, but it was the Empire that expanded them to provide the major part of the revenue needed to pay for the war. On the grounds of good financial practice, the burden of taxation was increasingly shifted from direct to indirect taxation – that is from the well-to-do property owners to the consumers, the majority of whom were poor. Taxes on land rose only slowly, while the yield of indirect taxes on commodities increased by 50 per cent in the decade to 1814. In 1806 a tax on salt, unpleasantly reminiscent of the **gabelle** of the *ancien régime*, was introduced, and four years later the old state monopoly on tobacco was re-established.

Gabelle
The tax on salt imposed during the *ancien régime*.

Key term

- Not surprisingly, therefore, several of his institutions represent a pragmatic compromise between the Revolution and the *ancien régime* – the Concordat, for example, officially abandoned the Revolutionary anti-clerical line and the strict separation of Church and State, while at the same time obtaining official Papal recognition that the sale of church lands was irrevocable.

Fraternity

One of the basic aims of the Revolution was to spread its ideals and principles beyond the frontiers of France. This goal was enshrined in the Decree of Fraternity, issued on 19 November 1792. The French promised support to the citizens of any country wishing to overthrow their rulers. Napoleon certainly sought to import some of the key structures of the Revolution into the territories he occupied. The French legal system, which established equality before the law and an end to feudalism, was introduced with various degrees of success into many parts of the Empire (see page 106). Yet the fraternity of the Napoleonic

Key question
What was the impact of French fraternity during the Napoleonic era?

Issue of the Decree of Fraternity:
19 November 1792

Key date

Empire came with a price. As the Italians found between 1796 and 1797, the benefits of the new structures had to be paid for in indemnities. Being an ally of France also meant that levies of troops had to be provided for the *Grande Armée*. The friendship of the Empire proved to be very much a two-edged sword; it brought benefits but at a high cost.

While the Napoleonic era marked a break with the Revolutionary period, there was also a measure of continuity with it. Under the Emperor there was a return to a much more authoritarian style of government. Many of the most significant gains made since 1789 were, however, maintained. The conclusion of historians Richard Cobb and Colin Jones is:

> Although Napoleon consolidated many of the Revolution's achievements, including administrative and legal changes, economic reforms and the abolition of feudalism, much of what was most distinctive and significant about those years perished at his hands. The Rights of Man were turned on their head as discipline, hierarchy and authoritarianism replaced the revolutionary device of liberty, equality and fraternity. Under his rule France passed into the hands of an autocrat with far more absolute power than Louis XVI had ever enjoyed.

Summary diagram: Napoleon and the Revolution

Did Napoleon preserve or destroy the gains of the French Revolution?	
Preserve: <ul><li>Ended tax exemptions for church and nobility</li><li>Ended feudalism</li><li>Equality before the law</li><li>Transfer of land</li></ul>	**Destroy:** <ul><li>Restoration of hereditary monarchy</li><li>The separation of Church and State established during the Revolution</li><li>Use of censorship and repression</li><li>Ended direct democracy and democratic republicanism</li><li>Restored honours system and nobility</li></ul>

2 | The Impact and Legacy of Napoleon's Rule on France

There is consensus that continuity between the Napoleonic era and the *ancien régime* was much greater than previously believed. It appears that under the Empire, France changed less than during the shorter Revolutionary period and that comparatively little of Napoleon's work outlasted his regime. Of course, there were major political, constitutional, legal and religious changes under Napoleon. These were intended by him to affect the way individuals thought and the way they lived.

Government and administration

Some features of the new political structure suggested parallels with the *ancien régime*. These were:

Key question
What similarities were there between Napoleon's political structure and that of the *ancien régime*?

- The Council of State, chosen by the First Consul – this was similar to the old Royal Council by which the kings of France had governed.
- Napoleon retained the *départements* of the Revolution, but reintroduced the 40,000 pre-1789 communes as his basic territorial and electoral unit.
- The role of the prefect was similar to that of the *intendant* of the *ancien régime*.

Once the Consulate was made hereditary it became to all intents and purposes a monarchy. In 1804, Napoleon became 'by the grace of God and the Constitution, Emperor of the French'. He seems to have decided against adopting the title 'King of France' in deference to revolutionary sensibilities, and to avoid a direct comparison with the monarchical past. In any case, his ambitions had outgrown the idea of a mere kingdom; he already saw himself at the head of a 'universal empire'. This might all seem a far cry from the doctrines of 1789. However, by retaining '*République française*' on official documents until 1804 and on the reverse of his coins until 1809, Napoleon was demonstrating to the people that his government, both Consulate and Empire, was a continuation of the Revolution.

On the other hand, when in 1804, after his consecration by the Pope, Napoleon took the crown from the altar, raised it above the congregation and placed it on his own head, he was showing that sovereignty no longer belonged to the people as in republican days but had been transferred absolutely to him and his heirs for ever. The presence of the Pope at Notre Dame certainly gave Napoleon a prestige he could not otherwise have acquired, while making it plain to the rest of the world that the church had given its blessing to an empire sprung from a revolution it had previously denounced. Indeed, on the eve of the Austrian marriage in 1810 (which itself was seen by many Frenchmen as a betrayal of the Revolution), Napoleon, entertaining what he called a 'garden of kings', presented himself to them as a fellow monarch welcoming his royal neighbours.

The lack of any popular representation in either of his regimes would not have worried Napoleon, for his view of sovereignty of the people had become far removed from that of Rousseau's *Social Contract*, the work that had influenced him as a young man. By 1804, Napoleon considered that sovereignty of the people did not imply their right to a say in government. What Napoleon believed it meant was the right of the people to have a ruler who governed them as the majority wished to be governed. In a way, the Napoleonic Empire was similar to an absolute monarchy but under another name.

It would be easy, however, to exaggerate the repressive nature of Napoleon's rule and to forget that he did maintain the great gains of the Revolution. He confirmed in the Constitution and the Civil Code the end of feudalism in France and the equality of Frenchmen before the law, and in the Concordat the irrevocability of the sale of the *biens nationaux*.

Social impact

Key question
What impact did Napoleon's rule have on French society?

As knowledge of social conditions is patchy and inconclusive, assessing the impact of Napoleon's rule on French society is difficult. Where local studies have been undertaken they appear to indicate that agricultural wages rose slowly in the years 1800–15. Wages for the most part did not keep pace with rents, which rose sharply due to the increased demand for land. The reasons for this increased demand are uncertain. It may have been a consequence of the increase in population. There was no **agricultural revolution** during the period 1800–15, and farming continued at a **subsistence level**. Until 1811, harvests were good and food was cheap and plentiful. It was not until the bad harvest of 1811, followed by the extra conscription burdens of 1812–14, that Napoleon was faced with any serious social unrest in the countryside. Despite the good harvests and the end of feudalism, there seems to have been at least as much rural poverty in the later years of the Empire as there had been before 1789.

Napoleon was very committed to ensuring that he maintained the support of the main beneficiaries of the Revolution, such as the *bourgeoisie* who had bought land. His social policies were conservative in relation to the rural and urban poor since he did not wish to upset the *bourgeoisie* by introducing costly reforms that they would have to pay for. He liked to speak of how the French people loved him as the 'people's king' or as the peasants' friend, but it is difficult to see why either he or they should have believed it. He did nothing for the mass of the people except conscript their sons for the army while taxing them heavily for the privilege. After 1815, the propaganda produced by Napoleon's supporters carefully crafted the mythical figure of the 'Emperor of the common man' as a reaction to Bourbon favouritism towards the aristocracy.

In the urban areas, conditions for workers were bad. Two measures combined to limit their freedoms:

- The Le Chapelier Law which banned trade unions was reaffirmed in 1803.
- The introduction of the *livret* (see page 66) threatened a worker's right to seek new employment.

Napoleon seems to have regarded the urban workers with the gravest suspicion, believing them to be troublemakers who needed firm handling and close police supervision.

In a much wider social context, Napoleon's long wars did have an impact on the population of France, but to a much lesser extent than was at one time believed. Of the two million men who found themselves in the army between 1800 and 1814 the number killed (dying of wounds, disease, hunger or cold, or who simply went missing believed killed) has been estimated at

Key terms

Agricultural revolution
The process by which agriculture is mechanised and new methods of food production are introduced.

Subsistence level
A backward type of agriculture producing only enough food to survive.

916,000. This figure is usually quoted as representing about seven per cent of the total population of France; but that is misleading because the losses were not spread evenly across the population. They fell heavily on the young men of marriageable age – a devastating 38 per cent of men born in the years 1790–5 were killed, the majority of them between 1812 and 1814. To the extent that this must have left many young women without husbands, and reduced further the already declining birth rate, these losses contributed to some extent to the slow growth of the population in nineteenth-century France.

Economic impact

Key question
What developments occurred in the French economy under Napoleon?

Opinions differ over whether or not the French economy expanded or stood still under Napoleon. In 1785 the economic development of Britain and France was comparable. But over the next 15 years, while industrial development in Britain was forging ahead, the upheavals of the Revolution were holding back the French economy. The view of the British social historian Alfred Cobban, that under Napoleon the only 'trade which flourished was smuggling', would appear to be rather harsh. The picture from the industrial sector during the Empire is mixed.

Some sectors of the French economy were probably on the edge of an industrial revolution by 1800. The cotton industry was certainly expanding. Two factors that contributed to this were:

- mechanisation, through the introduction of imitation British spinning machines, such as the 'mule-jennies'
- the protectionist effect of the Continental Blockade on domestic production that removed the competition from British cotton cloth.

There was a dramatic growth in the number of cotton-spinning firms in Paris, where between 1808 and 1811, 57 were in operation, employing over 12,000 workers. French imports of raw cotton more than doubled between 1803 and 1807, and a shortage of supplies from French colonies was made up until 1811 by overland shipments from the **Levant**. There was no similar advance in any of the other textile industries. Linen and hemp manufacturers found themselves facing declining demand and the silk and woollen industries suffered also from the fashionable preference for cotton dress materials during the Empire.

A number of other industries expanded slowly in the Napoleonic period. The chemical industry did make some progress, developing artificial dyes and new bleaching materials for the cotton spinners and weavers, and experimenting with the production of artificial soda for the soap manufacturers of Marseilles. The iron industry benefited from the demand for armaments needed for Napoleon's wars, but failed to modernise itself, preferring the old method of **smelting** the ore with charcoal rather than coal.

Levant
Land bordering the eastern Mediterranean.

Smelting
The process of melting an ore in order to extract metal from it.

Key terms

The economy of the countryside was equally stagnant. Despite official encouragement, land clearing and drainage made little headway. Crop yields did not increase and labour methods remained primitive. Landowners did not reinvest their rents in the land and no new agricultural techniques were developed. Any agricultural expansion that took place was simply an extension of the cultivated area. The only other development of any significance was a government programme for the growing of sugar-beet and chicory to fill gaps left by the colonially produced sugar and coffee, which were no longer available because French maritime trade was being blockaded by Britain.

The impact of the Continental Blockade 1806–13

Key question
How did the Continental Blockade affect France?

The Blockade was an ambitious plan to conquer Britain by economic means. British exports were to be prevented from entering Europe. The unsold goods, it was believed, would then build up to such an extent that British trade would be brought to a standstill and its economy disrupted. If, at the same time, *imports* into Britain were allowed, or even encouraged – in exchange for cash payment in gold – this would help to drain away its bullion reserves and weaken its economy further. Britain would be unable to fulfil its main role in the Coalition against France – that of paymaster, providing the money needed to maintain and equip the allied armies. It was hoped that this would make Britain sign a separate peace before its position as a trading nation had been totally undermined.

The basis of the Blockade was laid out in two decrees:

Key date
Berlin Decree launched the Continental Blockade: 21 November 1806

- The Berlin Decree of 21 November 1806 stated that the British Isles was officially in a state of blockade by land and sea and forbade any communication with them by France or any of its satellites.
- The Milan Decree (1807) extended the embargo on British goods to all neutral ships that complied with the new British demands.

Britain responded by insisting that all neutral ships be required to call at British ports for inspection, to pay duties and to obtain licences, before trading with French-controlled ports.

The Blockade was intended to protect French home industries from British competition and to provide them with new European markets in the satellite and annexed states. In return, these states would provide goods needed by France for home consumption or manufacture and re-export to the rest of the Empire. In this way Napoleon's European territories would form a self-sufficient commercial and trading enterprise, independent of foreign goods.

There were both positive and negative consequences for France from the Continental Blockade.

Negative
- The great ports of the Atlantic and Channel coasts did suffer severely from the loss of sea-borne trade, and from the British navy's **counter-blockading** activities.
- Shipbuilding and its associated maritime trades, such as rope-making and sail-making, declined, as did inland industries that depended on overseas markets.
- The long-established linen industries of the north and west of France were badly affected by the loss of exports.
- The loss of profits from overseas trade resulted in less capital for investment. Some investors moved their money out of commercial enterprises, such as trading, into what seemed to be more secure areas, such as land ownership. The lack of business confidence led to the collapse of a number of banks.
- Attempting to enforce the Blockade throughout Europe pushed France into disastrous new conflicts, notably in Spain and Russia, leaving the country weakened militarily, economically and politically and left Napoleon's fortunes in decline.

Positive
- In areas away from the coasts, many traders and producers benefited from the protection to home industries offered by the Blockade. It provided an opportunity to export goods across the Alps and the Rhine to outlying parts of the Empire. Consumers in those areas who were denied access to cheaper British goods had no choice but to pay the high prices demanded by French producers.
- As the British navy closed the sea-lanes to French goods, trade routes moved overland, away from the coast. Paris became an important trading centre for luxuries, and items of fashion, as did Lyons for silk goods. Strasbourg and other eastern frontier cities prospered as **entreports** as the Rhine traffic and the trade it provided in both legitimate and **contraband goods** more than doubled in the years 1806–10.

(see page 70)

Key terms

Counter-blockading
The prevention by the British navy of all ships entering or leaving French ports.

Entreports
Ports which receive, store and re-export goods.

Contraband goods
Smuggled items.

Cultural impact

Napoleon's cultural legacy to France was not great. He was not particularly concerned with the arts, literature, sculpture, painting or drama, except in so far as they could be used for propaganda purposes to glorify himself. His regime imposed censorship on books and periodicals and he closed down most of the theatres in Paris (see page 70). Napoleon did make some changes to the appearance of the city. He added or commissioned a small number of monuments and buildings in the classical style – among them the Arc de Triomphe Du Carrousel (1808), the column in the Place Vendôme (1814) and the planned rebuilding of La Madeleine church as a Greek temple. In general, however, Paris remained in appearance the city of Louis XVI.

One cultural feature that did have an impact relates to the style and fashion of the period 1800–15. The name given to it is 'Empire' (perhaps to emphasise the importance of official art). This is seen at its most distinctive in the context of interior decoration where it directly reflects Napoleon's own interests. Its inspiration was from the classical world of ancient Greece and Rome. Napoleon was also very interested in Egypt, where he campaigned in 1799 and concerned himself as much with

Key question
What was the cultural impact of Napoleon's rule?

Modern-day photographs of Paris showing the Arc de Triomphe Du Carrousel (top left), Place Vendôme (top right) and La Madeleine (bottom). These were clearly inspired by similar buildings and monuments in the ancient world.

deciphering the country's ancient heritage as with the process of conquering it. Inlaid furniture, decorated with mythological figures of all kinds and military emblems, was very much the rage, as were the new, tall looking-glasses seen everywhere. Antiquity, with a touch of the east, dominated not only furnishings but the Empire style of dress favoured by everyone in society except Napoleon. Without regard to fashion he continued to wear, except on state occasions, a battered hat, a long grey overcoat and the green jacket of the Imperial Guard.

Napoleon's legacy: what survived after 1815?

Key question
Did any of Napoleon's policies and achievements survive his defeat in 1815?

The restoration of the Bourbon monarchy in 1814 resulted in changes to the structure of government. Under pressure from the allies, Louis XVIII granted France a limited constitution. Napoleon's centralised and autocratic structure, therefore, disappeared, along with the imperial title, in favour of a (nominally) representative government. However, other institutions remained, including much of his **bureaucratic organisation**, which had increased rapidly in size by 1815. The Ministry of the Interior enjoyed very wide-ranging powers, overseeing provincial administration, trade, arts and crafts, prisons, public works, education, science, welfare and a host of other topics. It had proliferated into a number of departments and bureaux with an ever increasing staff to match. Other civil

Key term

Bureaucratic organisation
The government administration.

ministries had expanded equally rapidly to meet the needs of a government perpetually at war, doubling their staff to a total of around 4000 by the late Empire. On the basis of this well-organised civil service, headed by specially selected and trained auditors, Napoleon could be described as 'the originator of modern centralised bureaucracy in France'.

Among the other aspects of Napoleon's regime which have survived are the following:

- The Legion of Honour continued to be awarded.
- Frenchmen remained equal before the law.
- The land settlement was left untouched.
- The legal codes and much of their judicial organisation remained in being. Today, judges are still appointed for life and the *Code Napoléon* is still the foundation of modern French law, although it was recodified in 1958.
- The provincial administrative system of prefects, sub-prefects and mayors remained the basis of local government.
- Most of Napoleon's financial reforms survived, including the Bank of France.
- The *lycées*, in a demilitarised form, survived and the Baccalaureate examination introduced in 1809 is still sat by French children at the end of their school life.
- The Concordat, minus the imperial catechism, remained the basis of relations between the French government and the Roman Catholic Church until 1904 when it came to an end with an agreement that totally separated church and state.

Arguably Napoleon's greatest legacy to France was a civil one. From more than a decade of war he left his country no permanent reminder – except a few triumphal arches, civic names and the Legion of Honour. Whether the overall effect of Napoleon's rule on France was for good or ill is debatable – the strong government, the good order, the glory and prestige that he gave the country must be balanced against the restriction of freedom, and the cost of war, in terms of human suffering and economic hardship, that his regime imposed on the French people.

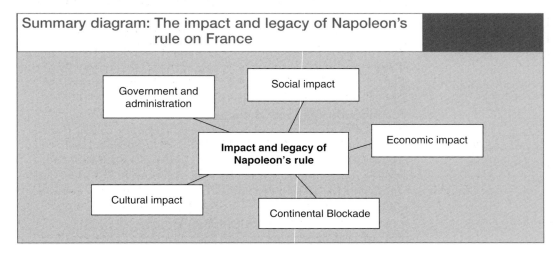

Summary diagram: The impact and legacy of Napoleon's rule on France

- Government and administration
- Social impact
- Economic impact
- Impact and legacy of Napoleon's rule
- Cultural impact
- Continental Blockade

3 | The Napoleonic Legend

Key question
What was the
Napoleonic legend?

From early on in his career, Napoleon went to great lengths to present as favourable an image of himself as possible. This practice continued and was refined when he attained power. He was possibly one of the earliest rulers to appreciate the power of propaganda. Following his final defeat and imprisonment on the island of St Helena on 17 October 1815, he set out to explain and justify his actions in a series of lengthy dictated recollections. When these were published, they formed the basis of the 'Napoleonic legend' of which he himself had been the chief architect, and on which others were to build after his death.

Key date
Arrival of Napoleon on
St Helena: 17 October
1815

Image and reality

Key question
What did Napoleon
consider to be the
benefits of
propaganda?

As far as Napoleon was concerned the benefits of propaganda were considerable. These included:

- ensuring the presentation of a favourable image of himself and the imperial dynasty
- presenting France and its revolutionary achievements in a positive way to the citizens of other European states
- spreading negative and hostile views of his enemies.

Napoleon used a number of methods to cultivate his image and to spread his propaganda. The two main methods used were:

- First, controlling the media. During the Empire, Napoleon imposed strict press censorship (see page 70) ensuring that only favourable material was published. He took a direct role in issuing Bulletins that were delivered to all prefects for display in their departments, providing carefully crafted updates of the latest military situation.
- Second, projecting a positive visual image. Napoleon employed painters to depict himself in a range of positive ways. These images variously showed the Emperor as heroic, brave, powerful, magisterial and compassionate.

Key terms

Personality cult
The elevation of an individual by means of propaganda to almost divine status.

Disinformation
The practice of spreading false information for the purpose of deception.

Both these methods went some way towards creating a **personality cult** and helped to sow the seeds of the Napoleonic legend.

The origin of the legend pre-dates the successful *coup* of Brumaire to his time in Italy during 1796–7. Napoleon's role in a string of dazzling victories at Castiglioni, Arcola, Lodi, Rivoli and Mantua was embellished and exaggerated both at the time and later by a range of writers and artists (see page 81).

Self-promotion

As well as making proclamations and issuing Orders of the Day, Napoleon published newsheets, full of **disinformation**, intended to boost army morale and dishearten the enemy. These newsheets were widely circulated, and their contents included exaggerated reports or Bulletins on the favourable progress of the war, written by Napoleon himself. He also sent senior officers to Paris in relays to report personally to the Directory, and also to brief the Paris press. When he returned to France in 1797 he was greeted as a hero. The *Institut de France*, the leading scientific association in Europe, honoured Napoleon by admitting him to their mathematics division, and everywhere he went he was feted. At a splendid ceremony in the Luxembourg Palace he personally handed over the Treaty of Campo Formio to the Directors.

This practice of issuing self-promoting Bulletins continued throughout Napoleon's career. His interpretation of the Battle of Eylau (1807) offers a good insight into his methods. It was the first battle in which some of his troops had run away, and where he sustained high losses. Napoleon managed by skilful manipulation of the facts to make it appear not a drawn encounter but a French victory. His technique was to:

- deny emphatically the Russian versions of the engagement
- dictate 'an eye-witness account, translated from the German' as the one he wished to go down into history
- send back to France specially commissioned pictures of the action
- issue Bulletins which initially falsified the number of French dead, substituting 2000 for the real figure of 20,000
- publish the almost certainly fictitious 'last words of a French officer killed in the battle'. They bore a close resemblance to other 'last words' used in earlier Bulletins. 'I die content, since victory is ours ... Tell the Emperor I have only one regret – that in a few moments I shall be beyond doing anything more in his service or for the glory of France.'

There could be no place in the legend for a drawn battle, any more than for a defeat.

Visual images

Napoleon fully appreciated the power of the visual image for propaganda purposes. Official painters were recruited to portray Napoleon and his regime in the most flattering light. To this end, he was aided by some of the greatest artists of the age. Two in particular stand out. **Gros** met Napoleon in 1796 during his Italian campaign and was responsible for producing a number of carefully honed images of the Emperor. In 1804 he completed *Bonaparte Visiting the Victims of the Plague at Jaffa* (see page 72). The painting depicts an incident from the Egyptian campaign when Napoleon, at his most compassionate, visited and comforted sick soldiers at a hospital. The heroic Emperor is the theme of another work by Gros. *Napoleon at the Battle of Eylau* was clearly intended as a work of propaganda (see page 165). It is a romanticised depiction of the indecisive battle, fought in a snowstorm in February 1807. Gros's version of the battlefield does not evoke the horrific reality of the 40,000 French and Russian dead; it shows, instead, Napoleon the inspirer, motivator and comforter, among his beloved troops.

The greatest of Napoleon's image-makers was **Jacques-Louis David**. He often used considerable **artistic licence** when painting official portraits or recording state events, in a way best suited for

Key figures

Antoine-Jean Gros 1771–1835 Prominent French painter. Met Napoleon during his first Italian campaign. Produced many large paintings of Napoleon at war.

Jacques-Louis David 1748–1825 The most famous French painter of the Revolutionary and Napoleonic periods. Appointed Napoleon's official court painter.

Key term

Artistic licence Where an artist interprets an event by stretching reality to fit his on her preconception.

Napoleon on the Battle Field of Eylau on 9th February 1807, painted in 1808 by Baron Antoine-Jean Gros (1771–1835).

use as propaganda. When commissioned to portray Napoleon's crossing of the Alps in the second Italian campaign of 1800, David was instructed to show the heroic First Consul 'calm, on a fiery horse' at the head of his men (see front cover). This he accomplished with considerable style, although it was common knowledge that Napoleon had travelled on a mule, plodding along some way to the rear of the main army. Napoleon had refused even to sit for David on this occasion, telling him that it was more important to immortalise his spirit of genius than to capture his exact likeness. It was not until long after Napoleon's death that a more realistic version of the scene was painted by the French artist Paul Delaroche (see page 166).

The emergence of the Napoleonic legend

Key questions
How did the legend develop? What were its main features?

During the six years that he was on St Helena (1815–21) in the custody of the British, Napoleon spent a great deal of his time perfecting his life story. From the very outset he seems to have been determined to make the most of his captivity to justify his actions. As he pointed out to his companions, 'Our situation here may even have its attractions; the whole word is looking at us; we are martyrs in an immortal cause.' This careful reworking of his career led the historian Tulard to conclude that 'the greatest of Napoleon's victories was over his detractors. It was at St Helena that the ogre became God.' It is possible that Napoleon's deteriorating mental condition, his growing megalomania,

Napoleon Crossing the Alps by Paul Delaroche, 1850.

became evident in his writings and conversation while in exile. He began by dictating his own *Memoirs*, but these, concerned largely with details of his early campaigns and of Waterloo, are conspicuously dull. Much more interesting are the reminiscences, diaries and journals written by Napoleon's companions on St Helena, which record in considerable detail his conversations with them against the background of everyday life at Longwood, the house where he lived on the island.

The first and most influential of these documentary sources, published in 1823, two years after Napoleon's death, was the *Mémoriale de Sainte-Hélène*. It was written by the Comte de Las Cases as a record of conversations he had with Napoleon between 1815 and 1818. This work is probably the most important single element in the later development of the legend. Despite being described after publication as 'an effusion of sentimental old French twaddle' it sold large numbers of copies, and has been extensively, and sometimes uncritically, used ever since as the

Publication of Las Cases' *Mémoriale de Sainte-Hélène*: 1823

Key date

A print of Napoleon on St Helena.

chief guide in evaluating Napoleon's own perception of his policies.

The *Mémoriale* and to some extent *A Voice from St Helena* (1822), the journals written by Napoleon's doctor on the island, B. Edward O'Meara, need to be used with caution. They are all to some extent limited in that they were intended from the outset for publication and were written by men devoted to Napoleon. They are essentially **hagiographical** studies and do not provide a balanced and critical evaluation of their subject. Three private journals, never meant for other eyes, present a much more unvarnished picture of Napoleon, but have only become available for study comparatively recently and have not so far been greatly used by historians and biographers. Napoleon encouraged his companions to write down word for word everything he said, or, more often, dictated to them, by promising quite correctly that the records they were compiling would make their fortunes when published after his death.

Las Cases, whose *Mémoriale* runs to around 500,000 words, based his work on notes made at the time, but seems to have edited them extensively before publication, smoothing Napoleon's usual abrupt phrases and fiery rhetoric into a well-rounded literary style. Opinions vary about how accurately Napoleon's actual words were recorded by any of the diarists; but even if every word *were* reproduced exactly as spoken, 'whether it is all true is quite another thing!' as an early critic said after reading O'Meara's journal.

Key term

Hagiographical
A biographical study which is very sympathetic and uncritical of its subject.

Napoleon's view of his rule

During his exile Napoleon set out to change the public perception of his rule and his role, from that of a military dictator to one of long-time, albeit unrecognised, champion of liberalism and nationalism. The political climate in Europe after 1815 following the restoration of the Bourbons was influenced by the **Holy Alliance** (Austria, Prussia and Russia). To many this was seen as a victory for the forces of reaction. The core of the Napoleonic legend was Napoleon's projection of himself as the champion of liberalism against the reactionary monarchies of old Europe.

Napoleon made a number of points to support his assertion that he was at heart a liberal monarch who had been forced into adopting war by his enemies. These had been:

- His granting of a liberal constitution – the *Acte Additionnel* – during the Hundred Days (see page 141).
- The declaration that his previous autocratic rule had been forced upon him by circumstances, and was in any case no more than a temporary measure needed to enable him as a true patriot to defend France against its enemies. 'If I had won in 1812, my constitutional reign would have begun then. Had I reigned 20 years longer I would have shown the difference between a constitutional emperor and a king of France.'
- As 'the natural mediator in the struggle of the past (i.e. the old ruling families of Europe) against the Revolution' he had brought together monarchy and liberalism.
- He was not warlike; he had always wanted peace. It was only the old dynasties who had imposed war upon him. He had been forced to stop them destroying the Revolutionary gains in France, and to liberate and unify the peoples of Europe who were still being oppressed by feudal governments. 'Each of my victories was a diplomatic step on my road towards restoring peace to Europe … after every victory I always offered a general peace.'
- Had he been given time, the 'people's Emperor' would have 'divided Europe into national states, freely formed and free internally … a United States of Europe would have become a possibility' in a new era of peaceful economic co-operation.
- He had been unable to deliver his ultimate vision for Europe due to the opposition of Britain – paymaster of the various anti-French coalitions.

The growth of the Napoleonic legend

After Napoleon's death in 1821, the legend gathered momentum in France. This was despite an official ban in the country until 1830 of the publication of any material favourable to him. Napoleon's downfall and lonely death in exile may well have contributed to the rapid growth of the legend in the 1820s and 1830s. While many poets and artists over time adopted a romantic and sentimental view of the Napoleonic era others focused on the reality of his rule. François-René Chateaubriand

Key question
How did Napoleon view his reign?

Key term

Holy Alliance
A reactionary alliance established in 1815 aimed at preventing future revolutions.

Key question
What contributed to the growth of the Napoleonic legend?

(1768–1848), one of the outstanding French literary figures of the early nineteenth century, who had always been extremely hostile to Napoleon, pointed out how easy it was to glorify Napoleon once he was dead and his dictatorship a thing of the past:

> It is the fashion of the day to magnify Napoleon's victories. Gone are the sufferers, and the victims' curses, their cries of pain, their howls of anguish are heard to more … no longer are parents imprisoned for their sons, nor a whole village punished for the desertion of a conscript … no longer are the conscription lists stuck up at street corners … It is forgotten that the people, the court, the generals, the friends of Napoleon had all become weary of his oppression and his conquests.

People *were* forgetting the negative aspects of Napoleon's rule, now that they were faced with life during the restoration – a dull Bourbon court, the pervasive influence of *émigrés* and priests and the end of any further glory for France. This 'bored generation', born too late to have fought in his wars, discovered in Napoleon a hero. His brilliant victories and conquests and the glory he brought France were in marked contrast to the dreariness of everyday life after 1815. The deaths and loss of political and cultural freedoms were conveniently ignored. By the 1830s the Romantics were mourning the so-called 'martyrdom' of Napoleon's last days on St Helena.

The accolade

Key question
How did the name Napoleon continue to exert an influence?

In his will Napoleon had requested that his remains be returned to France to, '… rest on the banks of the Seine, among the French people that I loved so well'. King Louis-Philippe, in a bid to court popularity, decided to fulfil Napoleon's wishes. In October 1840, almost 25 years to the day since Napoleon had landed on St Helena, a French ship arrived there, with British permission, to take his body back to Paris. On 15 December 1840 amid great ceremony the procession made its way to the Invalides, a former military hospital. With the final reinterment of the body in a magnificent sarcophagus below the golden dome of the Invalides, the Napoleonic legend reached its zenith. Surrounded by a range of Napoleonic relics, his hat, his sword worn at Austerlitz, his insignia of the Legion of Honour, hero-worship merged into almost religious veneration of the former Emperor.

Key dates

Napoleon's remains were buried in Paris: 15 December 1840

Death of Napoleon's son: 22 July 1832

Louis Napoleon elected President of the Second Republic: 10 December 1848

After the death of Napoleon's son, the King of Rome, on 22 July 1832, followers of the Emperor placed their faith in his nephew, the politically ambitious Louis-Napoleon, son of Napoleon's brother Louis. He staged unsuccessful *coups* in 1836 and 1840 against King Louis-Philippe, in the course of which he proclaimed that he 'represented … a principle, a cause and a defeat: the principle is the sovereignty of the people, the cause is the cause of the Empire, and the defeat is Waterloo'. The monarchy was overthrown by a revolution in 1848 and the Second Republic established. Although largely unknown, the name he shared with his illustrious uncle was certainly a factor in gaining

Napoleon's tomb in the Invalides in Paris.

Louis-Napoleon its Presidency on 10 December 1848. In his *Napoleonic Ideas* he set out in detail, as an example to be followed, the view of the First Empire outlined by his uncle while in exile. Louis-Napoleon seized power on 2 December 1851 and a year later established the Second Empire. As Napoleon III he declared that he stood for 'order and authority, religion, the welfare of the people and … for national dignity': many, therefore, expected that he would prove a reincarnation of the Napoleon of the legend. This did not happen, and with the collapse of his regime in 1870 the legend suffered an eclipse.

Key date
Louis Napoleon seized power and later declared himself Napoleon III. Start of the Second Empire: 2 December 1851

Napoleon in history

Key question
How has the study of Napoleon developed since his death?

When news of Napoleon's death was published in London on 6 July 1821, *The Times*, an establishment newspaper, attempted an instant summary of his impact on France and Europe. It described his life as 'the most extraordinary yet known to political history'. While generously conceding that 'He was steady and faithful in his friendships, and not vindictive where it was in his power to be', the paper went on to note that:

> Buonaparte will go down to posterity as a man who … applied his immense means to the production of a greater share of mischief and misery to his fellow-creatures, who carried on a series of aggressions against foreign states, to divert the minds of his own subjects from the sense of their domestic slavery; thus imposing on foreign nations a necessity for arming to shake off his yoke, and affording to foreign despots a pretext for following his example.

Despite the view of the British, however, Napoleon never seems to have had any serious doubts about the verdict of history on his career. This was not surprising as he took great pains to provide historians with records favourable to it, both before and after 1815. It was typical of him that, glancing through old copies of the official, government-sponsored newspaper, *Le Moniteur*, he expressed his approval: 'These are invariably favourable to me alone. Really talented and careful historians will write history with official documents. Now these documents are full of me; it is their testimony I solicit and invoke.'

From St Helena he attempted to pre-empt how historians might assess his life:

> I have no fear whatever about my fame. Posterity will do me justice. The truth will be known … From nothing I raised myself to be the most powerful monarch in the world … The historian of the Empire … will have an easy task, for the facts speak for themselves, they shine like the sun … On what point could I be assailed on which a historian could not defend me? For my intentions? As to these I can be absolved. For my despotism? But it can be demonstrated that dictatorship was absolutely necessary. Will it be said that I restricted liberty? It can be proved that licentiousness and anarchy still threatened liberty. Shall I be accused of being too fond of War? It can be shown I was always attacked first … Shall I be blamed for my ambition? … my ambition was of the highest and noblest kind that ever perhaps existed! that of establishing and consecrating the rule of reason and the exercise and enjoyment of all the human faculties! Here the historian will probably feel compelled to regret that such an ambition was not fulfilled.

During his confinement on St Helena, Napoleon's health deteriorated quite rapidly. In the second half of 1817 he suffered from severe swelling of the legs. In October of that year he was diagnosed by his doctor O'Meara with hepatitis – a liver disease, and was treated with mercury. The views that he expressed, and which were recorded by Las Cases, may well suggest a growing irrationality to the point of madness in the last years of his life. His version of history in the above example would appear to be delusional.

'For or against' Napoleon?

Key figure

Anne Louise Germaine, Madame de Staël 1766–1817 Prominent author and thinker. Daughter of Necker, a leading politician under Louis XVI. She was an outspoken critic of Napoleon.

Chateaubriand was one of the first critical commentators on Napoleon's career, publishing in 1814 a pamphlet denouncing him as a destroyer of men and a suppressor of freedom. Thousands of historians and writers who followed him produced works that were either 'for or against' Napoleon. Very few were neutral. **Madame de Staël**, whose account of Napoleon was published in 1818, within a year of her death, was just as critical, just as damning as Chateaubriand, but her work contained a historical perspective, setting Napoleon in his time and place, measuring him against events – and finding him wanting.

As Napoleon's death receded into the past, French histories of his life multiplied rapidly. One of the most important was by Adolphe Thiers. His monumental, 20-volume work – *Histoire du Consulat et de l'Empire* – appeared between 1845 and 1862. He was deeply influenced by the Napoleonic legend, yet from a political perspective he was a liberal, who served as a minister under King Louis-Philippe (1830–48) and later embraced republicanism. Thiers had a deep dislike of the English and he much admired Napoleon's stance against them. What determined the approach of many nineteenth-century writers was not so much that they were 'for or against' Napoleon but that they clearly shared a belief that he had shaped the course of history. Their writings can essentially be categorised as belonging to the 'great men' school of historical study. In essence they argued that events were shaped by the will of a single individual. More recently the tendency has been to focus on the forces and factors that caused these dramatic events.

One of the best **résumés** of the historical debate surrounding Napoleon was by the Dutch historian Pieter Geyl, whose classic *Napoleon: For and Against* was published in 1944. It was completed during the Nazi occupation of Holland while the author was under house arrest. Although Hitler is not mentioned in Geyl's book, he was clearly the inspiration for the work. To quote Geyl:

> We cannot see the past in a single communicable picture, except from a point of view, which implies a choice, a personal perspective. It is impossible that two historians, especially two living in different periods should see any historical personality in the same light. The greater the political importance of an historical character, the more impossible this is.

Developments in Napoleonic historiography

The vast addition to the literature on Napoleon could well be taken as evidence in support of this view. There remains a fascination with all aspects of the man and his life. His military achievements and campaigns in particular are an enduring source of study. According to the historian John Dunne, there have been two significant developments in Napoleonic **historiography** since 1945. These are:

- First, there has been a shift in focus away from studying Napoleon himself to examining aspects of the way he governed his various territories. Among the issues covered by this structural approach are the way élites such as the old aristocracy and the new nobility operated, the regional responses to conscription, and issues relating to law and order under the Empire. Many of these are based on carefully researched local studies.
- Second, against a backdrop of greater European integration, there has been interest in the wider continental experience under Napoleon. Historians have started to examine carefully

Key terms

Résumés
Summary of the views of other writers.

Historiography
The study of the views of historians.

the impact of Napoleonic rule on the occupied territories making up the Empire. The focus has been on whether or not they derived any benefits from the Empire, how they fared economically, and what, if any, were the legacies of the French legal and administrative systems that were imposed upon them.

Whether we find him fascinating or repellent, it is impossible to stand aside, unaffected by Napoleon. He dominated an age and a continent, and in many ways out-lasted his life. Almost two centuries after his death, the skills of legions of historians continue to be exercised in trying to unravel the life, career, impact and legacy of this extraordinary man. As Geyl observed, 'History is indeed an argument without end.'

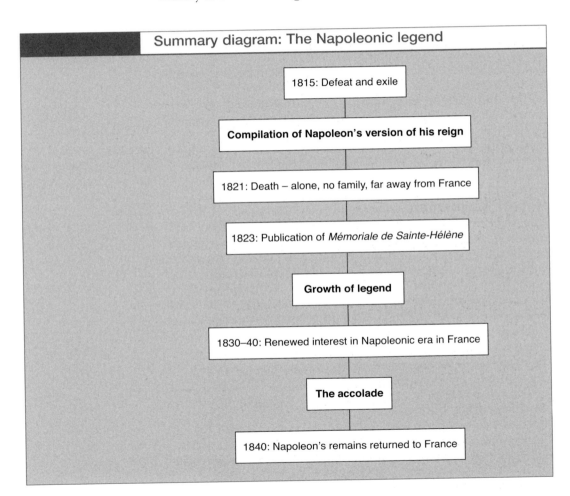

Summary diagram: The Napoleonic legend

1815: Defeat and exile

Compilation of Napoleon's version of his reign

1821: Death – alone, no family, far away from France

1823: Publication of *Mémoriale de Sainte-Hélène*

Growth of legend

1830–40: Renewed interest in Napoleonic era in France

The accolade

1840: Napoleon's remains returned to France

4 | The Key Debate

One aspect of the study of Napoleon that has generated a great deal of interest and comment among historians involves the nature of his legacy. The tangible reminders of his legacy have already been noted on page 161. The aim of this section is to consider whether there were other areas that survived the fall of his regime. The key issue examined here is:

What was the nature of Napoleon's legacy?

Georges Lefebvre

Lefebvre was one of France's most distinguished historians of the Revolutionary period. He was a committed Marxist who viewed the French Revolution as bringing about the downfall of feudalism and paving the way for the emergence to political power of the *bourgeoisie*. In his book *Napoléon* (Paris, 1935), Lefebvre provided what was essentially an unsympathetic portrait of Napoleon as an ambitious, driven general who seized power and established a dictatorship that resulted in 'eternal war'. While noting that Napoleon's personal ambition of creating a universal empire was not realised, traces of his other policies survive. Among the most important was administrative reorganisation of the state and hastening the destruction of the *ancien régime* in France.

Robert B. Holtman

The American historian Robert Holtman in his book *The Napoleonic Revolution* (Louisiana, 1967) believes that it is difficult to evaluate in which field Napoleon made the greatest impact and left the greatest legacy. The one area that Holtman considers would be high on any list is the change Napoleon made to the system of government and administration of France. In selecting this area he is to some degree mirroring Lefebvre's choice. Holtman argues that Napoleon's concept of the modern state, as a centralised entity which treated individuals as citizens rather than subjects, was to an extent embraced by those rulers who opposed him and survived his fall.

Geoffrey Ellis

Ellis has written many works on Napoleon covering both his domestic and foreign policies. Most people, according to Ellis, who have a general interest in the Emperor and his Empire will know of his military skills as a brilliant commander and his imperial conquest. They are less likely, however, to appreciate his domestic achievements. When his Empire was dismantled in 1815, Ellis considered that his lasting legacy was his civil rule. He pointed to some of the aspects that survived Napoleon's fall, for example the Bank of France, the prefecture, the Legion of Honour and the Civil Code. Napoleon's declared view of 'France first' did much to ensure that the territories he occupied and the satellite states he created were ruthlessly exploited. Despite what

Napoleon later suggested, his actions did not indicate the first tentative steps towards European integration.

D.G. Wright

Wright supported the view that it is possible to admire Napoleon as a key figure in the development of the modern state, one that wielded such enormous power over the lives of its citizens. However, he suggested that it is also very easy to exaggerate his influence and legacy on both France and Europe. Wright pointed out that arguably France changed much less between the years 1800 and 1815 than between the years 1785 and 1800. According to Wright's analysis, Napoleon's regime did not last long enough to achieve any real stability, which was always going to be a challenge given the almost continuous period of warfare throughout the duration of the Empire. One example suggested by Wright of an institution superficially reconciled to the regime was the Catholic Church. In the period after 1815, however, the church recovered its spirit of independence and abandoned its loyalty to the state.

Some key books in the debate

Geoffrey Ellis, *Napoleon. Profiles in Power* (Longman, 1997).
Robert B. Holtman, *Napoleonic Propaganda* (Louisiana State University Press, 1950).
Robert B. Holtman, *The Napoleonic Revolution* (J.P. Lippincott, 1967).
Georges Lefebvre, *Napoléon* (Paris, 1935).
D.G. Wright, *Napoleon and Europe* (Longman, 1984).

Study Guide: AS Question

In the style of OCR

To what extent did the French people benefit from Napoleon's rule?

Exam tips

The cross-references are intended to take you straight to the material that will help you answer to the question.

The question tells you to evaluate the impact of Napoleonic government on the people. There is no specific answer but, whatever line you argue, you must give clear evidence to back up what you say. Among the benefits, you might consider:

- the stabilisation of Revolution
- order and stability; effective government; legal reforms (page 50)
- educational reforms (page 52)
- the healing of religious divisions/problems (page 54).

However, you might want to question whether some of these were 'benefits'.

To evaluate properly, you must look at the other side, so to balance your investigation consider (arguably) negative aspects:

- the imposition of dictatorship, censorship, police state (pages 61–5)
- the loss of Revolutionary gains (popular sovereignty) (page 40)
- years of war and foreign hostility (page 86).

A strong answer will look further than evaluating a list of areas with a 'gain/loss' balance sheet to think about the degree of benefit to individual groups within French society (for example women, the notables, the peasants).

Napoleon and his family

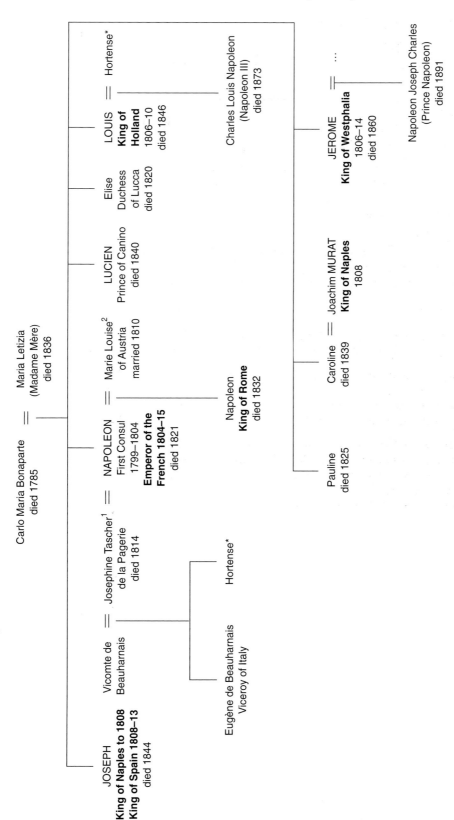

Napoleonic family tree. Note how Napoleon sought to place close members of his family on the thrones of countries he was seeking to control. [1] Josephine was Napoleon's first wife. [2] Marie Louise was Napoleon's second wife. * Hortense was Josephine's daughter from her first marriage, and married Napoleon's brother, Louis.

Further Reading

Chapter 1
Correlli Barnett, *Bonaparte* (London, 1978).
Vincent Cronin, *Napoleon* (London, 1971).
Philip Dwyer, *Napoleon. The Path to Power 1769–1799* (London, 2007).
H.A.L. Fisher, *Napoleon* (Oxford, 1971).
Felix Markham, *Napoleon* (Weidenfeld & Nicolson, 1963).

Chapter 2
R.S. Alexander, *Napoleon: Reputations* (Hodder Arnold, 2001).
Geoffrey Ellis, *Napoleon: Profiles in Power* (Longman, 1997).
Clive Emsley, *Napoleon* (Longman, 2003).
Peter Taaffe, *The Masses Arise. The Great French Revolution 1789–1815* (Fortress Books, 1989).

Chapter 3
Alfred Cobban, *A History of Modern France. Volume 2, 1799–1945* (Penguin, 1961).
George Rudé, *Revolutionary Europe 1783–1815* (Penguin, 1964).
D.M.G. Sutherland, *The French Revolution and Empire* (Blackwell, 2003).
Albert Vandal, *The Advent of Napoleon. Volume 1* (Paris, 1903).

Chapter 4
Jacques Bainville, *Napoléon* (Paris, 1931) and *Dictators* (London 1937).
Richard Cobb, *The Police and the People. French Popular Protest 1789–1820* (Oxford University Press, 1970).
Alfred Cobban, *Dictatorship: Its History and Theory* (Jonathan Cape, 1939).
Martin Lyons, *Napoleon Bonaparte and the Legacy of the French Revolution* (London, 1994).

Chapter 5
Michael Broers, *Europe Under Napoleon 1799–1815* (Arnold, 1996).
David G. Chandler, *The Campaigns of Napoleon* (Weidenfeld & Nicolson, 1993).
Philip Dwyer, *Napoleon: The Path to Power 1769–1799* (London, 2007).
Charles Esdaile, *Napoleon and the transformation of Europe* (London, 2003).

Chapter 6

R.S. Alexander, *Napoleon* (Arnold, 2001).

Michael Broers, *Europe Under Napoleon 1799–1815* (Arnold, 1996).

Geoffrey Ellis, *The Napoleonic Empire* (Palgrave, 1991).

Paul Kennedy, *The Rise and Fall of the Great Powers* (Fontana, 1988).

Martin Lyons, *Napoleon Bonaparte and the Legacy of the French Revolution* (Macmillan, 1994).

Derek McKay and H.M. Scott, *The Rise of the Great Powers 1648–1815* (Longman, 1983).

Chapter 7

R.S. Alexander, *Napoleon* (Hodder Arnold, 2001).

Michael Broers, *Europe Under Napoleon 1799–1815* (Arnold, 1996).

Vincent Cronin, *Napoleon* (Penguin, 1971).

Clive Emsley, *Napoleon: Conquest, Reform and Reorganisation* (Longman, 2003).

Charles Esdaile, 'The British Army and the Guerrilla War in Spain' in *The Road to Waterloo: The British Army and the Struggle against Revolutionary and Napoleonic France, 1793–1815*, edited by Alan J. Guy (Alan Sutton, 1990).

Charles Esdaile, *The French Wars 1792–1816* (Routledge, 2001).

Charles Esdaile, *The Peninsular War* (Penguin, 2002).

Charles Esdaile, *Napoleon's Wars* (Penguin, 2007).

Paul Kennedy, *The Rise and Fall of the Great Powers* (Fontana, 1988).

Felix Markham, *Napoleon* (Weidenfeld & Nicolson, 1963).

Paul W. Schroeder, *The Transformation of European Politics 1763–1848* (Clarendon Press, 1994).

D.M.G. Sutherland, *The French Revolution and Empire* (Blackwell, 2003).

Jean Tulard, *Napoleon: The Myth of the Saviour* (Methuen, 1984).

Chapter 8

John Dunne, 'Napoleon: For and Against … and Beyond', *History Review* (March, 1997).

Geoffrey Ellis, *Napoleon. Profiles in Power* (Longman, 1997).

Pieter Geyl, *Napoleon: For and Against* (Penguin, 1976).

Robert B. Holtman, *Napoleonic Propaganda* (Louisiana State University Press, 1950).

Robert B. Holtman, *The Napoleonic Revolution* (J.P. Lippincott, 1967).

Georges Lefebvre, *Napoléon* (Paris, 1935).

Martyn Lyons, *Napoleon Bonaparte and the Legacy of the French Revolution* (Macmillan, 1994).

Stendhal (Marie-Henri Beyle), *Vie de Napoleon* (1837).

J. Tulard (editor), *Napoléon à Sainte-Hélène* (Paris, 1981).

D.G. Wright, *Napoleon and Europe* (Longman, 1984).

Glossary

Abdicated   Gave up power.

Acte Additionnel   A supplement to Napoleon's previous constitution, granting some liberal reforms such as freedom of the press.

l'Agglomération   Bringing together people who share the same language, culture and traditions.

Agricultural revolution   The process by which agriculture is mechanised and new methods of food production are introduced.

Anarchists   In the context of the Revolution those who wished to create chaos and disorder.

Annexed   Taken over by a foreign power as of right.

Archbishop   A senior figure in the church with authority over bishops.

Armistice   Cessation of hostilities usually preceding a peace treaty.

Arrondissements   The sub-divisions making up each department.

Artistic licence   Where an artist interprets an event by stretching reality to fit his or her preconception.

Austrian Netherlands   Modern-day Belgium which the Austrians had ruled since 1713.

Battle of the Nations   Another name for the Battle of Leipzig – a large battle involving over 500,000 troops.

Bellerophon   A British warship on which Napoleon was held while awaiting transport to St Helena in 1815.

Biens nationaux   Royalist and church lands seized by the state early in the Revolution and sold off to anyone able to pay.

Blitzkrieg   A war of rapid movement where large numbers of forces are directed towards a very narrow front.

Body politic   The political nation – those groups and individuals who were active in the political life of the country.

Bourbon monarchy   The Spanish royal family, closely related to the deposed French royal family.

Bourgeoisie   The middle classes, for example lawyers, merchants and bankers.

Brigandage   Outbreaks of lawlessness and violence by armed groups of bandits.

Brigands   Gangs of outlaws roaming the countryside.

Brutus   One of Julius Caesar's assassins.

Bureaucratic organisation   The government administration.

Caesar   A reference to the Roman general Julius Caesar, who seized power in ancient Rome and was considered by many a military dictator.

Careers open to talents   Any person of ability irrespective of social status should be able to progress in their chosen field.

Catechism   A set form of question and answer, used by the church to teach the key aspects of its faith.

Censorship   The control or suppression by the state of media and culture considered critical.

Centralised   Political power dispensed from one central location or through one individual.

Chancellor   Head of the Austrian government.

Cidevant   List drawn up during the Revolution of former members of the nobility.

Clan system   A group of people, related in some way, who protect and look after one another.

Cockade   A tri-coloured cloth rosette comprising the red and blue of Paris and the white of the uniform of the French guards.

Committee of Public Safety   Effectively, the government of France during 1793–4 and one of the twin pillars of the Terror along with the Committee of General Security.

Conscription   Compulsory military service for all men between certain ages.

Conscription draft   All men who were eligible for compulsory military service.

Consul   The title given to the three new executive members.

Continental Blockade   An attempt to close all European ports to British ships.

Contraband goods   Smuggled items.

Conventionnels   Members of the Convention between 1792 and 1795.

Cossacks   Fierce Russian mounted soldiers from the southern region of the Ukraine.

Counter-blockading   The prevention by the British navy of all ships entering or leaving French ports.

Counter-revolutionaries   All who were hostile to the Revolution.

Coup d'état   Overthrowing a government and seizing power.

Coup **of Brumaire**   Brought about the overthrow of the Directory.

Coup **of Fructidor**   Napoleon deployed the army on behalf of Barras to expel newly elected royalists from the Assembly.

Coup **of Prairial**   The removal of two Directors who were considered to be ineffective.

Crusades   Attempts by Christian countries in western Europe to free the holy places in Palestine from Muslim control.

Dechristianisation   A policy aimed at the physical destruction of all religious features.

Decree of outlawry   Anyone accused of outlawry could be immediately arrested and summarily executed without a trial.

Departments   The local government divisions established by the National Assembly.

Despotic   The abuse and misuse of power by a ruler.

Dictator   A ruler who has total control or power over a state.

Direct taxes   Taxes imposed on all by the state, usually based on income or the ownership of property.

Disinformation   The practice of spreading false information for the purpose of deception.

Divide and rule   The attempt to ensure that potential enemies were kept apart.

The Donation   Charlemagne's gift of Rome and most of Italy to the Pope.

Dotations   Lavish gifts of land which accompanied the titles awarded by Napoleon.

Draconian measure   A severe or extreme law or policy.

Draft dodgers   Men attempting to avoid conscription to the army.

Élan   Enthusiasm and passionate commitment for the republican cause.

Elba   A small island off the north-western coast of Italy.

Émigrés   Former members of the aristocracy, royalists and priests who fled France fearing for their safety.

Entail   The procedure to control the inheritance of property by ensuring that it passed down the owner's line of descendants.

Entreports   Ports which receive, store and re-export goods.

Estates-General   Elected representatives from the clergy, nobility and everyone else.

Executive   The decision-making part of the government.

Federal revolt   The rejection of the authority of the government in Paris in favour of regional authority.

Feudal dues   Either financial or work obligations imposed on the peasantry by landowners.

First Coalition   Had been in existence since 1793 when Britain joined the war against France.

First Consul   The most important of the three consuls who headed the government after the 1799 *coup*.

Franc   On 7 April 1795 the Convention introduced the silver franc as the official unit of currency, replacing the *livre*.

Freehold property   Property fully owned by an individual.

Freemasonry   A secretive organisation that looks after the interests of its members.

Frost nail   A nail with a sharp head driven into the hoof of a horse to prevent it slipping in icy conditions.

Gabelle   The tax on salt imposed during the *ancien régime*.

Gendarmes   A police force set up in 1790 and modelled on the cavalry attached to the royal family during the *ancien régime*.

Grande Armée   The name used by Napoleon for his army in 1805.

Grapeshot   Canisters of small shot that spread widely when fired from cannon.

Guerrilla **fighters**   Irregular soldiers who draw supplies and support from the local population.

Guild system   The rigid control of entry into a range of professions and occupations in order to maintain high wages and prices.

Hagiographical   A biographical study which is very sympathetic and uncritical of its subject.

Hereditary principle   A system where an individual is succeeded by his nearest male relative – usually the eldest son. Such a system is used in monarchies.

Historiography   The study of the views of historians.

Holy Alliance   A reactionary alliance established in 1815 aimed at preventing future revolutions.

Holy Roman Empire   A union of states of various sizes, mostly German speaking, which existed between 962 and 1806, whose rulers recognised the authority of an Emperor.

Homme de guerre   Literally man of war, a reference to Napoleon as a military figure.

House arrest   When an individual is confined by the state to his or her house.

The Hundred Days   Napoleon's campaign in 1815 to try to regain the throne.

Iberian peninsula   The area encompassing Spain and Portugal.

Imperial Guard   The most élite regiment in the French army.

Imperialism   The process of creating an empire.

Indirect taxes   Taxes levied on selected goods.

Indoctrination   The process of imposing a set of beliefs and values on people.

Jacobin club   'The Society of the Friends of the Constitution', the most extreme of the political clubs in Paris.

Juntas   Local resistance committees.

La patrie   The fatherland – with which all passionate revolutionaries closely identified.

Land tenure The various legal ways in which land can be held.

Le Chapelier law A law passed by the National Assembly in 1791 that banned strikes and made trade unions illegal.

Le Moniteur A popular newspaper founded in 1789. It became the official government newspaper in 1799.

League of Armed Neutrality An agreement by Russia, Sweden, Denmark and Prussia to prevent Britain trading with the Baltic.

Left wing A position supporting extreme change to benefit the majority of the population.

Legion of Honour An élitist organisation created by Napoleon to bind powerful men to his regime through a system of rewards and titles.

Lettres de cachet A detention order signed by the King and a minister authorising the imprisonment without trial of a named individual.

Levant Land bordering the eastern Mediterranean.

Levée en masse A decree passed in 1793 which compelled the whole population to help defend the country.

Levies Soldiers raised by conscription.

Liberal Tolerant of the rights and views of others, including individual freedom and equality.

Lines of Torres Vedras A system of carefully constructed defensive fortifications protecting Lisbon.

Live off the land The expectation that an army would supply itself from the area in which it was located.

Livret A combined work permit and employment record, without which it was impossible legally to obtain a job.

Louvre The premier gallery and museum in Paris, on the site of a former royal fortress.

Luxembourg Palace The official residence of the Directory and then the Consuls.

Lycées Élite schools for the sons of the wealthy organised on strict military lines.

Marshal The highest rank in the French army. Napoleon promoted 26 generals to Marshal of the Empire.

Mercenaries Soldiers who hire out their services to anyone.

Mixed order Placing troops in a combination of lines and columns.

Musket A smooth-bored, muzzle-loading flintlock rifle, firing a single lead bullet and fitted with a bayonet.

Nation in arms The mobilisation of the entire nation to help in its defence.

Nationalism Close identification by a group of people with the language, history, traditions and culture of a territory.

Natural frontiers Natural features, such as rivers, mountains, lakes or the sea.

Neutral country One which takes no side in a conflict.

Non-juring priests Priests who refused to take the oath to the Civil Constitution of the Clergy.

Notables The most prominent men in any community.

Notre Dame The Catholic cathedral in Paris, located on an island in the river Seine.

'Old France' The France of the pre-Revolutionary period.

Ottoman Empire A vast declining empire controlling most of North Africa and the Middle East.

Pack the Senate Napoleon appointed his own nominees whose loyalty and support he could guarantee.

Patronage Using various means including bribery and rewards to gain support.

Perfidious Albion   A phrase coined during the French Revolution to describe the untrustworthiness of the British.

Personality cult   The elevation of an individual by means of propaganda to almost divine status.

Philosophes   Liberal intellectuals interested in analysing the relationship between government and society.

Plebiscite   A vote on a single issue where electors are asked whether they support or reject a proposal.

Political apathy   A lack of interest in politics.

Popular sovereignty   A belief that political power rests with the people and their chosen representatives.

Propaganda   Using the media to persuade the population to support the regime.

Puppet state   A state directly under the control of another state.

Purge   The forced removal of political opponents.

Rapprochement   When former enemies seal their differences and improve their relations.

Regency   A period when the authority of a child ruler is exercised by an adult until he or she comes of age.

Regicide   Someone who voted for the execution of Louis XVI.

Renaissance   Renewed interest in learning and the arts.

Representatives on mission   Highly placed politicians sent from Paris with the authority of the government to ensure generals were actively carrying out their orders.

Requisitioning   The forcible purchase of food and other supplies for the army from the civilian population.

Restoration   The return of the Bourbons to the throne of France.

Résumés   Summary of the views of other writers.

The right   In the context of the French Revolution, supporters of the monarchy.

Risorgimento   Mid-nineteenth-century movement to create a unified Italian state.

Roman law   A legal system created in ancient Rome over 2000 years ago which listed crimes and punishments in a series of tables.

Rump   A group of sympathetic deputies who remained after the others had been expelled or had fled.

Saint-Cloud   A royal palace on the outskirts of Paris.

Saint-Domingue   An important French colony in the Caribbean.

Sans-culottes   Working-class people living in towns and cities.

Sceptre   A symbolic rod held by a monarch to represent authority.

Schism   A deep division.

Scorched earth   The destruction of food supplies and shelter to deny the invaders any support or help as they advanced.

Second Coalition   An anti-French coalition comprised of Britain, Russia, Austria and the Ottoman Empire.

Senatoreries   Estates of land awarded to members of the Senate.

Senatus-consultum   A procedure that allowed the Senate to preserve and amend the constitution and to approve constitutional change and new laws.

Serfdom   A system where the population is tied to the land and not free to leave the control of their feudal lord.

Skirmishers   Small groups of soldiers operating independently, fighting minor engagements and living off the land.

Smelting   The process of melting an ore in order to extract metal from it.

Spanish ulcer An ulcer is a wound that weakens the victim but is rarely fatal.

St Helena A tiny British island in the south Atlantic over 1000 miles off the coast of Africa.

Stiletto A dagger with a very thin blade.

Strategy A plan of action designed to achieve the goal of victory in a war.

Subsidies Money paid by Britain to allies for funding their armies.

Subsistence level A backward type of agriculture producing only enough food to survive.

Subversives Those wishing to overthrow the state.

Tactics The methods used by generals and commanders to conduct battles.

Talavera Following this battle, Wellesley was created Viscount Wellington.

Temporal sovereigns Those who exercise political power over an area as opposed to spiritual power.

The Terror A ruthless system of government created by the Jacobins between 1793 and 1794 to defeat the enemies of the Republic.

Thermidor One of the months in the new Revolutionary calendar, 9 July–17 August.

Trajan's column Erected in 113AD to celebrate the victories of the Emperor Trajan and decorated with images of the Roman army.

Tribute monies Financial contributions to the French state.

Tsar The Russian Emperor.

Universal suffrage A vote for every man over a certain age regardless of wealth.

Vendée rebellion Anti-republican revolt covering several departments in western France including the Vendée.

Viceroy Napoleon's direct representative in Italy.

Vienna Congress A meeting of the great powers (1814–15) to agree a settlement in Europe after Napoleon's defeat.

Voix consultative The right merely to express an opinion.

Voix deliberative Each consul would have an equal vote in any decision making.

Volk People bound together by a common heritage and shared language.

Index